CONGRESS OF THE UNITED STATES: POWERS, STRUCTURE AND PROCEDURES

CONGRESS OF THE UNITED STATES: POWERS, STRUCTURE AND PROCEDURES

N.O. KURA (EDITOR)

Nova Science Publishers, Inc.
Huntington, NY

Senior Editors: Susan Boriotti and Donna Dennis
Office Manager: Annette Hellinger
Graphics: Wanda Serrano
Information Editor: Tatiana Shohov
Book Production: Cathy DeGregory, Kay Seymour, Lynette Van Helden
and Jennifer Vogt
Circulation: Ave Maria Gonzalez, Ron Hedges and Andre Tillman

Library of Congress Cataloging-in-Publication Data
Available Upon Request

ISBN 1-56072-914-7.

227 Main Street, Suite 100
Huntington, New York 11743
Tele. 631-424-6682 Fax 631-425-5933
E Mail Novascil@aol.com

Printed in the United States of America

CONTENTS:

LEGISLATIVE POWERS OF CONGRESS: A BRIEF REFERENCE GUIDE

George Costello

Summary

A House rule now requires that committee reports identify the constitutional source of power to enact the reported bill. This report is designed to assist in identification of Congress' legislative powers. It lists legislative powers, sets forth the constitutional text for each power, and provides brief commentary. Powers are grouped in the following broad subject matter categories: power to tax and spend, commercial powers, citizenship, civil rights and voting rights, elections, property and territory, war and related powers, federal-state relations, and checks on other branches. An introductory section is devoted to the scope of congressional powers.

Introduction

A House Rule now requires that a committee report on a bill "include a statement citing the specific powers granted to the Congress in the Constitution to enact the law proposed by the bill." House Rule XI, cl. 2(l). This report is designed to assist in the required identification and citation of congressional powers, and to that end catalogs and briefly describes such powers. The focus is on Congress' legislative powers, although certain of Congress' non-legislative powers (e.g., impeachment, and the power to judge elections and qualifications of members) are also cited. No effort is made to catalog all of the powers conferred on other branches, although these powers too can be of legislative significance due to the fact that Congress has the power to make all laws "necessary and proper" to carry into execution "all other Powers vested . . . in the Government of the United States, or in any Department or Officer thereof." Nor is any effort made to catalog the many limitations that the Constitution places on exercise of governmental power (e.g., those contained in Article I, section 9, and in the Bill of Rights); only limitations textually linked to grants of power are included. This report, therefore, can be useful only in helping to identify the source of congressional power to legislate in a particular area, and does not purport to offer additional guidance in determining the ultimate constitutional validity of specific legislation. For analysis of how particular powers or limitations have been interpreted, see *The Constitution of the United States of America: Analysis and Interpretation*, Senate Document 103-6, and cumulative supplements (the most recent being Sen. Doc. 104-14).

The selected congressional powers are grouped below under broad topical headings. Constitutional text is italicized.

Scope of Congressional Powers

Limited and Enumerated Powers

All legislative powers herein granted shall be vested in a Congress of the United States. Article 1, section 1.

The powers not delegated to the United States by the Constitution, nor prohibited by it to the States, are reserved to the States respectively, or to the people. Tenth Amendment.

Article I, section 1 does not grant to Congress "all legislative power," but rather grants to Congress certain specific powers, "herein granted" and enumerated in section 8 and elsewhere in the Constitution. The Tenth Amendment underscores this arrangement.

Broad and Elastic Powers

The Congress shall have power . . . To make all laws which shall be necessary and proper for carrying into Execution the foregoing Powers and all other Powers vested by this Constitution in the Government of the United States, or in any Department or Officer thereof. Article I, section 8, cl. 18.

That this clause enlarges rather than narrows the powers of Congress was established by Chief Justice Marshall's classic statement in *McCulloch v. Maryland* (1819): "Let the end be legitimate, let it be within the scope of the Constitution, and all means which are appropriate, which are plainly adapted to that end, which are not prohibited, but consist with the letter and spirit of the Constitution, are constitutional."

The clause has another important consequence: by authorizing Congress to enact legislation necessary and proper to carry into execution all powers vested in the United States, it gives Congress a share in the responsibilities of the other branches. In other words, legislation need not be limited to implementing powers that the Constitution confers directly on Congress; legislation also may implement powers conferred on the President and the courts.

Supremacy — Preemptive Scope of Federal Law

This Constitution, and the Laws of the United States which shall be made in Pursuance thereof; and all Treaties made, or which shall be made, under the Authority of the United States, shall be the supreme Law of the Land; and the Judges in every State shall be bound thereby, any Thing in the Constitution or Laws of any state to the Contrary notwithstanding. Article VI, cl. 2.

The "supremacy clause" directs that valid (constitutional) federal laws take precedence over conflicting state constitutional provisions and laws.

Power to Tax and Spend

The Congress shall have Power To lay and collect Taxes, Duties, Imposts and Excises, to pay the Debts and provide for the common Defence and general Welfare of the United States; but all Duties, Imposts and Excises shall be uniform throughout the United States. Article I, section 8, cl. 1.

No Capitation, or other direct Tax shall be laid, unless in Proportion to the Census of Enumeration . . . . Article I, section 9, cl. 4.

The Congress shall have power to lay and collect taxes on incomes, from whatever source derived, without apportionment among the several States, and without regard to any census or enumeration. Sixteenth Amendment.

The Congress shall have Power . . . To borrow Money on the credit of the United States. Article I, section 8, cl. 2.

No Money shall be drawn from the Treasury, but in Consequence of Appropriations made by Law. Article I, section 9, cl. 7.

Direct taxes (property taxes and capitation taxes) must be apportioned among the States, and indirect taxes (all other taxes) must be "uniform." A holding by the Supreme Court invalidating an income tax law enacted pursuant to Article I, § 8, cl. 1 led to adoption of the Sixteenth Amendment. The purposes for which Congress may tax and spend are very broad; the "general welfare" is not limited by the scope of other enumerated powers under which Congress may regulate. On the other hand, Congress has no power to regulate "for the general welfare," but may only tax and spend for that purpose. Article I, § 9, cl. 7 enhances congressional control over the executive branch by restricting spending to that authorized by an appropriation.

Commercial Powers

"The Congress shall have power . . .

To regulate commerce with foreign Nations, and among the several States, and with the Indian Tribes. Article I, section 8, cl. 3.

To establish ... uniform Laws on the subject of Bankruptcies throughout the United States. Article I, section 8, cl. 4.

To coin money, regulate the Value thereof, and of foreign Coin, and fix the Standard of Weights and Measures. Article I, section 8 cl. 5.

To provide for the Punishment of counterfeiting the Securities and current Coin of the United States. Article I, section 8, cl. 6.

To establish Post Offices and post Roads. Article I, section 8, cl. 7.

To promote the Progress of Science and useful Arts, by securing for limited Times to Authors and Inventors the exclusive Right to their respective Writings and Discoveries. Article I, section 8, cl. 8.

The "commerce clause" (cl. 3 above) is one of the most far-reaching grants of power to Congress. Interstate commerce covers all movement of people and things across state lines, including communication and transportation. The Supreme Court recently summarized, in *United States v. Lopez* (1995), three broad categories of the commerce power. Congress may regulate the use of the

channels of interstate commerce, may regulate and protect the instrumentalities of interstate commerce, and, in addition, may regulate those activities that substantially affect interstate commerce.

Citizenship

The Congress shall have power . . . To establish an uniform Rule of Naturalization. Article I, section 8, cl. 4.

All persons born or naturalized in the United States and subject to the jurisdiction thereof, are citizens of the United States and of the State wherein they reside. Fourteenth Amendment, section 1.

The power to establish uniform naturalization requirements means that Congress may define the circumstances under which immigrants may become citizens. The Fourteenth Amendment, adopted in 1868 as one of the Civil War Reconstruction amendments, had the effect of conferring citizenship on African Americans, and thereby reversing the Supreme Court's decision in the *Dred Scott* case (1857). Section 5 of the Fourteenth Amendment, reproduced in the next section, gives Congress explicit enforcement authority.

Civil Rights and Voting Rights

No State shall make or enforce any law which shall abridge the privileges or immunities of citizens of the United States; nor shall any State deprive any person of life, liberty, or property, without due process of law; nor deny to any person within its jurisdiction the equal protection of the laws. Fourteenth Amendment, section 1.

The Congress shall have power to enforce, by appropriate legislation, the provisions of this article. Fourteenth Amendment, section 5.

Both the due process clause and the equal protection clause have been interpreted broadly, and Congress' enforcement authority is correspondingly broad. The privileges and immunities clause, though it has been more narrowly construed by the Court, may nonetheless support (in conjunction with section 5) significant legislation. See, e.g., 42 U.S.C. § 1983. The due process clause has been interpreted by the Supreme Court as having substantive as well as procedural application, and as incorporating (i.e., applying to the states) most of the Bill of Rights. While the immediate impetus for the equal protection clause was to prohibit racial discrimination, the clause is not so limited by its terms, and applies across the board to all forms of discriminatory classifications by "state action."

Neither slavery nor involuntary servitude, except as punishment for crime . . . , shall exist within the United States. Thirteenth Amendment, section 1.

Congress shall have power to enforce this article by appropriate legislation. Thirteenth Amendment, section 2.

Congress has relied on the Thirteenth Amendment to legislate against slavery-like conditions, such as peonage.

The right of the citizens of the United States to vote shall not be denied or abridged by the United States or by any State on account of race, color, or previous condition of servitude. Fifteenth Amendment, section 1.

The Congress shall have power to enforce this article by appropriate legislation. Fifteenth Amendment, section 2.

Congress has relied on the Fifteenth Amendment for the several iterations of the Voting Rights Act. Nearly identical language extends the same protection to women, and to citizens who are at least 18 years of age:

The right of the citizens of the United States to vote shall not be denied or abridged by the United States or by any State on account of sex.
Congress shall have power to enforce this article by appropriate legislation.
Nineteenth Amendment.

The right of the citizens of the United States, who are eighteen years of age or older, to vote shall not be denied or abridged by the United States or by any State on account of age. Twenty-sixth Amendment, section 1.

The Congress shall have power to enforce this article by appropriate legislation. Twenty-sixth Amendment, section 2.

Elections

The Times, Places and Manner of holding Elections for Senators and Representatives, shall be prescribed in each State by the Legislature thereof; but the Congress may at any time by Law make or alter such Regulations, except as to the Places of chusing Senators. Article I, section 4, cl. 1.

While the Fifteenth Amendment and the other voting rights guarantees noted above protect only against state action, congressional authority under this clause includes protection of the electoral process against private interference. A variety of enactments can trace to this authority, including campaign finance laws and the Hatch Act (insofar as it applies to federal elections).

Each House shall be the Judge of the Elections, Returns and Qualifications of its own Members. Article I, section 5, cl. 1.

The House and the Senate act as judicial tribunals in resolving contested election cases.

The Congress may determine the Time of chusing the Electors, and the Day on which they shall give their Votes; which Day shall be the same throughout the United States. Article II, section 1, cl. 4.

Congress has exercised this authority to specify the day on which presidential elections are held (i.e., the day on which electors are chosen), the day on which electors gather to vote, and the day on which electoral ballots are counted.

The District constituting the seat of Government of the United States shall appoint in such manner as the Congress may direct: A number of electors of President and Vice President equal to the whole number of Senators and Representatives in Congress to which the District would be entitled if it were a State . . . . Twenty-third Amendment, section 1.

The Congress shall have power to enforce this article by appropriate legislation. Twenty-third Amendment, section 2.

Congress may implement the Twenty-third Amendment.

Representatives shall be apportioned among the several States according to their respective numbers, counting the whole number of persons in each State . . . . Fourteenth Amendment, section 2.

The actual enumeration shall be made . . . in such manner as they [Congress] shall by law direct. Article I, section 2, cl. 3.

Congress fixes by law the total number of Representatives, and provides for apportionment among the states in accordance with the Constitution's requirements. Congress also makes statutory provision for the taking of the decennial census.

. . . Congress may by law provide for the case wherein neither a President elect nor a Vice President elect shall have qualified, declaring who shall then act as President, or the manner in which one who is to act shall be selected . . . . Twentieth Amendment, section 3.

The Congress may by law provide for the case of the death of any of the persons from whom the House of Representatives may choose a President whenever the right of choice shall have devolved upon them, and for the case of the death of any of the persons from whom the Senate may choose a Vice President whenever the right of choice shall have devolved upon them. Twentieth Amendment, section 4.

These provisions supplement the Twelfth Amendment, which calls for selection of a President by the House, and selection of a Vice President by the Senate, in the event that no one receives a majority of electoral votes.

Whenever the Vice President and a majority of either the principal officers of the executive departments or of such other body as Congress may by law provide,

Representatives their written declaration that the President is unable to discharge the powers and duties of his office, the Vice President shall immediately assume the powers and duties of the office as Acting President. Twenty-fifth Amendment, section 4.

Congress performs other important, non-legislative functions under this Amendment by voting on confirmation of the President's nomination to fill a vacancy in the office of Vice President, and by resolving disputes over the President's fitness to discharge the powers and duties of his office.

The right of citizens of the United States to vote in any primary or other election for President or Vice President, for electors for President or Vice President, or for Senator or Representative in Congress, shall not be denied or abridged by the United States or by any State by reason of failure to pay any poll tax or other tax. Twenty-fourth Amendment, section 1.

The Congress shall have power to enforce this article by appropriate legislation. Twenty-fourth Amendment, section 2.

At the time of adoption of the Amendment in 1964, the poll tax, a remnant of Reconstruction era legislation in the South, was maintained by five states.

Note: other Amendments relating to the subject of elections have been set forth above under the heading "Civil Rights and Voting Rights."

Property and Territory

The Congress shall have power . . . To exercise exclusive Legislation in all Cases whatsoever, over such District . . . as may, by Cession of Particular States, and the Acceptance of Congress, become the Seat of the Government of the United States, and to exercise like Authority over all Places purchased by the Consent of the Legislature of the State in which the Same shall be, for the Erection of Forts, Magazines, Arsenals, dock-Yards and other needful Buildings. Article I, section 8, cl. 17.

This clause enables Congress to govern the District of Columbia, and also to govern forts and other places obtained from states for the federal government's purposes.

The Congress shall have power to dispose of and make all needful Rules and Regulations respecting the Territory or other Property belonging to the United States . . . . Article IV, section 3, cl. 2.

This is the authority by which Congress regulates the public lands and governs acquired territories such as Puerto Rico, the Virgin Islands, Guam, and American Samoa.

[N]or shall private property be taken for public use, without just compensation. Fifth Amendment.

Implicit in the Fifth Amendment's requirement that just compensation be paid for private property that is taken for a public use is the existence of the government's power to take private property for public use. The Supreme Court has called this power an "attribute of sovereignty." The power resides in Congress, and may be delegated to private as well as public entities so long as its exercise is limited to public purposes.

War and Related Powers

The Congress shall have power . . .

To define and punish Piracies and Felonies committed on the high Seas, and Offences against the Law of Nations. Article I, section 8, cl. 10.

To declare War, grant Letters of Marque and Reprisal, and make Rules concerning Captures on Land and Water. Article I, section 8, cl. 11.

To raise and support Armies . . . . Article I, section 8, cl. 12.

To provide and maintain a Navy. Article I, section 8, cl. 13.

To make rules for the Government and Regulation of the land and naval Forces. Article I, section 8, cl. 14.

To provide for calling forth the Militia to execute the Laws of the Union, suppress Insurrections and repeal Invasions. Article I, section 8, cl. 15.

To provide for arming, and disciplining, the Militia, and for governing such Part of them as may be employed in the Service of the United States, reserving to the States respectively, the Appointment of the Officers, and the Authority of training the Militia according to the discipline prescribed by Congress. Article I, section 8, cl. 16.

No State shall, without the consent of Congress . . . engage in War, unless actually invaded, or in such imminent Danger as will not admit of delay. Article I, section 10, cl. 3.

Treason against the United States, shall consist only in levying War against them, or in adhering to their Enemies, giving them aid and Comfort. No Person shall be convicted of Treason unless on the Testimony of two Witnesses to the same overt Act, or on Confession in open Court. Article III, section 3, cl. 1.

The Congress shall have Power to declare the Punishment of Treason, but no Attainder of Treason shall work Corruption of Blood, or Forfeiture except during the Life of the Person attainted. Article III, section 3, cl. 2.

Congress' war powers, Article I, § 8, cls. 11-14 above, are underscored by the power to declare war. Congress can also exercise control over military ventures through its power of the purse (see especially Art. I, § 8, cl. 1 and Article I, § 9, cl. 7 below). Under Article II, section 2, the President is Commander in Chief of the armed forces. The right of the states to maintain a militia — now the National Guard — is subject to control by Congress pursuant to clauses 15 and 16, above. The crime of treason is defined by the Constitution, but Congress has the power, as limited by the language of Article III, § 3, cl. 2, to declare the punishment for treason.

Federal - State Relations

This Constitution, and the Laws of the United States which shall be made in Pursuance thereof; and all Treaties made, or which shall be made, under the Authority of the United States, shall be the supreme Law of the Land; and the Judges in every State shall be bound thereby, any Thing in the Constitution or Laws of any state to the Contrary notwithstanding. Article VI, cl. 2.

The "supremacy clause," also set forth above under "Scope," directs that valid federal laws preempt conflicting state constitutional provisions and laws.

The powers not delegated to the United States by the Constitution, nor prohibited by it to the States, are reserved to the States respectively, or to the people. Tenth Amendment.

The Tenth Amendment, also set forth above under "Scope," reflects the fact that federal powers are enumerated and defined, and hence not all-encompassing; governmental powers not delegated to the Federal Government are reserved to the States.

No State shall, without the Consent of the Congress, lay any Imposts or Duties on Imports or Exports, except what may be absolutely necessary for executing it's inspection Laws: and the net Produce of all Duties and Imposts, laid by any State on Imports or Exports, shall be for the Use of the Treasury of the United States; and all such Laws shall be subject to the Revision and Control of the Congress. Article I, section 10, cl. 2.

This clause complements the congressional power under Article I, section 8, cl. 1 to impose imposts and duties on imports and exports.

No State shall, without the Consent of Congress, lay any Duty of Tonnage, keep Troops, or Ships of War in time of Peace, enter into any Agreement or Compact with another State, or with a foreign Power, or engage in War unless actually invaded, or inn such imminent Danger as will not admit of delay. Article I, section 10, cl. 3.

Here again, Congress may consent to States exercising powers otherwise prohibited. Clauses 2 and 3 of section 10 contrast with clause 1, which prohibits altogether specified actions by states and contains no provision for congressional consent. Interstate compacts are relatively common; under Supreme Court interpretations, congressional consent may take a variety of forms, express or implied, before or sometimes after the fact.

Full Faith and Credit shall be given in each State to the public Acts, Records, and Judicial Proceedings of every other State. And the Congress may by general Laws prescribe the Manner in which such Acts, Records, and Proceedings shall be proved, and the Effect thereof. Article IV, section 1.

This "Full Faith and Credit Clause" gives Congress what amounts to enforcement authority over the required recognition by each state of the judgments, records, and legislation of other states.

New States may be admitted by the Congress into this Union; but no new State shall be formed or erected within the Jurisdiction of any other State; nor any State be formed by the Junction of two or more States, or Parts of States, without the Consent of the Legislatures of the States concerned as well as of the Congress. Article IV, section 3.

Congress by legislation may admit new states on an equal footing with existing states.

The United States shall guarantee to every State in this Union a Republican Form of Government, and shall protect each of them against Invasion; and on Application of the Legislature, or of the Executive (when the Legislature cannot be convened) against domestic Violence. Article IV, section 4.

Exercising this authority, Congress has authorized Presidents to send federal troops into a state to guarantee law and order.

Checks on the Other Branches

The Executive Branch

The President, Vice President and all civil Officers of the United States, shall be removed from Office on Impeachment for, and Conviction of, Treason, Bribery, or other High Crimes and Misdemeanors. Article II, section 4.

The House of Representatives . . . shall have the sole power of Impeachment. Article I, section 2, cl. 5.

The Senate shall have the sole Power to try all Impeachments. . . . And no person shall be convicted without the Concurrence of two thirds of the Members present. Article I, section 3, cl. 6.

Judgment in cases of Impeachment shall not extend further than to removal from Office, and disqualification to hold and enjoy any Office of honor, Trust or Profit under the United States: but the Party convicted shall nevertheless be liable and subject to Indictment, Trial, Judgment and Punishment, according to Law. Article I, section 3, cl. 7.

The President . . . shall have Power to Grant Reprieves and Pardons for Offenses against the United States, except in Cases of Impeachment. Article II, section 2.

Congress may remove from office the President, Vice-President, and other "civil officers" (other executive officers and judges). The House initiates the impeachment process, and the Senate conducts a trial to determine whether to convict or acquit. Convicted persons can be barred from holding federal office in the future, and may be subject to criminal trial in the courts. The President's otherwise unlimited pardon power does not extend to impeachment convictions.

. . . [N]o Person holding any Office of Profit or Trust under [the United States] shall, without the consent of Congress, accept any present, Emolument, Office, or Title, of any kind whatever, from any King, Prince or foreign State. Article I, section 9, cl. 8.

This restriction complements denial to Congress of the power to grant titles of nobility. By statute, Congress requires that federal officials turn over to the government all but minimal gifts from foreign nations.

[The President] shall have Power, by and with the Advice and Consent of the Senate, to make Treaties, provided two thirds of the Senators present concur . . . . Article II, section 2.

The Senate's advice and consent role in treaties is one of several means by which Congress may influence foreign policy, the principal others being the war powers and the appropriations power noted above, and the confirmation authority listed below.

[The President] shall nominate, and by and with the Advice and Consent of the Senate, shall appoint Ambassadors, other public Ministers and Consuls, Judges of the supreme Court, and all other Officers of the United States, whose Appointments are not herein otherwise provided for, and which shall be established by Law: but the Congress may by Law vest the Appointment of such inferior Officers, as they think proper, in the President alone, in the Courts of Law, or in the Heads of Departments. Article II, section 2.

The requirement that the President obtain Senate approval of appointment of ambassadors, judges, and executive branch officers is an important check on the President's authority. Also significant are Congress' powers to create (and by implication abolish) offices (including executive departments and agencies), and to specify who shall have the appointment authority for "inferior" officers.

The Judicial Branch

Note: the impeachment power, set forth above as a check on the executive branch, applies as well to judges.

The judicial Power of the United States, shall be vested in one supreme Court, and in such inferior Courts as the Congress may from time to time ordain and establish. Article III, section 1.

The Congress shall have Power . . . To constitute Tribunals inferior to the supreme Court. Article I, section 8, cl. 9.

Congress may create inferior courts, and first did so in the Judiciary Act of 1789. By implication Congress may also abolish inferior federal courts, although in doing so Congress presumably must reassign judges, who have lifetime tenure.

In all Cases affecting Ambassadors, other public Ministers and Consuls, and those in which a State shall be a Party, the supreme Court shall have original Jurisdiction. In all the other Cases before mentioned, the supreme Court shall have appellate Jurisdiction, both as to Law and Fact, with such Exceptions, and under such Regulations as the Congress shall make. Article III, section 2, cl. 2.

The appellate jurisdiction of the Supreme Court, unlike its original jurisdiction, is subject to "exceptions" and "regulations" prescribed by Congress. Whether and to what extent Congress may deprive the Court of jurisdiction to hear constitutional issues is unsettled. Congress' authority to create and abolish "inferior" federal courts includes implicit authority to control jurisdiction of such courts.

The Trial of all Crimes . . . shall be held in the State where the said Crimes shall have been committed; but when not committed within any State, the Trial shall be at such Place or Places as the Congress may by Law have directed. Article III, section 2, cl. 3.

In all criminal prosecutions, the accused shall enjoy the right to a speedy and public trial, by an impartial jury of the State and district wherein the crime shall have been committed, which district shall have been previously ascertained by law . . . . Sixth Amendment.

Congress' broadest authority over the location of trials for federal crimes relates to crimes "not committed within any State" — i.e., crimes committed on the high seas, in territories of the United States, or at forts or other federal enclaves that are under the exclusive legislative jurisdiction of the United States.

The Privilege of the Writ of Habeas Corpus shall not be suspended, unless when in Cases of Rebellion or Invasion the public Safety may require it. Article I, section 9, cl. 2.

The power of Congress to suspend the writ of habeas corpus in cases of rebellion or invasion is generally conceded. The President's authority to do so is disputed; after initially suspending the writ on his own motion during the Civil War, President Lincoln sought and received congressional authorization.

Congress of the United States:
Powers,Structure, and Procedures

FOREIGN POLICY ROLES OF THE PRESIDENT AND CONGRESS

Richard F. Grimmett

Summary

The United States Constitution divides the foreign policy powers between the President and Congress so that both share in the making of foreign policy. The executive and legislative branches each play important roles that are different but that often overlap. Both branches have continuing opportunities to initiate and change foreign policy, and the interaction between them continues indefinitely throughout the life of a policy.

This report identifies and illustrates 12 basic ways to make U.S. foreign policy. The President or the executive branch can make foreign policy through:

1) — responses to foreign events
2) — proposals for legislation
3) — negotiation of international agreements
4) — policy statements
5) — policy implementation
6) — independent action.

In nearly all of these circumstances, Congress can either support the President's approach or seek to change it. In the case of independent Presidential action, it may be very difficult to change policy in the short term; in the case of a legislative proposal by the executive branch or treaties and international agreements submitted to the Senate or Congress for approval, Congress has a decisive voice. In most cases Congress supports the President, but it often makes significant modifications in his initiatives in the process of approving them.

Congress can make foreign policy through:

1) — resolutions and policy statements
2) — legislative directives
3) — legislative pressure
4) — legislative restrictions/funding denials
5) — informal advice
6) — congressional oversight.

In these circumstances, the executive branch can either support or seek to change congressional policies as it interprets and carries out legislative directives and restrictions, and decides when and whether to adopt proposals and advice.

The practices illustrated in this report indicate that making U.S. foreign policy is a complex process, and the support of both branches is required for a strong and effective U.S. foreign policy.

Introduction

The Constitution divides the foreign policy powers between the President and Congress but not in a definitive manner.[1] Edward S. Corwin wrote:

> What the Constitution does, *and all that it does*, is to confer on the President certain powers capable of affecting our foreign relations, and certain other powers of the same general kind on the Senate, and still other such powers on Congress; but which of these organs shall have the decisive and final voice in determining the course of the American nation is left for events to resolve.[2]

Events have confirmed that together the President and Congress make foreign policy, but they have not resolved the question of which branch originates or finally determines policy. The two branches share in the process and each plays an important but different role. The question of who makes foreign policy does not have a more precise answer for several reasons.

First, U.S. foreign policy is not created in a vacuum as some sort of indivisible whole with a single grand design. Rather, making foreign policy is a prolonged process involving many actors and comprising dozens of individual policies toward different countries, regions, and functional problems.

Second, the complex process of determining foreign policy makes it difficult to decide who should be credited with initiating or altering any particular foreign policy. The two branches constantly interact and influence each other. Under these circumstances, it is difficult to trace an idea back to its origin, determine when a proposal actually influences policy, and decide when a modification creates a new policy.[3]

Third, the roles and relative influence of the two branches in making foreign policy differ from time to time according to such factors as the personalities of the President and Members of Congress and the degree of consensus on policy. Throughout American history there have been ebbs and flows of Presidential and

---

[1]See appendix for excerpts from the U.S. Constitution relating to foreign policy powers.

[2]Corwin, Edward S. The President, Office and Powers, 1787-1957. New York, New York University Press, 1957. p. 171 (emphasis in original).

[3]Baldwin, David A. Congressional Initiative in Foreign Policy. The Journal of Politics, November 1966. p. 754-773.

congressional dominance in making foreign policy, variously defined by different scholars. One study classified the period 1789-1829 as one of Presidential initiative; 1829-1898 as one of congressional supremacy; and 1899 through the immediate post-World War II period as one of growing Presidential power.[4] Another study defined three periods of congressional dominance, 1837-1861, 1869-1897, and 1918-1936, with a fourth one beginning toward the end of the Vietnam War in 1973.[5] During the Reagan and Bush Administrations the pendulum swung back toward Presidential dominance, reaching its height in 1991 during Operation Desert Storm against Iraq.[6] In the post-Persian Gulf war era, both President and the Congress are confronted with issues in foreign policy that may well define which branch of government will play the dominant role during the first decade of the twenty-first century.

For many years a perception existed that the executive branch usually initiated foreign policy with the implication that this relegated Congress to an inconsequential role. Writing in 1950 Robert Dahl wrote, "Perhaps the single most important fact about Congress and its role in foreign policy, therefore, is that it rarely provides the initiative. Most often initiative springs from the executive-administrative branch."[7] In 1962 James A. Robinson studied 22 case studies of foreign policies over the previous 30 years and found three cases of congressional initiative: the 1943 repeal of the Chinese exclusion laws, the 1943 Fulbright resolution calling for postwar participation in an international organization, and the 1958 Monroney resolution proposing the International Development Association.[8] Francis O. Wilcox, who was Staff Director of the Senate Foreign Relations Committee from 1947-1955, and Assistant Secretary of State for International Organization Affairs from 1955-1961, has argued, however, that "some of the most imaginative and constructive foreign policies since World War II have originated in Congress."[9]

In the period after the Vietnam War, Congress reasserted its role in foreign policy. It on occasion initiated new policies and exerted decisive influence on policies initiated by the executive branch. One study on the subject concluded that "the fact remains that the President is still in charge of American foreign policy," but it noted also that "the American Congress has more power to influence foreign affairs than its counterpart in any other country."[10] Another study concluded: "For all the problems

---

[4]Cheever, Daniel S., and H. Field Haviland, Jr. American Foreign Policy and the Separation of Powers. Cambridge, Harvard University Press, 1952. 244 p.

[5]Franck, Thomas M., and Edward Weisband. Foreign Policy by Congress. New York, Oxford University Press, 1979. 357 p.

[6]U.S. Congress. House. Congress and Foreign Policy, 1991. Washington, G.P.O., 1992, p. 19.

[7]Dahl, Robert A. Congress and Foreign Policy. New York, Norton, 1950. p . 58.

[8]Robinson, James A. Congress and Foreign Policy-Making. Homewood, Ill., Dorsey Press, 1967. p. 66.

[9]Wilcox, Francis O. Congress, the Executive, and Foreign Policy. New York, Harper and Row, 1971, p.14.

[10]Crabb, Cecil V., Jr., and Pat M. Holt. Invitation to Struggle: Congress, the President and (continued...)

caused by a resurgent Congress with unprecedented resources and a will to be involved more directly in foreign policy, the system is working much more the way the Founding Fathers devised it than we have seen in some time."[11]

This report identifies and illustrates 12 major ways to make U.S. foreign policy, six utilized by the President or the executive branch, and six utilized by the Congress. No attempt has been made to measure how often the various practices are used. However, the findings of the report are consistent with Corwin's classic statement that:

> ...actual *practice* under the Constitution has shown that, while the President is usually in a position to *propose*, the Senate and the Congress are often in a technical position at least to *dispose*. The verdict of history, in short, is that the power to determine the substantive content of American foreign policy is a *divided* power, with the lion's share falling usually, though by no means always, to the President.[12]

This report does not attempt to define how a policy is made within a branch, as this is a complex and varied process and would require a detailed study of each case. Several case studies of this type are indicated in footnotes, and illustrations mentioned in the report highlight some of the many individuals and groups within each branch who contribute to policy formation.[13] Similarly, the report does not examine the influence of groups outside the executive and legislative branches, but the illustrations show that such groups, including the judiciary, interest groups, the press, and the public at large, can sometimes play an important role.

---

[10](...continued)
Foreign Policy. Washington, Congressional Quarterly Press, 1980. p. 3.

[11]Ornstein, Norman. The Constitution and the Sharing of Foreign Policy Responsibility. In The President, the Congress, and Foreign Policy. New York, Association of Former Members of Congress and the Atlantic Council of the United States, 1985. p.64.

[12]Corwin, The President, Office and Powers, p. 171(emphasis in original).

[13]For a collection of case studies, see the Congress and Foreign Policy committee prints, prepared by the Congressional Research Service and published by the House Foreign Affairs Committee, annually, from 1974 to 1992. These committee prints are subsequently cited as Congress and Foreign Policy, together with their pertinent year of coverage.

The President as Initiator

Following are six basic ways the President or executive branch can originate or initially shape foreign policy. In these circumstances, Congress is put in the position of either responding positively to the President's initiative or seeking to adjust or reverse the impact of his position.

Response to Foreign Events

Current events in foreign countries or a sudden action by a foreign government often challenge U.S. interests. As spokesman and head of the foreign service, the armed forces, the intelligence services, and the bureaucracy, the President usually responds to such events and thus initiates U.S. policy. Congress ordinarily supports the President, but on occasion seeks a change in policy.

For example, Congress supported President Reagan in the Falkland Islands crisis between Argentina and the United Kingdom. After Argentina in April 1982 seized and occupied the Falkland Islands, which the United Kingdom claimed as a crown colony, the U.S. executive branch sought to mediate the dispute. When Argentina refused one of the U.S. peace overtures, Secretary of State Alexander Haig announced that the United States would prohibit arms sales to Argentina and provide material support for British operations. Both Houses of Congress passed resolutions supporting the U.S. action siding with the United Kingdom.[14] The crisis ended in June 1982, and in December 1983 the Department of State lifted the ban on arms sales to Argentina.

Congress helped bring about a change in Administration-initiated policy in response to events in Lebanon.[15] In September 1983, Congress reached a compromise with the Reagan Administration, and agreed to authorize participation in the Multinational Force in Lebanon for 18 months[16]. After a terrorist bombing attack in Beirut on October 23, 1983, that killed more than 200 Marines, President Reagan first took the position that the United States had vital national interests in Lebanon and would continue to participate in the Multinational Force. Prominent Members of Congress questioned the policy, and some proposed an amendment to cut off funds for participation. While the amendment was defeated, criticism of the policy continued. The Subcommittee on Investigations of the House Armed Services Committee and a Department of Defense Commission headed by retired Admiral Robert Long both filed reports in December 1983 that questioned the U.S. ability to achieve its objectives by the use of the Marines. Public opinion polls also indicated that a majority of Americans thought the Marines should be withdrawn. On February 7, 1984, President Reagan announced that the Marines would be redeployed to ships

---

[14]U.S. Congress. House. Congress and Foreign Policy, 1982. p. 10.

[15]For further discussions see Preece, Richard M. Congress and the Conflict in Lebanon. Congress and Foreign Policy, 1983, p. 11-28; and Laipson, Ellen. Congress and the Withdrawal of the Marines from Lebanon. Congress and Foreign Policy, 1984, p. 11-20.

[16]Multinational Force in Lebanon Resolution , P.L. 98-119, signed October 12, 1983.

off the coast of Lebanon, and in March he reported that U.S. participation in the Multinational Force had ended.

On August 2, 1990, President Bush responded to the Iraqi invasion of Kuwait the previous day by immediately applying full economic sanctions against Iraq, and, within a week, deploying U.S. Armed Forces to help defend Saudi Arabia against potential attack. In October Congress supported continued action through the United Nations, and enacted the economic sanctions into law. In January 1991, Congress authorized the use of the U.S. Armed Forces to implement U.N. Security Council resolutions.[17]

President Bill Clinton authorized U.S. actions in support of U.N. and NATO operations aimed at halting the fighting in the former territory of Yugoslavia, particularly in Bosnia. Under President Clinton the United States participated in airlifts into Sarajevo, Bosnia, naval monitoring of sanctions, aerial enforcement of a "no-fly zone", and aerial enforcement of safe havens. In December 1995, President Clinton authorized the deployment of over 20,000 American combat troops to Bosnia as part of a NATO-led peacekeeping force to help enforce the Dayton peace accords aimed at resolving the Bosnian conflict. Subsequently, in December 1996, President Clinton agreed to provide up to 8,500 American ground troops to participate in a NATO-led follow-on force in Bosnia termed the Stabilization Force (SFOR). These actions were taken by the President in the absence of express congressional approval, and despite continuing disputes between the Congress and the President over the proper course of action for the U.S. in the Bosnian conflict.[18]

Following the seizure of Haiti's government by Haitian military leader Raul Cedras in July 1993 from its President Jean-Bertrand Aristide, the United Nations took a number of steps to support the restoration of Aristide to power, including an embargo, and in July 1994, authorizing a multinational force to facilitate the departure of the military leadership in Haiti. In mid September 1994, President Clinton sent a U.S. negotiating team to Haiti to urge the peaceful departure of the military junta, while ordering the U.S. military to prepare for an invasion of Haiti, if necessary, to restore President Aristide. The military junta agreed to leave Haiti peacefully in the face of an imminent U.S. invasion. Subsequently, the U.S. sent approximately 21,000 military forces to Haiti to disarm Haitian military and paramilitary forces, and to aid a U.N. peacekeeping operation in restoring civil government and order in Haiti. President Clinton undertook the Haiti operation without the prior approval of Congress and was criticized for this. Congress subsequently passed S.J. Res. 229 in October 1994 (signed as P.L. 103-423) which stated the sense of Congress that the

---

[17]See Mark, Clyde. Congress and Iraq, 1990, in Congress and Foreign Policy, 1990, p. 109-137, and Kenneth Katzman, War and Peace in the Middle East, Congress and Foreign Policy 1991, p. 21-53.

[18]See Grimmett, Richard F. War Powers Resolution: Presidential Compliance. CRS Issue Brief 81050. Woehrel, Steven and Julie Kim. Bosnia-Former Yugoslavia and U.S. Policy. CRS Archived Issue Brief 91089 and Bowman, Steven R. Bosnia: U.S. Military Operations. CRS Issue Brief 93056.

President should have sought congressional approval before deploying U.S. forces to Haiti and supported a prompt and orderly withdrawal as soon as possible.[19]

Administration Proposal for Legislation

On occasion, the executive branch wants to begin a foreign policy program that requires legislation or appropriations, and accordingly proposes legislation to Congress. Congressional approval in this situation is essential. Congress may play a more or less active role in the development of the legislation, modifying the Administration bill or developing entirely new legislation of its own.

The classic example of a policy proposed by the Administration but subsequently developed by both branches working together cooperatively is the Marshall plan.[20] On June 5, 1947, Secretary of State George Marshall proposed U.S. assistance for European recovery on condition that the European nations initiate and agree on plans for an aid program. The Western European governments responded with a proposal for a program based on 4 years of U.S. assistance. To allow sufficient time for consideration, President Truman requested an interim aid program that was passed by Congress in December 1947. He then submitted to Congress the proposal for the longer term European Recovery Program. Congress created a Select Committee on Foreign Aid that made an independent study of the needs in Europe. The Senate Foreign Relations and House Foreign Affairs Committees also held extensive hearings, and the legislation that emerged was widely considered to be the product of a bipartisan, joint effort of both branches.

Since then Presidents have annually proposed foreign assistance programs that Congress has authorized or appropriated after modifying as it saw fit, often using the legislation as a vehicle for initiatives of its own. In 1978, for example, Congress required a new emphasis in both bilateral and multilateral aid for programs designed to meet basic human needs, and also launched a Women in Development program to promote attention to women in the economic development process.[21] After democratic reforms occurred in Poland and Hungary during 1989, President Bush proposed an aid package and trade benefits for the two countries. As the year continued and all of Eastern Europe was transformed by the replacement of Communist governments with democratic reforms, Congress enlarged the package and urged more active U.S. support for the growing democratic movements.[22]

---

[19]See Taft-Morales, Maureen E. Haiti Under President Preval: Issues for Congress. CRS Issue Brief 96019.

[20]For further discussion see Hutchinson, Martha Crenshaw. The Marshall Plan Model: A Case Study of the Congressional Information Problem. In Executive-Legislative Consultation on Foreign Policy, Strengthening the Legislative Side. House Foreign Affairs Committee Print, April 1982. p. 77-85.

[21]See Sanford, Jonathan E. International Economic Assistance. In Congress and Foreign Policy, 1978. p. 73-100.

[22]See Miko, Francis. Congress and the Transformation of Eastern Europe in 1989, in Congress and Foreign Policy, 1989, p. 19-37.

President Clinton in April 1993 proposed a major increase in United States assistance to Russia following a summit at Vancouver, Canada, with Russian Prime Minister Boris Yeltsin. The $1.6 billion U.S. assistance package, using existing appropriated funds, included more concessional terms for agricultural loans and an increase in assistance targeted at privatization. Further, funding was targeted at resettling Russian officers and providing employment training to assist their return to civilian life, while facilitating their withdrawal from the Baltics. The President stated that 75% of the assistance would be used outside of Moscow to make it more highly visible to the average Russian citizen than earlier U.S. aid programs. All such assistance efforts were aimed at advancing democratization in Russia.[23]

Negotiation of International Agreements

The power of negotiation gives the executive branch a dominant role in making foreign policy through international agreements, but the President must take into account congressional opinion because often agreements must be approved by the Senate or Congress. Congress also influences agreements by placing in legislation instructions and views concerning international agreements, indicating through various means what kind of agreement would be acceptable, and attaching reservations or other conditions when approving an agreement.

A few international agreements might be called "sole executive agreements" because the President considers that he has the authority to conclude them under his own powers and does not submit them to the Senate as treaties nor to Congress for approval.[24] Examples are the Yalta Agreement of 1945, the Vietnam Peace Agreement of 1973, the Iranian Hostage Agreement of 1981, and the Afghanistan Settlement Agreement of April 14, 1988.

Most international agreements, however, have some form of congressional participation. The Senate must approve treaties by a two-thirds majority. The bulk of executive agreements are either authorized by Congress prior to their conclusion or approved after their conclusion, and might be called congressional-executive agreements. As an example of prior action, Congress has authorized the executive branch to conclude agreements on military and economic assistance, space and nuclear energy cooperation, and foreign trade, and has set forth goals, guidelines, and criteria in the authorizing legislation. As an example of action after conclusion, Congress approved the SALT I interim agreement of 1972 by a joint resolution, with the Jackson amendment which requested that the President seek a future treaty that would not limit the United States to levels of strategic forces inferior to Soviet levels.

---

[23]For further discussion see Tarnoff, Curt. U.S. Assistance to the Soviet Union and Its Successor States 1991-1996: A History of Administration and Congressional Action. CRS Report 98-43F. January 14, 1998. 31p.

[24]For further discussion of various types of international agreements, see Treaties and Other International Agreements: The Role of the United States Senate. A Study Prepared for the Committee on Foreign Relations by the Congressional Research Service. Washington, G.P.O., November 1993. S. Prt. 103-53. 384 p.

In the case of trade agreements such as the North American Free Trade Agreement (NAFTA) and agreements negotiated under the auspices of the General Agreement on Trade and Tariffs (GATT), Congress has authorized negotiations in advance but required that it approve the agreement prior to its implementation.[25] The implementing legislation for both the NAFTA and the GATT Uruguay Round agreements was considered under so-called "fast-track" procedures in 1993 and 1994 respectively. This process had been developed during the Nixon and Ford Administrations to protect a President's ability to negotiate trade agreements with some confidence that they would not be undermined later by Congress through the traditional rules applied to legislation. Under "fast-track" rules, Congress was given 90 days to take action on the implementing bill after its formal introduction. Congress could not amend the bill. Each congressional committee of jurisdiction was given 45 days to review the proposed legislation. The proposed bill was then only subject to a yes or no vote in the House and the Senate. Since Congress could not amend the final legislation, a practice developed over the years whereby informal committee markup sessions were held on the draft implementing bills to indicate to the President key areas of Congressional concern regarding the specific trade legislation. This process afforded the President the opportunity to address these concerns as he deemed appropriate prior to submitting a final bill to implement the trade agreement. The debates over the NAFTA and the GATT Uruguay Round agreements were very contentious. Following passage of the implementing vehicle for the latter in a lame duck session of Congress in late 1994, the President's authority to use "fast-track" procedures lapsed. A subsequent effort by the Clinton Administration to secure renewal of this authority was dropped in late 1997 due to insufficient bipartisan support for granting it. In the fall of 1998 a bill to restore "fast-track" authority failed to pass the House of Representatives[26]

Legislative-executive branch interchange has been especially complex in the treaties relating to strategic arms reductions. In preparation for the Strategic Arms Reduction Treaty (START), the Senate and House formed Observer Groups to monitor the negotiations. After the START Treaty was submitted to the Senate on November 25, 1991, the Soviet Union ceased to exist and Senators worked with the Administration in deciding how to handle the new situation. A new protocol amending the treaty was negotiated in Lisbon with the Soviet successor states. The Senate approved the START Treaty on October 1, 1992, with several conditions, including that Belarus, Kazakhstan, Russia, and Ukraine be legally bound to all the obligations of the Soviet Union in the treaty.

---

[25]Sek, Lenore. Congress and Trade Negotiating Authority. In Congress and Foreign Policy, 1991, p. 103-117.

[26]For additional background see: Grimmett, Jeanne J. Why Certain Trade Agreements Are Approved as Congressional-Executive Agreements Rather Than as Treaties. CRS Report for Congress 97-896A. September 29, 1997. 6p. Howe, Robert H. North American Free Trade Agreement (NAFTA) and Related Issues: A Checklist of CRS Products. CRS Report for Congress 97-907L. October 9, 1997. 4p. Wilson, Arlene. The GATT and the WTO: An Overview. CRS Report for Congress 95-424E. March 27, 1995. 6p. Pregelj, Vladimir N. Trade Agreements: Renewing the Negotiating and Fast-Track Implementing Authority. CRS Issue Brief 97016.

Policy Statements

The President also establishes U.S. foreign policy through unilateral statements or joint statements issued with other governments. Sometimes unilateral statements are broad descriptions of American goals and objectives. In an address to the United Nations on September 21, 1992, President Bush called for strengthening the peacekeeping capabilities of the United Nations. Other times, the President articulates policy on a specific issue. In the State of the Union Address of January 28, 1992, President Bush proposed that the United States and Russia eliminate all their land-based multiple warhead ballistic missiles. On April 5, 1991, President Bush announced the United States would join international efforts to airdrop relief supplies to Kurdish refugees along the Iraqi-Turkish border. In January 1994, the Clinton Administration proposed the expansion of the alliance at the NATO summit. With Congressional support over the next four years, a number of gradual steps were taken leading to the Senate giving its consent to the amendment of the North Atlantic Treaty on April 30, 1998, by a vote of 80-19, permitting the admission of Poland, the Czech Republic and Hungary to the alliance.[27]

Joint statements—policy statements made with other countries—are not legally binding international agreements, but they commit the President to a course of action. At the conclusion of the summit conference in Tokyo on May 5, 1986, for example, leaders of seven nations including the United States issued a joint statement pledging to fight terrorism through specified economic and diplomatic actions. At the conclusion of the economic summit of the Group of Seven on July 8, 1992, the leaders issued a communique embodying a wide range of policies including support for the strategy of cooperation between the Russian Government and the International Monetary Fund.

Congress may support the policy enunciated by the President, attempt to change it, or find a way to participate in the further development of the policy. After the Conference on Security and Cooperation in Europe in Helsinki, on August 1, 1975, President Ford and 34 other heads of state signed the Final Act of the Conference that provided for the freer flow of people and information between East and West Europe. Congress by legislation established a Commission on Security and Cooperation in Europe to monitor the implementation of the accords.[28] Since that time the Commission, 12 of whose 15 members are Members of Congress, has closely monitored the accords and played an active role in development of U.S. policy in this area.

The executive branch makes a policy statement when it casts the U.S. vote in international organizations. Most measures adopted by international organizations, such as United Nations General Assembly resolutions, are not legally binding, but they put the United States on record as for or against a proposed course of action. The executive branch also determines the U.S. position on resolutions of the United

---

[27]Katzman, Kenneth. War and Peace in the Middle East. Congress and Foreign Policy, 1991, p. 21-53. Gallis, Paul E. NATO: Congress Addresses Expansion of the Alliance. CRS Issue Brief 95076.

[28]P.L. 94-304, approved June 3, 1976.

Nations Security Council, which many authorities consider binding, such as Resolution 678 (1990) calling for nations to use "all necessary means" to uphold earlier resolutions aimed at getting Iraq to withdraw from Kuwait.

Congress sometimes influences the U.S. vote in international organizations. It has on several occasions directed U.S. representatives in international financial institutions to vote in a specified manner. For example, in 1992 Congress provided that the Secretary of the Treasury should direct the U.S. Executive Director of the Inter-American Development Bank to vote against funding for any project of the Multilateral Investment Fund if the project was likely to cause loss of jobs in the United States. Members of Congress also serve on inter-parliamentary groups such as the North Atlantic Assembly and the parliamentary assembly of the Organization on Security and Cooperation in Europe, where their views may affect the perspectives and votes of members from other participating nations.[29]

Whenever implementation of the measures promised by the executive in unilateral or joint statements requires legislation or appropriations, Congress has more power in deciding whether to support or modify U.S. policy. When the Administration pledges funds to the multilateral development banks, for example, the funds must be authorized and appropriated by Congress. The United States could not increase its quota in the International Monetary Fund for assistance to Russia in 1992 until Congress appropriated the necessary funds.[30]

Policy Implementation

Even when Congress establishes foreign policy through legislation, the Administration continues to shape policy as it interprets and applies the various provisions of law. This is illustrated in arms sales policy. Congress has established the objectives and criteria for arms sales to foreign countries in the Arms Export Control Act, and it has required advance notification of major arms sales and provided procedures for halting a sale it disapproves. But the executive branch makes the daily decisions on whether or not to sell arms to specific countries and what weapons systems to provide. As an example, on September 14, 1992, President Bush notified Congress of his intention to sell 72 F-15 fighter aircraft to Saudi Arabia, and after the 30-day congressional review period expired, the sale proceeded.

Congress has found it necessary to maintain close supervision to prevent sales, particularly to Middle Eastern countries, that it did not approve. In some cases its actions had the effect of halting sales, and it has frequently brought about changes in proposed arms sales packages.[31] In 1985 Congress passed a joint resolution (P.L. 99-162) prohibiting a proposed sale of certain advanced aircraft and air defense systems

---

[29]Foreign Operations Appropriations Act, Title I, P.L. 102-391, signed Oct. 5, 1992.

[30]P.L. 102-391, signed Oct. 6, 1992.

[31]For further information see Grimmett, Richard F. Executive-Legislative Consultations on U.S. Arms Sales. U.S. Congress. House. Committee on Foreign Affairs. Committee Print, December 1982. 39 p. See also Arms Sales, Congressional Review Process, by Grimmett, Richard F. CRS Report for Congress 96-971F. 6p.

to Jordan prior to March 1, 1986, unless direct and meaningful peace negotiations between Israel and Jordan were underway. After the date passed, the Administration did not propose the sale, apparently in the belief it would be disapproved by Congress. In 1986 both Houses passed a joint resolution disapproving a sale of advanced missiles to Saudi Arabia, and the President vetoed the resolution; the Senate sustained the veto by a 66-34 vote, but only after the Administration removed Stinger (hand-held) missiles from the package.

Since the 1980s various Administrations have used their authority to establish regulatory guidelines for the export of U.S.-origin dual-use technologies. In the case of exports to China since the 1989 Tiananmen Square crackdown, U.S. law has required that China cannot obtain commercial satellites or related technology from the United States unless the President issues a waiver of this restriction, on a case-by-case basis, on the grounds that such a transaction is in the U.S. national interest or because China has made reforms in its human rights or political practices. In March of 1996, President Clinton transferred authority for issuing export licenses from the State Department to the Commerce Department. Subsequently, when it was discovered that two U.S. companies had shared technical information regarding the cause of an explosion of a Chinese rocket launching a U.S. commercial satellite, without having secured a license to do so from the State Department, a Justice Department investigation was launched. In the wake of the controversy over this transfer of technical information regarding satellites to China and charges that insufficient scrutiny was being given to security issues involved in such prospective transfers, Congress by an amendment to the FY1999 National Defense Authorization Act (P.L. 105-261), transferred authority to license commercial satellite and related data exports from the Commerce Department back to the State Department, effective in March 1999.

Independent Action

Occasionally the President undertakes a dramatic or sudden foreign policy action before Congress is fully informed about it. Congress then is faced with the dilemma of supporting the action or being charged with undercutting the President before the world. Congress usually supports the President, but on occasion it tries to halt or reverse the policy or pass legislation to restrain the President from similar actions in the future.

When President Reagan launched a military invasion of Grenada on October 24, 1983, Congress essentially supported the President in his stated effort to prevent the formation of a Communist foothold there. Although both Houses of Congress passed separate measures that would invoke the War Powers Resolution, neither measure was passed by both Houses.[32] Congressional leaders apparently received assurances

---

[32]The War Powers Resolution, P.L. 93-148, was passed over the veto of President Nixon in November 1973 to assure that both the President and Congress participate in decisions that might involve the United States in war. It requires the President to consult with Congress in every possible instance prior to the introduction of armed forces into hostilities or situations of imminent hostilities, and establishes a time limit of 60-90 days for U.S. forces to remain

(continued...)

from the White House that the troops would be out within 60 days, and public opinion strongly supported the action. Congress also supported the President's action by approving $15 million for grant economic assistance programs to Grenada.

Similarly, when President Reagan ordered the bombing of Libya on April 15, 1986, to counter state-supported terrorism, and when President Bush ordered the invasion of Panama on December 20, 1989, to apprehend General Manuel Noriega, most Members supported the President's effort. Widespread public support greeted the President's action and was also a factor in determining the congressional response.

In another instance, President Clinton addressed a financial crisis in Mexico, after a devaluation of the peso in late December 1994. In an effort to prevent Mexican default on billions of dollars worth of debt obligations, in early 1995, the President's economic advisors crafted a package of support for Mexico that did not require a Congressional vote on the controversial proposal. This action was taken when it appeared possible that Congress would not enact the Administration's legislation to deal with the crisis. The independent initiative by President Clinton included $20 billion in credits from the Exchange Stabilization Fund (ESF) of the Treasury Department, which is normally used to stabilize the U.S. dollar's value; $10 billion in credits from the Bank for International Settlements, and $17.8 billion from the International Monetary Fund (IMF). The Clinton Administration's independent intervention in the Mexican peso crisis led to significant criticism in Congress, but efforts to modify or block it were either defeated or abandoned.[33]

Occasionally, however, Congress significantly refines or alters a policy independently undertaken by the President. This was the case in the 1979 policy change toward the People's Republic of China and Taiwan. On December 15, 1978, President Carter announced suddenly that the United States would establish diplomatic relations with the People's Republic of China on January 1, 1979, and terminate the defense treaty with the Republic of China on Taiwan after the one year's notice required by the treaty. The Administration also submitted legislation to govern future relations with Taiwan.

While few Members of Congress opposed the establishment of relations with China, a move anticipated since President Nixon's trip to China in 1972, many Members sought to modify the practical implications of the new policy and reassure allies in the Pacific. Congress added sections to the Taiwan Relations Act to affirm that the United States would consider any nonpeaceful effort against Taiwan as a threat to the Western Pacific and would provide Taiwan with defensive arms to maintain a sufficient self-defense capability. Congress also made modifications in the

---

[32](...continued)
in such situations without congressional authorization.

[33]For background see Storrs, K. Larry. Mexico-U.S. Relations: Issues for Congress. Issue Brief 97028, and "Clinton Leads Mexico Bailout Effort," Congressional Quarterly Almanac 1995, pp. 10-16 and 10-17.

legislation aimed at continuing economic ties and placing Taiwan-U.S. relations on a firmer legal basis.[34]

Senator Barry Goldwater and other Members of Congress filed suit against the President for terminating the security treaty with the Republic of China without the approval of two-thirds of the Senate or a majority of both Houses of Congress. Senator Goldwater also introduced legislation to bar the President from terminating other defense treaties without congressional participation. While neither effort was successful, they illustrated that in undertaking independent action, the President risks punitive action by Congress that may reduce future flexibility in foreign policy actions.

The Congress as Initiator

Following are six basic ways in which Congress can originate or shape foreign policy. In these circumstances, the executive branch is put in the position of responding positively to the congressional initiative or seeking to adjust or reverse its impact on the course of foreign policy.

Resolutions and Policy Statements

Every year Members of Congress introduce large numbers of simple or concurrent resolutions stating the sense of the House, Senate, or Congress on foreign policy, and many such resolutions are adopted. Many observers are skeptical about the effectiveness of these sense of the House, Senate, or Congress resolutions. Like Presidential policy statements, they express the policy of a single branch of government, but their effect is often weaker because Congress does not execute policy. Since simple and concurrent resolutions are not legally binding, the executive branch often ignores them in carrying out foreign policy.

Nevertheless, sometimes such resolutions play a significant role in foreign policy by launching a new idea or promoting a new policy. S. Res. 264, introduced by Senator A. S. Mike Monroney, and adopted July 23, 1958, led to the establishment of the International Development Association as an affiliate of the World Bank designed to make low-interest, long-term loans. In 1973 the Senate adopted S. Res. 71, introduced by Senator Claiborne Pell, calling for an international agreement "prohibiting environmental or geophysical modification activity as a weapon of war." Such an agreement was subsequently negotiated and ratified by the United States in 1979. In 1979 the House passed H. Res. 321 urging the United Nations to convene an emergency session of the General Assembly to deal with the refugee crisis in Southeast Asia. This added to other calls for such a conference and subsequently a United Nations Conference was convened in July 1979. H.Con. Res. 248, adopted September 17, 1990, called for a higher priority for environmental concerns and urged increased attention to the linkage between the environment and national security.

---

[34]For further discussion see Sutter, Robert. Congress and U.S. Policy in Asia: New Relationships with China and Taiwan. In Congress and Foreign Policy, 1979, p. 54-71, and Executive-Legislative Consultations on China Policy, 1978-1979. House Foreign Affairs Committee Print, June 1980. 42 p.

Holding hearings on resolutions has occasionally given impetus to a policy even though the resolution itself did not pass. In 1967 Senator Pell introduced S. Res. 172 relating to international regulation of ocean activities. The Administration opposed the resolution and it was not adopted, but later the concept came to fruition in the seabed arms control treaty of 1971.

Simple and concurrent resolutions also serve as a channel of communication between Congress and foreign countries. While often the communications to foreign governments are formal messages of sympathy, congratulations, and appreciation, at other times they are more substantive. H. Con. Res. 484 of August 8, 1988, called on President Zia of Pakistan, consistent with his pledge of May 29, 1988, to hold free and fair elections not later than November 16, 1988. H. Con. Res. 136 of May 24, 1989, called on the Chinese Government to resolve the political crisis in China without violence. Congress annually passed resolutions calling for Baltic Freedom and commemorating "Captive Nations Week" from 1959 until independence was achieved by Lithuania, Latvia, and Estonia in 1991.

Sense of the Congress resolutions also provide a vehicle for support or advice to the President on foreign policy. After the U.S. military intervention in the Dominican Republic in 1965, for example, the House passed H. Res. 560 supporting the President in any action he deemed necessary to prevent Communist subversive aggression in the Western Hemisphere.[35] On May 5, 1986, the House adopted H. Res. 424 supporting the President's policy in Libya by expressing gratitude to the United Kingdom for allowing U.S. bombers stationed there to participate in the April 14, 1986, raid aimed at terrorist bases in Libya.

Congressional concerns over United States involvement in the developing internal conflicts in former Yugoslavia—Bosnia and Kosovo in particular—led to passage of sense of the Congress resolutions. Section 8100 of the Defense Appropriations Act for fiscal year 1995 (P.L. 103-335, signed September 30, 1994) stated the sense of Congress that DoD funds should not be made available for the purpose of deploying U.S. armed forces to participate in implementation of a peace settlement in Bosnia, unless previously authorized by Congress. On March 11, 1999, the House passed H.Con. Res. 42 by a vote of 219-191, expressing the sense of Congress that the President was authorized to deploy U.S. troops to Kosovo as part of a NATO peacekeeping operation, subject to conditions and various reporting requirements. On March 23, 1999, the Senate by a vote of 58-41 passed S. Con. Res. 21 expressing the sense of the Congress that the President was authorized to conduct "military air operations and missile strikes in cooperation with our NATO allies against the Federal Republic of Yugoslavia (Serbia and Montenegro). This Senate concurrent resolution was passed in reaction to the Serbian military actions in Kosovo and President Clinton's request, on March 23, 1999, for "legislative support" of his actions to deal with the Kosovo crisis. Subsequently, on April 28, 1999, the House

---

[35]For additional information see: Hutchinson, Martha Crenshaw. The Dominican Republic Intervention in 1965: A Case Study of the Congressional Information Problem. In U.S. Congress. House. Committee on Foreign Affairs. Executive-Legislative Consultation on Foreign Policy: Strengthening Foreign Policy Information Sources for Congress. Committee Print, February 1982. Washington, G.P.O., 1982. p. 73-84.

by a tie vote of 213-213 defeated S.Con. Res. 21, as well as a joint resolution, H.J. Res. 44, declaring war against Yugoslavia. Through these votes at least one house of the Congress indicated its skepticism of current Administration policy toward resolving the Kosovo conflict[36]

Legislative Directives

Congress sometimes initiates a foreign policy by using legislation to establish a new program, set objectives and guidelines, authorize and direct the executive branch to undertake specified activities, and by earmarking appropriations to be used in a specified way. The executive branch influences this kind of policy initiative because Members regularly seek Administration views in the process of formulating legislation, the President must approve legislation unless it is passed over a Presidential veto, and the executive branch implements the legislation.

As examples, in 1991 Congress took the lead in using defense funds to provide assistance to the former Soviet Union, authorizing and appropriating funds to dismantle Soviet nuclear weapons and provide military transportation for humanitarian assistance.[37] In 1992 Congress placed new sanctions and controls against Iran, Iraq, and nations or persons who assisted them in acquiring weapons of mass destruction.[38]

In 1997 and 1998, Congress was principally responsible for advancing legislation aimed at elevating the importance of combating religious persecution worldwide among U.S. foreign policy objectives. On October 27, 1998, the International Religious Freedom Act was signed into law (H.R. 2431, P.L. 105-292). This act established within the State Department an Office of International Religious Freedom headed by an Ambassador at Large, subject to confirmation by the Senate. This Ambassador is charged with , among other things, recommending appropriate U.S. government responses where the right to religious freedom abroad is violated, including preparing an annual report on country practices regarding religious freedoms. This law specifies sanctions against countries if they are determined to have engaged in or tolerated particularly severe violations of religious freedom.[39]

---

[36]For background see: Kim, Julie and Steven J. Woehrel. Bosnia-Former Yugoslavia and U.S. Policy. CRS Issue Brief 91089 and Woehrel, Steven and Julie Kim. Kosovo and U.S. Policy. CRS Issue Brief 98041. U.S. Congress. Congressional Record, Senate, March 23, 1999, p.S3101 and Congressional Record, House, April 28, 1999, pp. H2440-H2441, H2451-H2452 (daily edition).

[37]Conventional Armed Forces in Europe Treaty Implementation Act, P.L. 102-228, December 12, 1991. For case study, see Congress and the Transformation of the Soviet Union, by Nichol, James P. in Congress and Foreign Policy, 1991, p. 55-81.

[38]Iran-Iraq Arms Non-Proliferation Act of 1992, Title XVI of National Defense Authorization Act for Fiscal Year 1993, P.L. 102-484, signed October 23, 1992.

[39]For background see: Bite, Vita. Religious Persecution Abroad: Congressional Concerns and Actions. CRS Report 97-968F.

Legislative Pressure

Sometimes Congress pressures the executive branch into a new direction in foreign policy by threatening to pass legislation, even though the legislation is not enacted, or by continuing to exhort a policy through many means.

An example is the congressional effort in the 1980s to pass legislation imposing economic and other sanctions against South Africa. The effort was widely seen to have prodded the Reagan Administration to establish limited economic sanctions. Dissatisfied with the Administration's policy of "constructive engagement" and quiet diplomacy to bring an end to apartheid in South Africa, the House in 1983 approved legislation applying sanctions against South Africa as part of an extension of the Export Administration Act, but the bill was rejected by the Senate. Toward the end of 1984, American civil rights leaders began daily protests at the South African Embassy in Washington to focus greater attention on racial violence in South Africa and the repressive policies of the white minority government in South Africa. In June 1985 the House passed H.R. 1460 imposing sanctions and threatening a future cutoff of U.S. investment. The Senate followed with S. 995 providing military sanctions. The conference report called for a compromise that included a ban on U.S. import of South African Krugerrands. Before the Senate voted on the final bill, on September 9, 1985, President Reagan issued an executive order imposing sanctions that banned computer sales to the South African police and military and other government agencies that enforce apartheid, exports of nuclear technology to South Africa, and further bank loans to the South African Government. Later the President banned the importation of South African Krugerrands. Nonetheless in 1986 Congress enacted comprehensive sanctions against South Africa over the veto of President Reagan.[40]

Congress for several years pressured President Bush to take a greater leadership role in protecting the international environment. In 1989 many Members criticized the President for not leading a world effort to deal with global warming. After numerous congressional efforts to persuade the administration, including letters, hearings, and a Senate amendment calling for a global conference on the environment in 1989, the President offered to host an international meeting as a step toward negotiations on an international agreement to deal with global warming. Congress also pressed other countries to take environmentally beneficial action in foreign aid legislation.[41]

On June 9, 1998, Congress passed the Iran Missile Proliferation Sanctions Act (H.R. 2709) which would have imposed various sanctions on foreign entities that aided Iran's efforts to develop ballistic missiles. This legislation was vetoed by President Clinton on June 23, 1998. Nevertheless, passage of this bill may have

---

[40]Comprehensive Anti-Apartheid Act of 1986, P.L. 99-440, signed October 2, 1986. See The 99th Congress and South African Sanctions, by Shepard, Robert B. in Congress and Foreign Policy, 1985-86, p. 13-36.

[41]See Congress and International Environmental Issues in 1989, by Tarnoff, Curt in Congress and Foreign Policy, 1989, p. 121-139.

induced the Clinton Administration to act more forcefully with Russia in order to get it to curtail its technological assistance to Iran's ballistic missile program.[42]

Another example of legislative pressure is the reaction of various Senators to the Kyoto Protocol to the United Nations Framework Convention on Climate Change. This protocol is the implementation vehicle for the Climate Change Convention. The Kyoto Protocol was concluded on December 10, 1997 by delegates of 161 nations and sets binding targets for reduction of emissions of greenhouse gases by developed nations. The United States signed it on November 12, 1998, but it has not been submitted to the Senate for its advise and consent, as of this writing, due, in part, to indications given by some Senators that it would be rejected unless their key concerns are addressed first. The Clinton Administration has been attempting to secure actions from various nations that would assist in convincing the Senate that the Kyoto Protocol should be approved.[43]

Legislative Restrictions/Funding Denials

Congress has been most visible in its foreign policy role when it has placed legislation prohibitions or other limitations on the President's freedom of action in foreign affairs. Often these measures have been amendments to legislation authorizing or appropriating funds that the President was unlikely to veto. The use of funding restrictions or denials by Congress is a classic illustration of the "power of the purse" under the Constitution. Unlike other legislative action by Congress, its use is not subject to serious challenge by the President as an unconstitutional infringement on the President's foreign policy powers. Major legislative-executive confrontations have occurred when such restrictions have been passed despite the opposition of the President. Some examples follow.

On January 23, 1973, President Nixon announced the signing of the Paris peace accords to end U.S. involvement in the Vietnam war, but attacks by the Khmer Rouge in Cambodia continued and the United States resumed bombing in Cambodia. The Administration wanted to maintain freedom of U.S. action if North Vietnam or its Communist associates violated the accords. But Congress effectively halted such military action when it passed over the President's opposition amendments to funding legislation stating that after August 15, 1973, no funds under any legislation could be used to finance combat activities by United States military forces in, over, or from off the shores of North Vietnam, South Vietnam, Laos or Cambodia.[44]

---

[42]For background see: Katzman, Kenneth. Iran: Current Developments and U.S. Policy. CRS Issue Brief 93033.

[43]For background see: Fletcher, Susan R. Global Climate Change Treaty: The Kyoto Protocol. CRS Report for Congress 98-2ENR; Ackerman, David M. Global Climate Change: Selected Legal Questions About the Kyoto Protocol. CRS Report for Congress 98-349A; Morrissey, Wayne A. and John R. Justus, Global Climate Change. CRS Issue Brief 89005 by and Fletcher, Susan R. Global Climate Change Treaty: Negotiations and Related Issues. CRS Report for Congress 97-1000ENR.

[44]For further discussion see chapter, The Legislated Peace, in Franck, Thomas M. and Edward Weisband. Foreign Policy by Congress. New York, Oxford University Press, 1979.

(continued...)

In 1974 the Nixon Administration was pursuing a policy of normalizing trade relations with the Soviet Union as part of the broader policy of detente. Against the wishes of the Administration, Congress passed amendments to the Trade Act of 1974 which limited the amount of Export-Import Bank credits to the Soviet Union to $300 million and made the granting of most-favored-nation treatment conditional upon Soviet adoption of more liberal emigration policies. Subsequently the Soviet Union stated that because of such restrictions it would not put into force the trade agreement which the United States signed in 1972.

In early 1976, when the United States was supplying covert assistance through the Central Intelligence Agency to factions in Angola against an Angolan movement supported by Cuban troops and Soviet military assistance, Congress prohibited any kind of U.S. assistance to Angola unless expressly authorized by Congress.[45] This provision, known as the Clark amendment, forced the Administration to end U.S. aid. Congress repealed the amendment in 1985.

Throughout the Reagan Administration, Congress legislated numerous restrictions and limitations on military assistance to Central American countries. In 1983, for example, it limited the amount that could be spent on U.S. intelligence activities supporting military or paramilitary activities in Nicaragua.[46] In 1987, after the Central American governments signed a peace accord, Congress cut off military assistance to the Nicaraguan Contras (anti-Sandinista guerillas), and in 1988 permitted only non-lethal assistance.[47]

In 1992, Congress prohibited the testing of any nuclear weapon until July 1, 1993, and permitted using funds for nuclear tests after that time only in accord with strict guidelines and conditions, including a plan for achieving a multilateral comprehensive test ban.[48]

In 1993, Congress established a deadline for U.S. troops to leave Somalia. No funds could be used for military action after March 31, 1994, unless the President requested an extension from Congress and received legislative authority.[49]

---

[44](...continued)
p. 13-33.

[45]See chapter, Teaching the President a Lesson: Angola. In Franck, Thomas M., and Edward Weisband. Foreign Policy by Congress. New York, Oxford University Press, 1979. p. 46-57.

[46]See chapter, Congress and the Central American-Caribbean Region, in Congress and Foreign Policy, 1983.

[47]See Congress and Policy Toward Central American and Panama, by Taft-Morales, Maureen and Mark P. Sullivan, in Congress and Foreign Policy, 1988, p. 51-87.

[48]Section 507, Energy and Water Development Appropriations Act, 1993, P.L. 102-377, signed October 2, 1992.

[49]107 Stat. 1476, sec. 8151(b)(2)(B) (1993).

On March 12, 1996, President Clinton signed into law, H.R. 927, the Cuban Liberty and Democracy Solidarity Act (P.L. 104-114), often referred to as the Helms-Burton Act. This legislation, among other things, codifies all existing Cuban embargo Executive orders and regulations. This law does not provide for a Presidential waiver of any of these codified embargo provisions. The legislation also allows U.S. nationals to sue for money damages in U.S. Federal Court those persons that traffic in property confiscated in Cuba. The President can waive this provision for six month periods of time. The legislation further denies admission to the U.S. of aliens involved in the confiscation of U.S. property in Cuba or in the trafficking of confiscated U.S. property in Cuba. The Helms-Burton legislation has a direct and important effect on U.S. Cuban policy and was strongly opposed by the Clinton Administration prior to its enactment.[50]

In 1996, Congress passed H.R. 3107, legislation that would impose U.S. sanctions on foreign companies that invested in energy production in Libya or Iran, or sold certain products to Libya. The legislation, the Iran and Libya Sanctions Act of 1996, was signed into law by President Clinton on August 5, 1996 (P.L. 104-172).[51]

Informal Advice

Often Members of Congress shape foreign policy by providing advice to the executive branch in informal contacts. Such advice can also be given at meetings between the President and Members where no formal decision-making is contemplated, but where general reactions to prospective policy initiatives may be solicited by the President.

An example is President Eisenhower's decision not to intervene militarily in Indochina in 1954. At a meeting on April 3, 1954, Secretary of State Dulles and other executive branch officials met with congressional leaders including Senate Majority Leader William Knowland, Minority Leader Lyndon Johnson, Speaker Joseph Martin, Jr. and Minority Whip John McCormack. Secretary Dulles said a unanimous congressional opinion developed in the meeting that there should be no congressional action on a resolution to support involvement until commitments for support were obtained from other nations. Without assurance of either congressional or allied support, President Eisenhower decided against intervention.[52]

Another example is the proposal for U.S.-Soviet nuclear risk reduction centers. The idea had been advanced by Senators Henry Jackson, John Warner, and Sam Nunn in 1980, and Congress had endorsed the concept in the 1985 defense authorization

---

[50]For background see: Sullivan, Mark P. Cuba: Issues for Congress. CRS Issue Brief 94005 and Congressional Quarterly Almanac 1996, pp. 9-6, 9-7 and 9-8.

[51]For background see: Katzman, Kenneth. Iran: Current Developments and U.S. Policy. CRS Issue Brief 93033 and Congressional Quarterly Almanac 1996 pp. 9-5 and 9-6.

[52]For further discussion see: Gibbons, William. The Government and the Vietnam War, Executive and Legislative Roles and Relationships, Part I, 1945-1961. Senate Print 95-185 Pt. 1. Washington, G.P.O., 1984. p. 175-227.

act. Senators Warner and Nunn apparently persuaded President Reagan to bring up the idea at the summit conference of 1985 with Soviet Secretary General Gorbachev, and the two leaders agreed to negotiations on the subject. An agreement on nuclear risk reduction centers was signed September 15, 1987.

Congressional letters helped bring about a change in U.S. policy toward Cambodia. 162 House Members and 26 Senators wrote Secretary of State Baker a letter on November 29, 1989, questioning administration policy on Cambodia. On July 24, 1990, 66 Senators wrote President Bush taking issue with past U.S. support for representatives of three resistance groups including the Khmer Rouge to be the legitimate representative of Cambodia in the United Nations. Congressional critics also contended that the administration was placing too much emphasis on the need for compromise by the Vietnamese and the State of Cambodia, and not enough on restricting the Khmer Rouge. As a result of congressional pressure, administration officials stressed more their opposition to the Khmer Rouge, and the aid program was changed from a covert to an overt one which could be more openly debated.[53]

Oversight of Policy

Congress shapes foreign policy through regular oversight of executive branch implementation of foreign policy. This involves such mechanisms as hearings and investigations. In particular, hearings on annual authorizations and appropriations of funds for executive branch agencies carrying out foreign policy provide an opportunity for committee members to question and influence activities and policies. The Senate Foreign Relations and House International Relations Committees oversee the Department of State and other foreign affairs agencies; the Armed Services Committees oversee the Defense Department; the Intelligence Committees oversee the Central Intelligence Agency, and other parts of the intelligence community.

Hearings and investigations may be on any subject within a committee's jurisdiction and raise questions about policy for public discussion. Senate Foreign Relations Committee hearings on the Vietnam War and national commitments in the late 1960s and early 1970s, for example, contributed to public opinion against continued U.S. participation in the war. In 1987 special House and Senate committees investigated revelations that staff of the National Security Council had entered secret negotiations that linked the sale of U.S. arms to Iran with the release of American hostages, and that part of the proceeds from the sale had been used to assist the Nicaraguan rebels known as "Contras."[54]

Other frequently used oversight mechanisms are reporting requirements and requirements that certain decisions or international agreements be submitted to Congress in advance of the date they would be effective. The Freedom Support Act of 1992, for example, required several annual reports, including one on the effectiveness of the assistance provided to each of the independent states of the

---

[53]See Support for Third World Resistance Movements: Changing Priorities, by Copson, Raymond W.and Robert G. Sutter, in Congress and Foreign Policy, 1990, p. 77-107.

[54]See Congress and the Iran-Contra Affair, by Woldman, Joel M. in Congress and Foreign Policy, 1987, p. 15-33.

former Soviet Union, an analysis of programs to assist U.S. companies in transacting business with the independent states, and the activities of the Democracy Corps. It required semiannual reports on Soviet weapons destruction and numerous one-time reports. It also required reports of proposed obligations of funds for nonproliferation activities in advance of actual obligation, and a certification that a state was meeting certain criteria, such as forgoing excessive military modernization, prior to obligating funds for nonproliferation and disarmament programs.[55]

Since the early 1970s, Congress has used oversight mechanisms to advance human rights as an important factor in U.S. foreign policy. The House International Relations and Senate Foreign Relations Committees have held hearings on human rights in various geographic regions and specific countries, and cases involving violations of human rights of individuals in foreign countries. In 1975, Congress established machinery in the State Department to carry out the human rights policy and required annual reports from the Department on human rights observance by each recipient of U.S. foreign aid. In 1979 it required that the report cover all members of the United Nations. Congress has monitored the reports and executive branch policies toward countries with poor human rights records, frequently inserting in legislation conditions or restrictions aimed at improving human rights policies. The foreign operations appropriation act for FY1993, for example, prohibited aid to Zaire because of continued reports of human rights abuses in that country.[56]

In the mid-1990s, the Indonesian government's use of military force to deal with internal political dissension in East Timor, a province it took over by force from Portugal in the mid-1970s, led to criticism in the Congress of Indonesia's human rights practices. This led to inclusion of a restriction in the Foreign Operations Appropriation Act for FY1995 (P.L. 103-306, signed August 23, 1994) against the sale or licensing of "small or light arms and crowd control items" by the U.S. for Indonesia, pending a report to the Appropriations Committees of Congress by the Secretary of State that there had been significant progress made on human rights practices in East Timor and elsewhere in Indonesia. Funding for grant military assistance training of the Indonesian military was also denied in this legislation. The restriction on funding for participation in grant military funding for the Indonesian military has also been placed in recent appropriations acts.[57]

Conclusion

The practices illustrated in this report show that making U.S. foreign policy is a complex process. Both the legislative and executive branches play important roles; the roles are different, although frequently overlapping. Both branches have

---

[55]P.L. 102-511, signed October 24, 1992.

[56]P.L. 102-391, signed October 5, 1992. See House Committee on Appropriations Report 102-108, June 12, 1991, p. 39.

[57]Foreign Operations, Export Financing and Related Appropriations Act, FY1998 (P.L. 105-118, November 26, 1997. Omnibus Consolidated and Emergency Supplemental Appropriations Act, FY1999. (P.L. 105-277, October 21, 1998).

continuing opportunities to initiate and change foreign policy, and the interaction between them continues indefinitely throughout the life of a policy.

The President as the chief spokesman of the Nation, directs Government officials and machinery in the daily conduct of diplomacy, and has the principal responsibility for taking action to advance U.S. foreign policy interests. Congress in its oversight responsibility can affect the course of policy through enactment of legislation governing foreign relations and through the appropriation or denial of funds. Experience has shown that cooperation between the two branches is necessary for a strong and effective U.S. foreign policy.

Appendix: Division of Foreign Policy Powers between the President and Congress

Excerpts from the Constitution

ARTICLE I. Section 7. All Bills for raising Revenue shall originate in the House of Representatives, but the Senate may propose or concur with Amendments as on other Bills....

Section 8. The Congress shall have Power To lay and collect Taxes, Duties, Imposts, and Excises, to pay the Debts and provide for the common Defense....

To regulate Commerce with foreign Nations...

To establish an uniform Rule of Naturalization...

To coin Money, regulate the Value thereof, and of foreign Coin...

To define and punish Piracies and Felonies committed on the high Seas, and Offences against the Law of Nations;

To declare War, grant Letters of Marque and Reprisal, and make Rules concerning Captures on Land and Water;

To raise and support Armies, ...To provide and maintain a Navy;...

To make Rules for the Government and Regulation of the land and naval Forces;

To provide for calling forth the Militia to execute the Laws of the Union, suppress insurrections and repel invasions;....

To make all Laws which shall be necessary and proper for carrying into Execution the foregoing Powers, and all other Powers vested by this Constitution in the Government of the United States, or in any Department or Officer thereof....

Section 9. No Money shall be drawn from the Treasury, but in Consequence of Appropriations made by law;....

ARTICLE II. Section 1. The executive Power shall be vested in a President of the United States....

Section 2. The President shall be Commander in Chief of the Army and Navy of the United States, and of the Militia of the several States, when called into the actual Service of the United States;....

He shall have Power, by and with the Advice and Consent of the Senate, to make Treaties, provided two thirds of the Senators present concur; and he shall nominate, and by and with the Advice and Consent of the Senate, shall appoint Ambassadors, other public Ministers and Consuls,....and all other Officers of the United States, whose Appointments are not herein otherwise provided for....

Section 3. ...he shall receive Ambassadors and other public Ministers; he shall take Care that the Laws be faithfully executed, and shall Commission all the Officers of the United States. ....

Congress of the United States:
Powers,Structure, and Procedures

Conference Committee and Related Procedures: An Introduction

Stanley Bach

Summary

The House and Senate must pass the same bill or joint resolution in precisely the same form before it can be presented to the President. Once both houses have passed the same measure, they can resolve their differences over the text of that measure in one of two ways: either through an exchange of amendments between the houses or through the creation of a conference committee.

The House and Senate each have an opportunity to amend the other house's amendments to a bill; thus, there can be House amendments to Senate amendments to House amendments to a Senate bill. If either house accepts the other's amendments, the legislative process is complete. Alternatively, each house may reach the stage of disagreement at any time by insisting on its own position or by disagreeing to the position of the other chamber. Having decided to disagree, they then agree to create a conference committee to propose a single negotiated settlement of all their differences.

Conference committees generally are free to conduct their negotiations as they choose, but they are to address only the matters on which the House and Senate have disagreed. Moreover, they are to propose settlements that represent compromises between the positions of the two houses. When they have completed their work, they submit a conference report and joint explanatory statement, and the House and Senate vote on accepting the report without amendments. Sometimes conference reports are accompanied by amendments that remain in disagreement. Only after the two houses have reached complete agreement on all provisions of a bill can it be sent to the President for his approval or veto.

Introduction

This report is a brief summary of House and Senate procedures for reaching agreement on legislation. It discusses the provisions of House Rule XXII and Senate Rule XXVIII as well as other applicable rules, precedents, and practices. The report focuses on the most common and customary procedures. There are many exceptions, complications, and possibilities that are not addressed, and the House and Senate may modify or waive their procedures by unanimous consent or by other means.

The report is based upon the author's interpretation of the rules and published precedents of the two houses and his analysis of the application of these rules and precedents in recent practice. Readers may wish to study the provisions of House and Senate rules and examine the applicable precedents, especially in the sections on “Senate Bills; Amendments Between the Houses” and “Conferences Between the Houses” in *House Practice: A Guide to the Rules, Precedents and Procedures of the House*, and the corresponding sections on "Amendments Between Houses" and "Conferences and Conference Reports" in *Riddick's Senate Procedure* (Senate Document No. 101-28). There also is more detailed information on this subject in *Resolving Legislative Differences in Congress: Conference Committees and Amendments Between the Houses*, CRS Report 98-696, updated periodically.

Acting on the Same Bill

The House and Senate must pass the same bill or joint resolution and they must reach full and precise agreement on its text before it is submitted to the President for his approval or veto. The same requirements apply to a concurrent resolution and a joint resolution proposing a constitutional amendment, although neither receives presidential action.

At some stage of the legislative process, therefore, the House must pass a Senate bill or the Senate must pass a House bill. The simplest way of meeting this requirement is for one house to pass its own bill and send it to the "other body," which then considers and passes it, with or without amendments. Frequently, however, House and Senate committees each develop their own bill on the same subject. In these cases, one house often debates and amends the bill reported by its committee, but then amends and passes the corresponding bill that the other chamber already has passed.

For example, after the House passes a bill, it frequently takes up a bill on the same subject that it already has received from the Senate. The House then amends the Senate bill by striking out the text passed by the Senate (striking out all after the enacting clause) and replacing it with the text of the House bill it has just passed. The House then passes the amended Senate bill also. In this way, the House passes two bills with exactly the same text, but the Senate bill is the one likely to become law because both houses now have passed it, although with different provisions. Much the same thing happens in the Senate, except that the Senate does not actually pass its own bill before taking up the House bill. Instead, the Senate debates and amends the bill reported by its committee and, after third reading and engrossment (which ends the amending process), the Senate takes up and passes the House bill after amending it with the amended text of the Senate bill. Under these circumstances, the Senate never does pass its own bill even after considering it at length.

This process usually is routine but it can become more complicated. For instance, the Senate may pass one bill on several related matters before the House passes two bills of its own which address the same subjects. After the House passes its two bills, it may take up the one Senate bill and replace the text of that bill with the texts of both of its own bills. In other instances, the House and Senate may confront different political and procedural situations that make it convenient for them to include their versions of legislation on one subject as amendments to some third bill on an unrelated subject which serves as a convenient "vehicle." Such arrangements can be necessary because the House and Senate cannot begin the formal process of resolving their policy differences until these differences are embodied as amendments by one house to the version of the same bill as passed by the other.

Amendments Between the Houses

After one house passes a bill and the other then passes it with amendments, the House and Senate attempt to resolve the differences between their positions. When confronted with a major bill, the two houses usually create a conference committee for this purpose. However, a conference may not be necessary if they can reach an agreement through an exchange of amendments between the houses.

The amendments of one house to a bill from the other may be amended twice as the bill is sent ("messaged") back and forth between the House and Senate. Suppose, for example, that the Senate passes a House bill with amendments. The House can accept (concur in) the Senate amendments, in which case the differences are resolved. Alternatively, the House can amend the Senate amendments (concur in the Senate amendments with amendments). These House amendments are first degree amendments between the houses. The Senate then can accept (concur in) the House amendments to the Senate amendments, which would produce agreement. Or the Senate can concur in the House amendments to the Senate amendments with further Senate amendments, which are amendments in the second degree.

At this stage, the House can concur in the most recent Senate amendments, but it cannot propose new House amendments to them because they would be third degree amendments that are not permitted. (Of course, exactly the same process can occur in reverse if the House passes a Senate bill with amendments.) If the House and Senate adamantly defend their last amendments, they can send the bill back and forth several more times as each chamber first insists on and then adheres to its position. In the unlikely event that neither House retreats from its last position or is willing to discuss a compromise in conference, the bill ultimately dies. It cannot be shuttled back and forth indefinitely.

This process rarely results in stalemate because the two houses either reach agreement or they decide to submit their differences to a conference committee. However, an exchange of amendments sometimes takes the place of a conference. Once the two houses pass their versions of the same bill, the members and staff of the House and Senate committees of jurisdiction often meet informally to compare the two versions and discuss a compromise. If they reach an agreement that other concerned Representatives and Senators also accept, the House can, for example, concur in the Senate amendment with a House amendment that embodies the negotiated agreement. If the Senate then accepts (concurs in) this House amendment, the House and Senate have resolved their differences through the informal equivalent of a conference committee.

Considering Amendments From the Other House

House amendments to a Senate bill (or House amendments to Senate amendments to a House bill) are privileged for floor action by the Senate. The Senate usually decides to consider them by unanimous consent; if necessary, however, the Senate can vote for a non-debatable motion to take them up. Motions to dispose of the House amendments—such as motions to concur or to concur with amendments—are debatable and, therefore, subject to filibusters. In practice, however, the Senate rarely debates House amendments for very long. Either all the interested Senators agree to accept or amend the House amendments or they agree to go to conference instead.

The procedural situation in the House is somewhat more complicated, although, like the Senate, the House often acts on Senate amendments by unanimous consent. Until the House officially disagrees to Senate amendments to a House bill (or Senate amendments to House amendments to a Senate bill), these amendments usually are not privileged for consideration on the House floor. No motion is in order to concur in the Senate amendments, with or without amendments. When there is little or no controversy, the House often accepts or amends the Senate amendments by unanimous consent. Otherwise, the House usually can do so only through a motion to suspend the rules or under a special rule recommended by the Rules Committee and adopted by the House. The one motion that a Representative can make is to disagree to the Senate amendments and go to conference, but this motion must be made at the direction of the committee that originally reported the bill to the House.

Both houses cannot consider the same bill at the same time because the House or Senate can only act if it has the "papers"—the official copy of the bill as passed by the house in which it originated, the official copies of amendments by either house, and the messages by which each house informs the other of the actions it has taken. After one house acts on a bill or amendments from the other, it returns all the papers with an accompanying message describing its action. Thus, the House and Senate always act in sequence as custody of the papers changes hands.

Going to Conference

Before a conference committee is created to resolve disagreements between the two houses, the House and Senate each must state its disagreement over a bill, either by disagreeing to the amendments of the "other body" or by insisting on its own amendments. So long as one house concurs in the amendments of the other with amendments, there is no formal disagreement. But at any point during an exchange of amendments between the House and Senate, either house can propose that they can go to conference instead.

The two houses usually decide in one of two ways to establish a conference committee. When the Senate passes a House bill with amendments, for example, it can immediately insist on its amendments and request a conference with the House. This is likely to happen on major bills and any others for which a conference committee is certain to be necessary. The House almost always agrees to the conference although it need not do so—for example, it could simply agree to the Senate amendments instead. At other times, however, when the Senate passes a House bill with amendments, it may merely send back the bill and the amendments in the hope that the House will accept the Senate's amendments, making a conference unnecessary. If the House does not accept the amendments, it can disagree to them and request a conference. The Senate normally then insists on its amendments and agrees to the conference, after which it informs the House and returns the papers. Of course, the equivalent of either sequence of events may occur after the House passes a Senate bill with amendments.

A House decision to disagree to the Senate's position or insist on its own position is also important for two other reasons.

First, once the House reaches the "stage of disagreement," later action on the Senate's amendments is privileged. Representatives then can make motions on the floor to recede and concur, with or without amendments (stated more fully, motions that the House recede from its disagreement to a Senate amendment and either concur therein or concur in the Senate amendment with an amendment).

Second, the precedence among motions changes when the House reaches the stage of disagreement. Before disagreement, House precedents give priority to motions that perfect the bill. For example, a Representative can move that the House concur in the Senate amendments with amendments before the House votes on a motion already made by another Representative that the House simply concur in the Senate amendments. After disagreement, however, House precedents give priority to motions that promote agreement between the houses. For example, a Representative can move that the House recede and concur in a Senate amendment before the House votes on a motion already offered that the House recede and concur with an amendment.

Representatives usually cannot make motions to concur, with or without amendments, before the House reaches the stage of disagreement. So the precedence among motions is most likely to be important after a conference committee has met and reported its recommendations.

Appointing and Instructing Conferees

Each house usually appoints its conferees (also known as managers) immediately after deciding to go to conference. The Speaker appoints House conferees. The Senate can elect its conferees although it almost always decides, by unanimous consent, to authorize the Presiding Officer to appoint "the managers on the part of the Senate."

The chairman and ranking minority member of the committee or subcommittee that reported the bill are almost always conferees. They also play a major part in deciding who else is appointed. The committee or subcommittee leaders usually prepare a list of conferees from their chamber that the Speaker normally accepts and the Presiding Officer of the Senate always accepts. The party leaders also may become involved in selecting conferees, especially if the bill is particularly important, if it was reported by two or more committees, or if amendments to the bill from the other house touch the jurisdiction of more than one committee.

Most conferees are members of the committee that reported the bill. In the case of a bill that involves the jurisdiction of more than one committee, members of each committee often are appointed as conferees with authority only to negotiate an agreement with respect to the subjects or provisions of the bill that fall within the jurisdiction of their committees. Thus, some members may be designated as conferees for purposes of the entire bill while others are appointed only to address a specific section or title. Representatives also may appointed as conferees for limited purposes when the Senate adds to a House bill a non-germane amendment that is within the jurisdiction of another House committee. In addition, the Speaker may appoint other Representatives who, for example, offered important floor amendments. The list of conferees generally reflects the party balance in each house.

The House and Senate do not have to appoint the same number of managers, and they frequently do not. House conferees vote as a delegation, as do Senate conferees, and a majority of each delegation must sign the conference report. Thus, three Representatives have the same voting power in conference as thirty Senators. Each house is likely to appoint a larger number of conferees when the bill involves the jurisdiction of more than one of its standing committees. Some conference committees have only a handful of members from each chamber; at the other extreme, the conference on a reconciliation bill can have more than 250 members.

A Representative or Senator may move to instruct the conferees from his or her chamber immediately after that house agrees to go to conference but just before the conferees are appointed. For example, the House can instruct its managers to insist on the House position on a particular amendment, or the Senate can instruct its managers to recede to the House position on another amendment. However, instructions to conferees are never binding; no point of order lies against a conference report that is inconsistent with House or Senate instructions to its conferees. The House also can instruct its conferees if they do not report within twenty days after being appointed (or thirty-six hours after being appointed during the last six days of a session).

Conference Rules and Reports

Conference committee meetings are open to the public unless the conferees vote to close them, and the House must vote to authorize its conferees to do so. Beyond this requirement, there are virtually no House or Senate rules governing conference meetings. Conferees select their own chairman and usually work without formal rules on quorums, proxies, debate, amendments, and other procedural matters. Conferences are negotiating forums, and the two chambers allow conferees to decide for themselves how best to conduct their negotiations.

However, the House and Senate have important, and roughly the same, rules governing what decisions conferees can make. Conference committees are established to resolve disagreements between the House and Senate over their versions of the same bill. Therefore, the authority of conferees is limited to matters in disagreement. As a general rule, they may not change a provision on which both houses agree, nor may they add anything that is not in one version or the other. Furthermore, conferees are to reach agreements within the "scope" of the differences between the House and Senate positions. For example, if the House appropriates $10 million for some purpose and the Senate amends the bill by increasing the appropriation to $20 million, the conferees exceed their authority if they agree on a number that is less than $10 million or more than $20 million.

It is much harder to determine the scope of the differences when they are qualitative, not quantitative. Also, conferees have more latitude under some circumstances than under others. When one house passes a bill and the other then passes it with a series of separate amendments—each making a change in a different provision of the bill—these amendments usually are numbered, and it is relatively easy for the conferees to determine the scope of the differences over each amendment. This is generally not true, however, when the Senate passes a House bill (or the House passes a Senate bill) with an amendment in the nature of a substitute that totally replaces the text of the bill. In this situation, which arises very frequently, there is only one amendment in conference—for example, a Senate substitute for the House version of a bill. The two versions of the bill can take very different approaches to the same subject, making it difficult for the conferees to isolate every point of agreement and disagreement and to identify the scope of each disagreement. Under these circumstances, the conferees may write their own conference substitute, so long as it is a germane modification of the House and Senate versions.

When the conferees reach full agreement, their staffs prepare a conference report that states how they propose to resolve each of the disagreements. Accompanying the report itself is a joint explanatory statement (or statement of managers) which describes the various House and Senate positions and the conferees' recommendations in more detail. A majority of the House managers and a majority of the Senate managers must sign both the conference report and the joint explanatory statement. Each chamber then debates and votes on the conference report in turn.

If a conference agreement exceeds the scope of the differences or deals with a matter that is not in disagreement, the entire conference report is subject to a point of order when the House or Senate considers it. However, members rarely make such points of order for at least three reasons: first, conferees generally are careful not to exceed their authority; second, the Senate interprets the authority of its conferees generously, especially when they develop a conference substitute; and third, conferees sometimes can protect their recommendations against points of order by reporting amendments in technical disagreement.

Amendments in Disagreement

If the conferees cannot agree at all, they can file a conference report in disagreement. By the same token, if they can resolve some, but not all, of the amendments in disagreement, they can file a partial conference report on the agreements they have reached, accompanied by one or more amendments that remain in disagreement. But when conferees negotiate over the version of a bill passed by one house and a complete substitute for it passed by the other, they can report only in full agreement or full disagreement. In this case, there is only one amendment in conference, and conferees cannot report in disagreement on part of an amendment.

Conferees also report individual amendments in disagreement, rather than as part of their conference report, when they wish to resolve the differences over those amendments with proposals that exceed the scope of their authority. In this case, they report the amendments in technical disagreement to protect the conference report itself against a point of order. Acting in turn, the House and Senate first vote to approve the partial conference report and then act on each amendment in technical disagreement and the conferees' recommendation for disposing of it.

In addition, conferees on general appropriations bills may report certain amendments in technical disagreement because of another restriction that the rules of the House place on their authority. House rules are stricter than Senate rules in prohibiting both unauthorized appropriations and changes in existing law ("legislation") as provisions of general appropriations bills. Because of this difference, clause 5 of House Rule XXII forbids House conferees from including either kind of Senate provision in an appropriations conference report without a House vote authorizing them to do so. However, amendments in disagreement are not part of conference reports, and so they are not subject to this requirement. When appropriations conferees accept a legislative provision or an unauthorized appropriation proposed by the Senate, therefore, they usually report that Senate amendment in technical disagreement. Otherwise, a Representative could make a point of order against the conference report as a whole. Conference reports on general appropriations bills often are accompanied by many amendments in disagreement; in most cases, the disagreements are technical.

Until recently, appropriations conferees often reported partial conference reports that were accompanied by many amendments in technical disagreement. During the most recent Congresses, however, the more common practice has been for appropriations conferees to include all (or almost all) of their agreements in their conference reports. The House then adopts resolutions, reported by the House Rules Committee, that waive all points of order against the reports and against their consideration. If the House adopts such a waiver resolution, appropriations conferees can include unauthorized appropriations and legislative provisions in their report without the report being subject to points of order on the House floor.

Floor Action on Conference Reports

At the conclusion of a successful conference, the papers usually change hands. The conferees from the house that requested the conference bring the papers into conference and then turn them over to the conferees from the other house. Thus, the house that agreed to the conference normally acts first on the conference report. However, this is a practice that is not required by House or Senate rules.

The Senate usually considers a conference report by unanimous consent although, if necessary, a Senator can make a non-debatable motion to consider it. The report may be called up at any time after it is filed, and Senators then can debate it at length. If the Senate agrees by unanimous consent to limit the time for debate, the time is equally divided between the majority and minority parties.

In the House, the conference report cannot be considered until three days after being filed, and then only if the report and the joint explanatory statement have been printed in the *Congressional Record* for the day it was filed. Copies of the report and the statement also must be available to Representatives for at least two hours before they consider it. If the report meets these requirements, it is considered as having been read. Otherwise, the report is to be read before debate begins. Instead, the House typically agrees by unanimous consent to have the joint explanatory statement read and then to dispense with the reading. These availability requirements do not apply during the last six days of a session.

The House debates a conference report under the one-hour rule, with control of the hour equally divided between the two parties. However, if both floor managers support the report, a Representative opposed to it may claim one-third of the time for debate. At the end of the first hour, the House normally votes to order the previous question, which precludes additional debate. If Representatives could make points of order against a report, sometimes the House first considers and agrees to a resolution, recommended by its Rules Committee, that protects the report by waiving the points of order.

Conference reports are not amendable. Each report is a compromise proposal for resolving a series of disagreements; the House prevails on some questions, the Senate on others. If the House and Senate were free to amend the report, they might never reach agreement. At the end of debate, therefore, each house votes on whether to agree to the report as a whole. However, the house that considers the report first also has the option of recommitting it to conference. But when one chamber agrees to the report, it automatically discharges its conferees. As a result, the other house cannot vote to recommit because the conference committee has been disbanded.

If the conferees reach full agreement and the House and Senate agree to the conference report, the bill is enrolled (printed on parchment in its final form) and presented to the President for his approval or disapproval. However, if the conferees file a partial report and one or more amendments in disagreement, the two houses must agree on a way to dispose of each of these amendments before the bill can become law. Congress cannot present part of a bill to the President.

In the case of a partial conference report accompanied by amendments in disagreement, the House or Senate first debates and votes on the report and then takes up the remaining amendments. After a clerk reads one of these amendments, the floor manager makes a motion to dispose of it—moving, for example, to recede and concur in the amendment, to recede and concur in the amendment with an amendment, or to insist on its disagreement to the amendment. At this point, another member may offer a preferential motion. If the floor manager moves to insist, for example, another member may move to recede and concur instead. (In the House, a Representative sometimes demands that this motion be divided; if the House then votes to recede, he or she now may offer a new preferential motion that the House concur with an amendment.) The House or Senate votes first on any preferential motion.

When the clerk reaches an amendment in technical disagreement, the floor manager frequently moves to recede and concur with an amendment. This amendment embodies the agreement that the conferees reached but could not include in their report because it exceeded the scope of the differences. Now the agreement can be proposed in the form of an amendment because the restrictions of "scope" apply to conference reports, not to amendments between the houses. Similarly, when the House clerk reports a Senate appropriations amendment in technical disagreement, the floor manager moves that the House recede and concur, with or without an amendment, and approve the agreement that Rule XXII prohibited the conferees from including in their report.

If the floor manager intends to move that his or her house take the same action—e.g., recede and concur—on a number of amendments, he may ask unanimous consent that they be considered together (en bloc). The Senate frequently acts on most or all amendments in disagreement en bloc. Otherwise, amendments in disagreement are considered one at a time.

After one house agrees to the partial report and disposes of all the amendments in disagreement, the other house takes similar action. If the House and Senate approve the report and dispose of all the amendments in the same way, the bill is ready to be enrolled. If not, the two houses can try to resolve their remaining disagreements through a further exchange of amendments or positions or by creating a new conference committee. But if the House and Senate do agree to a new conference committee, the conference may only consider whatever disagreements remain; it may not re-open other issues because the House and Senate have resolved them.

Rejecting Non-germane Provisions

The House also has a special procedure in Rule XXII for dealing with non-germane Senate amendments that conferees sometimes include in their reports. This procedure protects the House from having to vote for or against a conference report that includes a Senate provision that the House did not and could not have considered because it would not have been germane to the bill as the House passed it.

Before the House begins to debate the report, a Representative can make a point of order that a particular provision of the report would not have been germane if it had been offered as an amendment to the bill in the House. If the Speaker sustains the point of order, the Representative then can move that the House reject the non-germane matter. The House votes on this motion after no more than forty minutes of debate. If the House defeats the motion, it then debates and votes on the conference report, including the non-germane matter. However, if the House votes to reject, it next votes on one of two motions, depending on the circumstances: to insist on the House amendment; or to recede and concur in the Senate amendment with an amendment consisting of the rest of the conference report, minus the non-germane provision. The Senate can then accept the House amendment or propose a new Senate amendment (again, depending on the circumstances), or it can request a new conference with the House. The same House rule includes a comparable procedure for dealing with non-germane matter in Senate amendments that the House considers after reaching the stage of disagreement—for instance, a Senate amendment reported from conference in disagreement.

Congress of the United States:
Powers,Structure, and Procedures

Committees of the United States Senate

Carol Hardy Vincent

SUMMARY

This report presents a profile of each Senate committee. For each committee, the information includes a jurisdictional summary, a list of subcommittees, the number of members of each party on the committee, and brief historical notations.

At the organization of the 105th Congress, there were 20 full committees—16 standing committees and 4 others. In addition, there were 68 Senate subcommittees. These numbers are unchanged from the 104th Congress.

Introduction

This report presents selected information for each Senate committee—information on its jurisdiction, subcommittees, current membership, and history. Senate Rule XXV, paragraph 1, identifies the 16 Senate standing committees and their legislative and oversight jurisdictions. For each standing committee, this report lists the topics of legislative jurisdiction and the oversight statements, identified as areas for "comprehensive study and review." The Senate also has four non-standing committees (two select, one special, and one other) which tend to have more narrow jurisdictions than the standing committees or lack legislative jurisdiction (the authority to consider referred bills and to report bills to the chamber). The jurisdiction/responsibility statement of each such non-standing committee is taken primarily from the resolution pertaining to the panel as contained in the *Senate Manual* (S. Doc. No. 104-1). Senate Rule XXV and these resolutions, not this report, are the authorities for statements of committee legislative and oversight jurisdiction.

The names of subcommittees and current membership figures are drawn from a February 14, 1997 publication of the Secretary of the Senate (S. Pub. 105-6) entitled *The Senate of the United States: Committee and Subcommittee Assignments*. In general, the history section for each committee notes its date of creation. This section may also include the names of other panels that were merged with the committee and the merger dates. For standing committees, it may list selected issues acquired (principally from other committees) after the codification of standing committee jurisdictions in 1946. For other committees, it may list the date the committee became permanent.

Finally, in cases where a committee is known to have prepared a published history of itself, a bibliographic citation is provided. This report does not identify committee documents with historical material where the primary focus is not committee evolution, nor other sources containing historical information such as articles, books, and agency reports.

Committee on Agriculture, Nutrition, and Forestry

Jurisdiction:

Agricultural economics and research; agricultural extension services and experiment stations; agricultural production, marketing, and stabilization of prices; agriculture and agricultural commodities; animal industry and diseases; crop insurance and soil conservation; farm credit and farm security; food from fresh waters; food stamp programs; forestry, forest reserves, and wilderness areas other than those created from the public domain; home economics; human nutrition; inspection of livestock, meat, and agricultural products; pests and pesticides; plant industry, soils, and agricultural engineering; rural development, rural electrification, and watersheds; and school nutrition programs.

Comprehensive study and review of matters relating to rural affairs, and to food, nutrition, and hunger, both in the United States and in foreign countries.

Subcommittees:

1. Forestry, Conservation, and Rural Revitalization
2. Marketing, Inspection, and Product Promotion
3. Production and Price Competitiveness
4 Research, Nutrition, and General Legislation

Membership:

Majority:	10
Minority:	8
Total:	18

History:

Created as Committee on Agriculture in 1825
Abolished in 1857, and reestablished in 1863
Renamed Committee on Agriculture and Forestry in 1884, and to current name in 1977
Added jurisdiction from Senate Select Committee on Nutrition and Human Needs, and jurisdiction over school lunch legislation in 1977

Printed History:

U.S. Congress, Senate Committee on Agriculture, Nutrition, and Forestry, *A Brief History of the Committee on Agriculture, Nutrition, and Forestry, United States Senate, and Landmark Agricultural Legislation, 1825-1986*, committee print, 99th Cong., 2nd sess. (Washington: GPO, 1986), 76 p.

Committee on Appropriations

Jurisdiction:

Appropriation of revenue for the support of the government, (except as provided in Rule XXV, subparagraph 1(e) pertaining to the Committee on the Budget); rescission of appropriations contained in appropriation acts; the amount of new spending authority described in section 401(c)(2) (A) and (B) of the Congressional Budget Act of 1974 which is to be effective for a fiscal year; certain measures pertaining to new spending authority as specified in the Congressional Budget Act of 1974.

Subcommittees:

1. Agriculture, Rural Development, and Related Agencies
2. Commerce, Justice, State, and the Judiciary
3. Defense
4. District of Columbia
5. Energy and Water Development
6. Foreign Operations
7. Interior
8. Labor, Health and Human Services, and Education
9. Legislative Branch
10. Military Construction
11. Transportation
12. Treasury, Postal Service, and General Government
13. VA [Veterans' Administration], HUD [Housing and Urban Development], and Independent Agencies

Membership:

Majority:	15
Minority:	13
Total:	28

History:

Created in 1867

Added jurisdiction over new spending authority as described in section 401(c)(2) of the Congressional Budget Act in 1974

Printed History:

U.S. Congress, Senate Committee on Appropriations, *Committee on Appropriations, United States Senate: 126th Anniversary, 1867-1993,* S. Doc. 103-17, 103rd Cong., 1st sess. (Washington: GPO, 1995), 163 p.

Committee on Armed Services

Jurisdiction:

Aeronautical and space activities peculiar to or primarily associated with the development of weapons systems or military operations; the common defense; the Departments of Defense, Army, Navy, and Air Force generally; maintenance and operation of the Panama Canal, including administration, sanitation, and government of the Canal Zone; military research and development; national security aspects of nuclear energy; naval petroleum reserves, except those in Alaska; pay, promotion, retirement, and other benefits and privileges of members of the Armed Forces, including overseas education of civilian and military dependents; selective service system; and strategic and critical materials necessary for the common defense.

Comprehensive study and review of matters relating to the common defense policy of the United States.

Subcommittees:

1. Acquisition and Technology
2. Airland Forces
3. Personnel
4. Readiness
5. Seapower
6. Strategic Forces

Membership:

Majority:	10
Minority:	8
Total:	18

History:

Committee on Naval Affairs and Committee on Military Affairs created in 1816

Independent Committee on Militia from 1816 through 1857; a combined Committee on Military Affairs and the Militia from 1857 through 1869; Committee renamed Committee on Military Affairs in 1869

Committee on Military Affairs and Committee on Naval Affairs merged by the Legislative Reorganization Act of 1946

Added jurisdiction over military aspects of atomic energy in 1977

Printed History:

None

Committee on Banking, Housing, and Urban Affairs

Jurisdiction:

Banks, banking, and financial institutions; control of prices of commodities, rents, and services; deposit insurance; economic stabilization and defense production; export and foreign trade promotion; export controls; federal monetary policy, including the Federal Reserve System; financial aid to commerce and industry; issuance and redemption of notes; money and credit, including currency and coinage; nursing home construction; public and private housing (including veterans' housing); renegotiation of government contracts; and urban development and urban mass transit.

Comprehensive study and review of matters relating to international economic policy as it affects United States monetary affairs, credit, and financial institutions; economic growth; urban affairs; and credit.

Subcommittees:

1. Financial Institutions and Regulatory Relief
2. Financial Services and Technology
3. Housing Opportunity and Community Development
4. International Finance
5. Securities

Membership:

Majority:	10
Minority:	8
Total:	18

History:

Created as Committee on Banking and Currency in 1913

Acquired jurisdiction of Committee on National Banks (created 1912) in 1921

Renamed to current name effective 1971

Added jurisdiction over foreign commerce and over veterans' housing in 1977

Printed History:

U.S. Congress, Senate Committee on Banking and Currency, *Committee on Banking and Currency, United States Senate: 50th Anniversary, 1913-1963*, S. Doc. 88-15, 88th Cong., 1st sess. (Washington: GPO, 1963), 100 p.

Committee on the Budget

Jurisdiction:

All concurrent resolutions on the budget, as defined in section 3(a)(4) of the Congressional Budget Act of 1974, and all other matters required under titles III and IV of the act.[1]

The Committee is to report the required matters under titles III and IV of the 1974 Act[2]; make continuing studies of the effect on budget outlays of relevant existing and proposed legislation and report the results of such studies to the Senate on a recurring basis; request and evaluate continuing studies of tax expenditures, devise methods of coordinating tax expenditures, policies, and programs with direct budget outlays, and report the results of such studies to the Senate on a recurring basis; review, on a continuing basis, the conduct by the Congressional Budget Office of its functions and duties.

Subcommittees:

None

Membership:

Majority:	12
Minority:	10
Total:	22

History:

Created by the Congressional Budget Act of 1974

Printed History:

None

---

[1] Such matters include reconciliation and other enforcement measures as described.

[2] A second source of the Committee's jurisdiction is the standing order of August 4, 1977, on the referral of budget process legislation. The Senate requires joint referral to the Committees on Budget and Governmental Affairs of all legislation affecting the congressional budget process, as described in the standing order.

Committee on Commerce, Science, and Transportation

Jurisdiction:

Coast Guard; coastal zone management; communications; highway safety; inland waterways, except construction; interstate commerce; marine and ocean navigation, safety, and transportation, including navigational aspects of deepwater ports; marine fisheries; merchant marine and navigation; nonmilitary aeronautical and space sciences; oceans, weather, and atmospheric activities; Panama Canal and interoceanic canals generally, except the maintenance and operation of the Panama Canal, including administration, sanitation and government of the Canal Zone; regulation of consumer products and services, including testing related to toxic substances, other than pesticides, and except for credit, financial services, and housing; regulation of interstate common carriers, including railroads, buses, trucks, vessels, pipelines, and civil aviation; science, engineering, and technology research and development and policy; sports; standards and measurement; transportation; and transportation and commerce aspects of outer continental shelf lands.

Comprehensive study and review of all matters relating to science and technology, oceans policy, transportation, communications, and consumer affairs.

Subcommittees:

1. Aviation
2. Communications
3. Consumer Affairs, Foreign Commerce, and Tourism
4. Manufacturing and Competitiveness
5. Oceans and Fisheries
6. Science, Technology, and Space
7. Surface Transportation and Merchant Marine

Membership:

Majority:	11
Minority:	9
Total:	20

History:

Created as Committee on Commerce and Manufactures in 1816

Acquired jurisdiction of Committees on Improvement of Mississippi River (created 1879); Fisheries (created 1884); Standards, Weights, and Measures (created 1909); Conservation of Natural Resources (created 1909); Coast and Insular Survey (created 1899) in 1921

History: (Continued)

Acquired jurisdiction of Committees on Pacific Railroads (created 1863), Railroads (created 1873), Transportation Routes to the Seaboard (created 1879), Transportation and Sale of Meat Products (created 1909), and Interoceanic Canals (created 1899), by the Legislative Reorganization Act of 1946

Acquired jurisdiction of Committee on Aeronautical and Space Sciences (created 1958) in 1977

Renamed Committee on Interstate and Foreign Commerce by Legislative Reorganization Act of 1946, Committee on Commerce in 1961, and to current name in 1977

Printed History:

U.S. Congress, Senate Committee on Commerce, Science and Transportation, *A Brief History of the Senate Committee on Commerce, Science, and Transportation and Its Activities Since 1947,* S. Doc. 95-93, 95th Cong., 2nd sess. (Washington: GPO, 1978), 138 p.

Committee on Energy and Natural Resources

Jurisdiction:

Coal production, distribution, and utilization; energy policy, regulation, and conservation; energy related aspects of deepwater ports; energy research and development; extraction of minerals from oceans and outer continental shelf lands; hydroelectric power, irrigation, and reclamation; mining education and research; mining, mineral lands, mining claims, and mineral conservation; national parks, recreation areas, wilderness areas, wild and scenic rivers, historical sites, military parks and battlefields, and on the public domain, preservation of prehistoric ruins and objects of interest; naval petroleum reserves in Alaska; nonmilitary development of nuclear energy; oil and gas production and distribution; public lands and forests, including farming and grazing thereon, and mineral extraction therefrom; solar energy systems; and territorial possessions of the United States, including trusteeships.

Comprehensive study and review of matters relating to energy and resources development.

Subcommittees:

1. Energy Research and Development, Production and Regulation
3. Forests and Public Land Management
3. National Parks, Historic Preservation, and Recreation
4. Water and Power

Membership:

Majority:	11
Minority:	9
Total:	20

History:

Created as Committee on Public Lands in 1816

Acquired jurisdiction of Committees on Geological Survey (created 1899), Indian Affairs (created 1820), Territories (created 1844), Mines and Mining (created 1865), Irrigation and Reclamation (created 1891) in 1921

Renamed Committee on Public Lands and Surveys in 1921, Committee on Public Lands effective 1947, Committee on Interior and Insular Affairs in 1948, and to current name in 1977

Added jurisdiction, in particular over naval petroleum reserves and oil shale reserves in Alaska, and over water power, in 1977

Printed History:

U.S. Congress, Senate Committee on Energy and Natural Resources, *History of the Committee on Energy and Natural Resources, United States Senate,* S. Doc. 100-46, 100th Cong., 2nd sess. (Washington: GPO, 1989), 391 p.

Committee on Environment and Public Works

Jurisdiction:

Air pollution; construction and maintenance of highways; environmental aspects of outer continental shelf lands; environmental effects of toxic substances, except pesticides; environmental policy; fisheries and wildlife; environmental research and development; flood control and improvements of rivers and harbors, including environmental aspects of deepwater ports; noise pollution; nonmilitary environmental regulation and control of nuclear energy; ocean dumping; public buildings and improved grounds of the United States generally, including federal buildings in the District of Columbia; public works, bridges, and dams; regional economic development; solid waste disposal and recycling; water pollution; and water resources.

Comprehensive study and review of matters relating to environmental protection and resource utilization and conservation.

Subcommittees:

1. Clean Air, Wetlands, Private Property, and Nuclear Safety
2. Drinking Water, Fisheries, and Wildlife
3. Superfund, Waste Control, and Risk Assessment
4. Transportation and Infrastructure

Membership:

Majority:	10
Minority:	8
Total:	18

History:

Created as Committee on Public Buildings in 1838, renamed Committee on Public Buildings and Grounds in 1857

Renamed Committee on Public Works, and jurisdiction enhanced to include roads, rivers, and harbors, by the Legislative Reorganization Act of 1946

Renamed to current name in 1977

Enhanced environmental jurisdiction, and acquired jurisdiction over most aspects of atomic energy and over wildlife and fisheries (except marine) in 1977

Printed History:

U.S. Congress, Senate Committee on Environment and Public Works, *History of the Committee on Environment and Public Works, United States Senate,* S. Doc. 100-45, 100th Cong., 2nd sess. (Washington: GPO, 1988), 161 p.

Committee on Finance

Jurisdiction:

Both the bonded debt of the United States and revenue measures generally, except as provided in the Congressional Budget Act of 1974; customs, collection districts, and ports of entry and delivery; deposit of public moneys; general revenue sharing; health programs under the Social Security Act and health programs financed by a specific tax or trust fund; national social security; reciprocal trade agreements; revenue measures relating to insular possessions; tariffs and import quotas, and matters related thereto; and transportation of dutiable goods.

Subcommittees:

1. Health Care
2. International Trade
3. Long-Term Growth, Debt, and Deficit Reduction
4. Social Security and Family Policy
5. Taxation and IRS Oversight

Membership:

Majority:	11
Minority:	9
Total:	20

History:

Created in 1816

Printed History:

U.S. Congress, Senate Committee on Finance, *History of the Committee on Finance,* S. Doc. 97-5, 97th Cong., 1st sess. (Washington: GPO, 1981), 138 p.

Committee on Foreign Relations

Jurisdiction:

Acquisition of land and buildings for embassies and legations in foreign countries; boundaries of the United States; diplomatic service; foreign economic, military, technical, and humanitarian assistance; foreign loans; international activities of the American National Red Cross and the International Committee of the Red Cross; international aspects of nuclear energy, including nuclear transfer policy; international conferences and congresses; international law as it relates to foreign policy; International Monetary Fund and other international organizations established primarily for international monetary purposes (except that any proposed legislation relating to such subjects reported by the Committee on Foreign Relations is to be referred to the Committee on Banking, Housing, and Urban Affairs, at the latter's request); intervention abroad and declarations of war; measures to foster commercial intercourse with foreign nations and safeguard American business interests abroad; national security and international aspects of trusteeships of the United States; oceans and international environmental and scientific affairs as they relate to foreign policy; protection of United States citizens abroad and expatriation; relations of the United States with foreign nations generally; treaties and executive agreements, except reciprocal trade agreements; United Nations and affiliated organizations; and the World Bank group, regional development banks, and other international organizations established primarily for development assistance purposes.

Comprehensive study and review of matters relating to national security policy, foreign policy, and international economic policy as it relates to foreign policy of the United States, and matters relating to food, hunger, and nutrition in foreign countries.

Subcommittees:

1. African Affairs
2. East Asian and Pacific Affairs
3. European Affairs
4. International Economic Policy, Export, and Trade Promotion
5. International Operations
6. Near Eastern and South Asian Affairs
7. Western Hemisphere, Peace Corps, Narcotics, and Terrorism

Membership:

Majority:	10
Minority:	8
Total:	18

History:

Created in 1816

Acquired jurisdiction of Committee on Relations with Canada (created 1892) and Committee on Relations with Cuba (created 1899) in 1921

Printed History:

U.S. Congress, Senate Committee on Foreign Relations, *Committee on Foreign Relations, 170th Anniversary, 1816-1986,* S. Doc. 99-21, 99th Cong., 2nd sess. (Washington: GPO, 1986), 91 p.

Committee on Governmental Affairs

Jurisdiction:

Archives of the United States; budget and accounting measures, other than appropriations, except as provided in the Congressional Budget Act of 1974; census and collection of statistics, including economic and social statistics; congressional organization, except for matter amending the Senate's rules or orders; federal civil service; government information; intergovernmental relations; municipal affairs of the District of Columbia, except appropriations therefor; organization and management of United States nuclear export policy; organization and reorganization of the executive branch of the government; Postal Service; status of officers and employees of the United States, including their classification, compensation, and benefits.

The Committee also is to receive and examine reports of the Comptroller General of the United States and submit any desired or necessary recommendations to the Senate in connection with the subject matter of such reports; study the efficiency, economy, and effectiveness of all agencies and departments of government; evaluate the effects of laws enacted to reorganize the legislative and executive branches of government; and study intergovernmental relationships between the United States and the States and municipalities, and between the United States and international organizations of which it is a member.

Subcommittees:

1. Investigations
2. International Security, Proliferation, and Federal Services
3. Oversight of Government Management, Restructuring, and the District of Columbia

Membership:

Majority:	9
Minority:	7
Total:	16

History:

Created as Committee on Expenditures in the Executive Departments, replacing more than ten separate "Expenditure" Committees in 1921

Renamed Government Operations in 1952 and to current name in 1977

Added jurisdiction, in particular over post office, civil service, and District of Columbia, in 1977

Printed History:

U.S. Congress, Senate Committee on Government Operations, *Committee on Government Operations, United States Senate, 50th Anniversary History, 1921-1971,* S. Doc. 92-31, 92nd Cong., 1st sess. (Washington: GPO, 1971), 194 p.

Committee on the Judiciary

Jurisdiction:

Apportionment of Representatives; bankruptcy, mutiny, espionage, and counterfeiting; civil liberties; constitutional amendments; federal courts and judges; government information; holidays and celebrations; immigration and naturalization; interstate compacts generally; judicial proceedings, civil and criminal, generally; local courts in the territories and possessions; claims against the United States; national penitentiaries; Patent Office; patents, copyrights, and trademarks; protection of trade and commerce against unlawful restraints and monopolies; revision and codification of the statutes of the United States; and state and territorial boundary lines.

Subcommittees:

1. Administrative Oversight and the Courts
2. Antitrust, Business Rights, and Competition
3. Constitution, Federalism, and Property Rights
4. Immigration
5. Technology, Terrorism, and Government Information
6. Youth Violence

Membership:

Majority:	10
Minority:	8
Total:	18

History:

Created in 1816

Acquired jurisdiction of Committees on Claims (created 1816), Patents (created 1837), and Immigration (created 1899), by the Legislative Reorganization Act of 1946

Printed History:

U.S. Congress, Senate Committee on the Judiciary, *History of the Committee on the Judiciary, 1816-1981*, S. Doc. 97-18, 97th Cong., 1st sess. (Washington: GPO, 1982), 215 p.

Committee on Labor and Human Resources

Jurisdiction:

Education, labor, health, and public welfare; aging; agricultural colleges; arts and humanities; biomedical research and development; child labor; convict labor and the entry of goods made by convicts into interstate commerce; domestic activities of the American National Red Cross; equal employment opportunity; Gallaudet College, Howard University, and Saint Elizabeth's Hospital; handicapped individuals; labor standards and labor statistics; mediation and arbitration of labor disputes; occupational safety and health, including the welfare of miners; private pension plans; public health; railway labor and retirement; regulation of foreign laborers; student loans; and wages and hours of labor.

Comprehensive study and review of matters relating to health, education and training, and public welfare.

Subcommittees:

1. Aging
2. Children and Families
3. Employment and Training
4. Public Health and Safety

Membership:

Majority:	10
Minority:	8
Total:	18

History:

Created as Committee on Education in 1869, and renamed Committee on Education and Labor in 1871

Acquired jurisdiction of Committee on Epidemic Diseases (created 1885), renamed Public Health and National Quarantine in 1896, in 1921

Renamed Labor and Public Welfare by the Legislative Reorganization Act of 1946

Renamed Human Resources in 1977 and to current name in 1979

Printed History:

U.S. Congress, Senate Committee on Labor and Human Resources, *History of the Committee on Labor and Human Resources, United States Senate, 1869-1979,* S. Doc. 96-71, 96th Cong., 2nd sess. (Washington: GPO, 1981), 531 p.

Committee on Rules and Administration

Jurisdiction:

Administration of the Senate Office Buildings and the Senate wing of the Capitol, including the assignment of office space; congressional organization relative to rules and procedures, and Senate rules and regulations including floor and gallery rules; corrupt practices; credentials and qualifications of Members of the Senate, contested elections, and acceptance of incompatible offices; federal elections generally, including the election of the President, Vice President, and Members of Congress; Government Printing Office, and the printing and correction of the Congressional Record, as well as matters under Senate Rule XI;[3] meetings of Congress and attendance of Members; payment of money out of the contingent fund of the Senate or creating a charge upon the same (except that any resolution relating to substantive matter within the jurisdiction of any other Senate standing committee is to be first referred to such committee); presidential succession; purchase of books and manuscripts and erection of monuments to the memory of individuals; Senate Library and statuary, art, and pictures in the Capitol and Senate Office Buildings; services to the Senate, including the Senate restaurant; and the United States Capitol and congressional office buildings, the Library of Congress, the Smithsonian Institution (and the incorporation of similar institutions), and the Botanic Gardens.

The Committee also is to make a continuing study of, and recommend improvements regarding, the organization and operation of Congress, with a view towards strengthening it, simplifying its operations, improving its relationships with other branches of government, and enabling it to better meet its responsibilities under the Constitution; and is to identify, and call to the Senate's attention, any court proceeding or action which it feels is of vital interest to Congress as a constitutionally established institution of the federal government.

Subcommittees:

None

Membership:

Majority:	9
Minority:	7
Total:	16

---

[3] Senate Rule XI identifies items to be printed that are within the Committee's purview, including documents, reports, and other matter transmitted by the executive departments, memorials, petitions, accompanying documents, and other papers except bills, Senate resolutions, and communications from state legislatures and conventions. Requests for printing additional copies of items also are within the Committee's purview.

History:

Created January 2, 1947, by Legislative Reorganization Act of 1946, merging Committees on Enrolled Bills (created 1789 as joint committee), Library (created 1806 as joint committee), Audit and Control of the Contingent Expenses of the Senate (created 1819 as standing committee), Printing (created 1841 as standing committee), Privileges and Elections (created 1871 as standing committee), and Rules (created 1874 as standing committee)

Printed History:

U.S. Congress, Senate Committee on Rules and Administration, *History of the Committee on Rules and Administration*, S. Doc. 96-27, 96th Cong., 1st sess. (Washington: GPO, 1980), 153 p.

Committee on Small Business

Jurisdiction:

Small Business Administration (SBA). Any legislation reported by the Committee which relates to matters other than the functions of the SBA, at the request of the chair of any standing committee having jurisdiction over the subject matter extraneous to the SBA's functions, is to be considered and reported by such standing committee prior to its consideration by the Senate. Likewise, measures reported by other committees directly relating to the SBA, at the request of the chair of the Committee on Small Business, are to be referred to the Committee for consideration of any portions of the measure dealing with the SBA, and are to be reported by the Committee prior to their consideration by the Senate.

Study and survey by means of research and investigation all problems of American small business enterprises.

Subcommittees:

None

Membership:

Majority:	10
Minority:	8
Total:	18

History:

Predecessor Select Committee on Small Business, created 1950
Acquired legislative jurisdiction in 1977
Created as standing committee in 1981

Printed History:

None

Committee on Veterans' Affairs

Jurisdiction:

Compensation of veterans; life insurance issued by the government on account of service in the Armed Forces; national cemeteries; pensions of all wars of the United States, general and special; readjustment of servicemen to civil life; solders' and sailors' civil relief; veterans' hospitals, medical care, and treatment of veterans; veterans' measures generally; and vocational rehabilitation and education of veterans.

Subcommittees:

None

Membership:

Majority:	7
Minority:	5
Total:	12

History:

Created by Legislative Reorganization Act of 1970

Printed History:

None

Special Committee on Aging

Jurisdiction:

To conduct a continuing study of any and all matters pertaining to problems and opportunities of older people, including, but not limited to, problems and opportunities of maintaining health, assuring adequate income, finding employment, engaging in productive and rewarding activity, securing proper housing, and, when necessary, obtaining care or assistance. The Committee is to report to the Senate from time to time (not less than once each year) the results of such study, together with such recommendation as it considers appropriate.

No proposed legislation is referred to the committee, and the committee does not have the power to report by bill, or otherwise have legislative jurisdiction.

Subcommittees:

None

Membership:

Majority:	10
Minority:	8
Total:	18

History:

Created as temporary committee in 1961
Became permanent in 1977

Printed History:

None

Select Committee on Ethics

Jurisdiction:

Receive complaints and investigate allegations of improper conduct which may reflect upon the Senate, violations of law, violations of the Senate Code of Official Conduct, and violations of rules and regulations of the Senate, relating to the conduct of individuals in the performance of their duties as Members of the Senate, or as officers or employees of the Senate, and to make appropriate findings of fact and conclusions with respect thereto.

Recommend to the Senate by report or resolution by a majority vote of the full committee disciplinary action (including, but not limited to, in the case of a Member: censure, expulsion, or recommendation to the appropriate party conference regarding such Member's seniority or positions of responsibility; and, in the case of an officer or employee: suspension or dismissal) to be taken with respect to such violations which the Select Committee shall determine, after according to the individuals concerned due notice and opportunity for hearing, to have occurred.

Recommend to the Senate, by report or resolution, such additional rules or regulations as the Select Committee shall determine to be necessary or desirable to insure proper standards of conduct by Members of the Senate, and by officers or employees of the Senate, in performance of their duties and discharge of their responsibilities.

Report violations by a majority vote of the full committee of any law to the proper federal and state authorities.

Provide assistance and counsel in connection with franked mail, and prescribe regulations governing the proper use of the franking privilege; investigate any unauthorized disclosure of intelligence information by a Member, officer, or employee of the Senate and report to the Senate on any substantiated allegation; issue regulations governing the acceptance by Senators and staff of gifts, trips, and decorations from foreign governments; administer the Senate financial disclosure requirements contained in the Ethics in Government Act of 1978, as amended; review, upon request, decisions on discrimination complaints of the Office of Fair Employment Practices (OFEP).[4]

Subcommittees:

None

---

[4] This paragraph contains a summary of duties, whereas the above paragraphs restate responsibilities contained in S.Res. 338 creating the Committee, as amended.

Membership:

Majority:	**3**
Minority:	**3**
Total:	**6**

History:

Created as Select Committee on Standards and Conduct in 1964
Added responsibility for franked mail in 1973
Added responsibility over disclosure of intelligence information in 1976
Renamed to current name in 1977
Added reference to Code of Official Conduct, and responsibility for foreign gifts, trips, and decorations in 1977
Added responsibility for administering the financial disclosure requirements in 1979
Added responsibility to review decisions on discrimination complaints by OFEP in 1991

Printed History:

None

Committee on Indian Affairs

Jurisdiction:

Conduct a study of any and all matters pertaining to problems and opportunities of Indians, including but not limited to, Indian land management and trust responsibilities, Indian education, health, special services, and loan programs, and Indian claims against the United States.

Report to the Senate from time to time, by bill or otherwise, recommendations with respect to matters referred or otherwise within the Committee's jurisdiction.

Subcommittees:

None

Membership:

Majority:	8
Minority:	6
Total:	14

History:

Created as temporary committee, with jurisdiction transferred from the then Committee on Interior and Insular Affairs (now Committee on Energy and Natural Resources), in 1977

Became permanent in 1984

"Select" removed from name in 1993[5]

Printed History:

None

[5] Although S. Res. 71 (103rd Congress) removed the term "select" from the Committee's name, it did not make the panel a standing committee.

Select Committee on Intelligence

Jurisdiction:

The Central Intelligence Agency and the Director of Central Intelligence; intelligence activities of all other departments and agencies of the government, including, but not limited to, intelligence activities of the Defense Intelligence and National Security Agencies, and other agencies of the Department of Defense; the Departments of State, Justice, and the Treasury; the organization or reorganization of any department or agency of the Government to the extent that the organization or reorganization relates to a function or activity involving intelligence activities; authorizations for appropriations, both direct and indirect, for the following: (1) the Central Intelligence Agency and Director of Central Intelligence; (2) the Defense Intelligence Agency; (3) the National Security Agency: (4) the intelligence activities of other agencies and subdivisions of the Department of Defense; (5) the intelligence activities of the Department of State; (6) the intelligence activities of the Federal Bureau of Investigation, including all activities of the Intelligence Division; 7) any department, agency, or subdivision which is the successor to any agency named in clause (1), (2) or (3), and the activities of any department, agency, or subdivision which is the successor to any department, agency, bureau, or subdivision named in clause (4), (5), or (6) to the extent that the activities of such successor department, agency, or subdivision are activities described in clause (4) (5) or (6).

Subcommittees:
None

Membership:

Majority:	10
Minority:	9
Total:	19

History:
Predecessor temporary Select Committee to Study Governmental Operations with Respect to Intelligence Activities (1975-1976)
Created as permanent Select Committee on Intelligence in 1976

Printed History:
U.S. Congress, Senate Select Committee on Intelligence, *Legislative Oversight of Intelligence Activities: The U.S. Experience,* committee print, 103-88, 103rd Cong., 2nd sess. (Washington: GPO, 1994), 157 p.

Congress of the United States:
Powers,Structure, and Procedures

THE AMENDING PROCESS IN THE SENATE

Stanley Bach

Summary

A bill is subject to amendment as soon as the Senate begins to consider it on the floor. Any committee amendments are considered first; then Senators can offer amendments to any part of the bill in any order. Senators may debate each amendment without limit unless the Senate (1) agrees to a motion to table (kill) the amendment, (2) agrees to a unanimous consent request to limit debate on the amendment, or (3) invokes cloture, thereby limiting debate on the amendment or on the bill and all amendments to it.

There are several different types of amendments. A first degree amendment proposes to change the text of the bill; a second degree amendment proposes to change the text of a first degree amendment that the Senate is considering. Third degree amendments are not allowed. An amendment may propose to strike out language from a bill (or a first degree amendment), to insert new language, or to replace language by striking out and inserting. In general, an amendment that proposes to replace the entire text of a bill is known as an amendment in the nature of a substitute; an amendment to replace the entire text of a first degree amendment is known as a substitute amendment. An amendment, especially in the second degree, that makes some lesser change is known as a perfecting amendment.

Depending on the kinds of amendments that Senators offer and the order in which they are recognized to offer their amendments, Senators can offer anywhere from three to 11 amendments before the Senate has to vote on any of them. The graphic ways of depicting these possibilities often are called the Senate's "amendment trees."

The Senate only requires that amendments be germane when amendments are offered (1) to general appropriations bills and budget measures, (2) under cloture, or (3) under certain unanimous consent agreements and rulemaking statutes. Otherwise, Senators can offer amendments on any subject to any bill. There are several general restrictions on the amending process. For example, it is not in order to propose an amendment that proposes only to amend language in a bill that already has been amended. However, it is possible to re-amend that language in the process of amending a larger portion of the bill. There also are special provisions in Senate rules to limit amendments to appropriations bills if those amendments propose unauthorized appropriations or changes in existing law. The Senate can, and sometimes does, choose not to enforce these restrictions.

The Senator who has offered an amendment may withdraw or modify it at any time until the Senate has taken some action on it, such as by amending it or by ordering a rollcall vote on it. Senators also may demand that certain amendments be divided into two or more parts. A rollcall vote on an amendment is ordered at the request of at least eleven Senators.

The Senate's cloture procedure makes several changes in the amending process. For example, no amendment can be offered under cloture unless a Senator submitted it in writing before the cloture vote occurred.

Introduction

This report summarizes many of the rules, precedents, and practices of the Senate affecting the consideration of amendments to measures on the floor. Much of the information presented here has been extracted from *Riddick's Senate Procedure*(Senate Document No. 101-28) the sole published collection of Senate precedents.

This report should be read with several caveats in mind. First, no report of this length can take account of every ruling that has been made and every contingency that can arise. Second, the Senate conducts much of its business by unanimous consent, and may thereby change or set aside its rules or customary procedures for specific and limited purposes. Third, Senate procedures are not static; the accuracy of this report will be affected by future changes the Senate makes in its formal rules or informal practices. Although this report may provide useful background information, it should not be considered a substitute for consultation with the parliamentarian and his associates on specific procedural problems and opportunities. This report should not be cited as authority in Senate proceedings.

Offering and Debating Amendments

When the Senate agrees to consider a bill or resolution (either by motion or by unanimous consent), the title of the measure is read. If there are committee amendments printed in the measure as reported, the first of these amendments then is pending automatically. Debate usually begins with opening statements about the measure as a whole by its majority and minority floor managers and other Senators. This is a customary practice of the Senate; its rules do not set aside a time for these opening statements. The Senate then acts on the committee amendments, after which Senators may offer their own amendments to any part of the measure in any order. In the House, measures often are read for amendment by sections or titles; in that case, Representatives may offer amendments only to the one section or title that is then open to amendment. In the Senate, by contrast, measures are considered to be open to amendment at any point.

The first amendments that the Senate considers are amendments recommended by the committee or committees that reported the measure. Senators do not have to call up these amendments for consideration. They are considered automatically, one by one, and in the order in which they are printed in the measure as reported (except by unanimous consent). However, individual Senators may offer second degree amendments to each committee amendment (or first degree amendments to that part of the measure that a committee amendment proposes to strike out or replace—see "The Amendment Trees"), and the Senate considers and disposes of any such amendments before acting on the committee amendment itself.

This means that the Senate usually considers each committee amendment before Senators offer other unrelated amendments from the floor. But the Senate may not dispose of all committee amendments at the beginning of the amending process. In fact, when a committee reports a measure with an amendment in the nature of a substitute for the entire text of the bill, the vote on that committee amendment normally concludes the amending process and immediately precedes the vote on passing the bill (see "The Amendment Trees").

When a Senate committee reports a bill with a series of separate amendments, the Senate often decides not to consider the amendments individually. Instead, the Senate may agree, by unanimous consent, to consider and agree to all the committee amendments *en bloc*, and then to consider the measure, as thus amended, as original text for the purpose of further amendment. Under such an agreement, Senators may offer amendments in two degrees to the text of each committee amendment that now has been made part of the measure. The effect of this arrangement is to create the same opportunities for Senators to propose amendments to each of the committee's recommendations that Senators enjoy when a committee reports a single text that includes all of its recommendations—either in the form of either a complete substitute for a measure referred to it or in the form of a new original measure that is introduced at the same time the committee reports it to the Senate. From time to time, one or more committee amendments may be excluded from such a unanimous consent agreement, leaving that amendment or those amendments to be considered separately.

When the Senate begins consideration of an appropriations measure that the House already has passed, the majority floor manager typically proposes this kind of unanimous consent agreement. The agreement normally includes a stipulation that Senators retain their rights to make points of order against any of the committee amendments that are to be incorporated into the measure under the terms of the agreement. The Appropriations Committee is the only Senate committee that often has reported important measures to the Senate with a series of separate committee amendments. Most other Senate committees usually consolidate all their amendments to a major bill into a single complete substitute amendment for the text of the bill as introduced, or they incorporate their amendments into the text of an original bill that the committee chairman introduces on behalf of the committee.

Paragraph 5 of Rule XV prohibits the consideration of a substantive committee amendment "which contains any significant matter not within the jurisdiction of the committee proposing such amendment." However, this prohibition does not apply if a committee chooses to incorporate that committee amendment into the text of an original bill it orders reported.

After disposing of individual committee amendments, the Senate considers additional first degree amendments, and amendments thereto, in whatever order Senators wish to offer them (absent some unanimous consent agreement to the contrary). In the case of a committee amendment in the nature of a substitute for the entire text of the bill, both that amendment and the text of the underlying measure are open to amendment at any point.

To offer an amendment, a Senator must have the floor, and paragraph 1 of Rule XIX directs the presiding officer "to recognize the Senator who shall first address him." As a matter of established practice, however, preference in recognition is accorded to the majority and minority leaders when either leader and another Senator are seeking recognition at the same time. The chair also may give preference in recognition to either floor manager of the measure the Senate is considering. Technically, a Senator loses the floor after offering an amendment (or making any motion) unless recognized again. In practice, the Senator offering an amendment normally is recognized to begin the debate on it.

With the exception of committee amendments, the order in which first degree amendments are offered is determined not by rule or precedent, but by the convenience of Senators. A second degree amendment, of course, must be offered while the first degree amendment it would affect is pending. The form of first and second degree amendments determines what additional amendments may be offered and pending simultaneously. (See "Types of Amendments" and "The Amendment Trees.") Normally, amendments are offered and considered individually, but Senators may request unanimous consent that two or more related amendments be considered *en bloc*, that is, as if they were one amendment. This is a useful practice when, for example, a Senator needs to amend a bill in two non-contiguous places in order to accomplish a single policy change.

An amendment must be in writing and, when offered, is to be read before debate begins. The reading of an amendment usually is dispensed with by unanimous consent when the floor managers and other interested Senators already are familiar with the amendment's purpose and provisions.

For the information and convenience of the Senate, Senators often submit proposed amendments to be printed in the *Congressional Record* a day or more before they are to be called up for consideration. If an amendment is submitted for printing in the *Record*, it is assigned a number at that time. Otherwise, the amendment is numbered at the time it is offered and read on the floor. In this way, all floor amendments are numbered sequentially throughout the course of a Congress. The text of each amendment usually appears in the *Congressional Record* at the point at which it is called up, even if it had been printed in an earlier issue of the *Record*.

Except under cloture, an amendment printed in advance in the *Record* enjoys no special standing (see "Amendments under Cloture"); it must be called up by a Senator in the same manner as any other amendment. However, a printed amendment may be called up by any Senator, not just by the Senator who submitted it for printing. This does not occur often.

The Senate can (but rarely does) adopt a motion that postpones to a time certain further action on an amendment that it has been considering. More commonly, a pending amendment may be laid aside temporarily, by unanimous consent, in order to permit consideration of another amendment instead. Once the second amendment is disposed of, the first amendment is back before the Senate automatically. When an amendment is laid aside temporarily, it is usually for one of two reasons: either to accommodate another Senator who wishes to offer an amendment at a certain time, or to permit interested Senators to discuss, and perhaps to agree on changes in, a pending amendment without occupying the time of the full Senate.

After the Senate agrees to consider a measure, amendments to it are in order at any time, subject to limitations on the number and types of amendments that may be pending simultaneously, until the measure has been read a third time by title. Except under cloture, Senate rules and precedents impose no limits on the number of amendments that may be offered. By the same token, there is no limit on how long Senators may debate one amendment or all amendments, except (1) by unanimous consent, (2) under cloture, or (3) under the provisions of certain rule-making statutes, such as the Congressional Budget Act of 1974 which imposes a time limit for Senate floor action on budget resolutions and reconciliation bills. Rule XIX states that "no Senator shall speak more than twice upon any one question in debate on the same day without leave of the Senate," but the length of each speech is not controlled.

A Senator may stop debate on an amendment by being recognized and then moving to lay it on the table. If the Senate agrees to this non-debatable motion, the amendment is considered to be rejected. (The Senate may vote to table a first degree amendment while a second degree amendment to it is pending.) If the tabling motion is defeated, debate on the amendment may resume. However, the vote on a motion to table an amendment often is considered to be a decisive test vote on the amendment; if the tabling motion is defeated on a roll call vote, the amendment itself may be agreed to by voice vote shortly thereafter. Moving to table an amendment is essentially a negative action, and there is no other motion available in the Senate to bring the body to an immediate vote to dispose of a pending amendment. Unlike the

House, the Senate does not permit its members to move the previous question or to move the close debate.

The Senate frequently does impose limitations on itself in the form of unanimous consent agreements that specify parliamentary conditions for considering and amending a particular measure. In their most comprehensive form, these agreements can impose a time limit for debating each first and second degree amendment and indicate how the time in each case is to be divided and controlled. A standard period of time may be provided for debating each amendment—for example, one hour for each first degree amendment and 30 minutes for each second degree amendment and any other debatable question—but the agreement may permit lengthier debates on certain specific amendments. The time for debating each amendment usually is divided between its proposer and the majority floor manager (or the minority floor manager, if the majority floor manager supports the amendment).

Such comprehensive unanimous consent agreements (or time agreements, as they often are called) also provide a period of time for debate on the question of final passage—debate on the measure as a whole, that may be used or yielded by the majority and minority floor managers at any time that the Senate is considering the measure. In addition, these agreements normally require that all amendments must be germane, although specific amendments may be exempted from this requirement.

Instead of approving a comprehensive time agreement when it begins debate on a bill, today the Senate is more likely to debate and amend a major bill for some time before developing an agreement that identifies the remaining amendments that may be offered to the bill and the amount of time available for debating each of those amendments. That agreement even may specify the order in which the remaining amendments are to be offered. The Senate also may reach agreements during the course of debate that apply only to individual amendments—for instance, an agreement limiting how long the pending amendment will be debated and which amendment will be the next one to be considered.

Unanimous consent agreements affect the amending process in another important respect. Under such an agreement, covering one or all amendments to a measure, it is not in order to move to table a pending amendment, or to offer another amendment that has precedence, or to make a point of order against the amendment, until all the time for debating it has expired or has been yielded back, at least by the proponent of the amendment. In the absence of a unanimous consent agreement, any Senator who is recognized may take any of these actions at any time after an amendment has been called up.

A unanimous consent agreement to limit debate on a specific amendment also constitutes action by the Senate on that amendment. Once such an agreement is reached, the Senator offering the amendment may modify or withdraw it only by unanimous consent. (See "Modification, Withdrawal and Division of Amendments.")

Through unanimous consent agreements, the Senate imposes an order and some limits on the amending process that are not required by Senate rules and precedents. However, these agreements require the explicit or implicit concurrence of every Senator. If a single Senator objects, the amending process may continue indefinitely or until the measure is fully amended, and without limitations on debate unless the Senate invokes cloture.

Types of Amendments

Some aspects of the amending process in the Senate are predicated upon several distinctions among types of amendments. Amendments may be distinguished in terms of their *degree, form,* and *scope*.

As a general rule, a measure being considered on the Senate floor is open to amendment in two degrees. Unless the Senate agrees otherwise by unanimous consent, it is in order to offer an amendment to the text of any measure (an amendment in the *first degree*), and it is also in order to offer an amendment to that amendment (an amendment in the *second degree*) while the first degree amendment is pending. It is not in order to offer an amendment in the third degree—an amendment to an amendment to an amendment—except by unanimous consent. (There are parliamentary conditions under which, in principle, as many as 11 amendments may be pending simultaneously; see "The Amendment Trees.")[1]

Amendments also differ in their form. First, an amendment may propose to *insert* additional language in a measure or pending first degree amendment without changing anything that already is in the text it would amend. Second, an amendment may take the form of a motion to *strike out* part of a measure or pending first degree amendment without inserting anything in its place. Or third, an amendment may propose to *strike out and insert*—to replace one or more words or provisions of a measure or pending first degree amendment with one or more different words or provisions.

Finally, amendments differ in scope. A *substitute amendment* in the first degree proposes to replace some part of the text of a measure. A *complete substitute* (denoted in this report as an *amendment in the nature of a substitute*) is a special form of substitute amendment that proposes to replace the entire text of the measure—to strike all after the enacting clause and insert "in lieu thereof" a different text.[2] A substitute amendment in the second degree proposes to replace the entire text of a pending first degree amendment with a different text. By their very nature, all

---

[1] Technically, there may be only one amendment pending before the Senate at any moment. The "pending amendment" is the amendment on which the Senate is to act first. For the sake of convenience in this report, however, the term "pending amendments" is used more generally to refer to all the amendments that have been offered and that have not been laid aside temporarily, withdrawn, or disposed of by the Senate in some fashion.

[2] Unlike the House, the Senate does not use the phrase "amendment in the nature of a substitute" to refer consistently and exclusively to an amendment that proposes to strike out all after the enacting clause of a bill (or resolving clause of a resolution) and replace that text with a different text. For purposes of clarity, the phrase will be used only in that sense in this report; but it should be borne in mind that Senators may use the same phrase in a broader sense.

substitute amendments are motions to strike out and insert; but not all motions to strike out and insert are characterized as substitutes.

On the other hand, *perfecting amendments* may take different forms. A first degree amendment to insert or a first degree motion to strike out is a perfecting amendment. In addition, a first degree amendment in the form of a motion to strike out and insert is considered to be a perfecting amendment if it would replace less of the measure than a pending first degree substitute amendment. A perfecting amendment in the second degree may take any of the three possible forms so long as it proposes to alter or "perfect," rather than to replace entirely, the text of a pending first degree amendment.

Whether a first degree amendment is considered to be a perfecting or a substitute amendment may depend on the parliamentary circumstances in which it is offered. When a Senator offers a first degree amendment in the form of a motion to strike out and insert, that amendment is considered to be a substitute amendment if no other such first degree amendment is already pending. However, the same first degree amendment to strike out and insert may be considered to be a perfecting amendment instead if it is offered while there is already pending a substitute for some larger portion of the measure. Any motion to strike out and insert in the first degree—even an amendment that would replace an entire title of the measure—is a perfecting amendment if it is offered while the Senate is considering an amendment in the nature of a substitute that would replace the text of the measure altogether.

By the same token, the distinction between perfecting and substitute amendments can depend on the way in which the amendments are drafted, not on the significance of the legislative changes they propose. With regard to second degree amendments, for example, any amendment is a substitute amendment so long as it proposes to insert something in the measure in place of the matter that the pending first degree amendment proposes to insert—without regard to whether the first degree amendment proposes only to insert or to strike out and insert. On the other hand, a second degree amendment is a perfecting amendment so long as it proposes to alter, but not replace entirely, the matter proposed to be inserted by the pending first degree amendment.

As a result, a second degree perfecting amendment may propose major changes in a first degree amendment, while a second degree substitute amendment may be identical to the text it would replace except for one word or number. It is sometimes possible, and useful, for the same second degree amendment to be drafted both as a perfecting amendment and as a substitute amendment so that the amendment may be offered under the widest range of parliamentary circumstances.

Precedence Among Amendments

The distinctions among types of amendments are not merely analytical; they can be of considerable practical importance because of the relations of *precedence* among amendments.

For purposes of the amending process in the Senate, "precedence" has two related meanings. If one amendment has precedence over another, (1) it may be offered while the other is pending, and (2) it is disposed of first. Thus, if amendment A has precedence over amendment B, amendment A may be offered even though amendment B already has been offered and is still pending before the Senate. And if both amendments are pending at the same time, the Senate acts on amendment A before it acts on amendment B. Precedence also has negative consequences: amendment B may not be offered while amendment A is pending and if both are pending at the same time, the Senate may not act on amendment B before it acts on amendment A (except by unanimous consent).

Three principles of precedence among amendments that are directed to the same text may be derived from Senate precedents, as follows:

1. a second degree amendment has precedence over a first degree amendment;
2. a motion to insert and a motion to strike out and insert have precedence over a motion to strike out; and
3. a perfecting amendment (and an amendment to it) has precedence over a substitute amendment (and an amendment to it).

The first of these principles is axiomatic. A second degree amendment is an amendment to a first degree amendment, and it must be offered while the first degree amendment is pending—that is, after the first degree amendment has been offered but before the Senate has disposed of it. The Senate also acts on an amendment to a first degree amendment before it acts on the first degree amendment itself. So this principle conforms to Senate practice under both meanings of precedence.

The other two principles are less obvious but their practical applications are similar. For example, if a first degree substitute amendment is pending (including an amendment in the nature of a substitute), an amendment may be offered to perfect the part of the measure that the substitute proposes to replace. If that perfecting amendment is offered, the Senate votes on the perfecting amendment to the measure before it acts on the substitute. By the same token, while a motion to strike out part of a measure is pending, an amendment may be offered to the text proposed to be stricken, and the Senate acts on the latter amendment before it votes on the motion to strike out. Because of these principles of precedence among amendments, a number of amendments may be pending at the same time (see "The Amendment Trees").

Precedence controls what amendments *may* be offered at any given time, but it has no effect on the order in which Senators are recognized to offer amendments. If two Senators wish to offer amendments, the order in which the amendments are called up for consideration, assuming both are in order, depends on which Senator seeks recognition first, not on the relative precedence of the two amendments. If two Senators seek recognition at the same time, the relative precedence of their two amendments does not determine which Senator will be recognized first.

The notion of precedence has another important effect on the amending process. Paragraph 1 of Rule XXII specifies an order of precedence among motions, including the motion to amend. Under the terms of this paragraph, a motion to adjourn or recess is in order while an amendment is pending. It is in order also to move to lay a pending amendment on the table. In fact, all the other motions listed in Rule XXII have precedence over the motion to amend.

The Amendment Trees

Under certain parliamentary circumstances, a number of amendments may be pending at the same time. The graphic display of the amendments that are in order at any one time sometimes is referred to as an "amendment tree."

There are at least two ways of depicting the amendment trees, both of which are presented in this section. The official system is the one used in *Riddick's Senate Procedure*. The four diagrams in this section that are labeled "charts" are taken directly from this source and are explained in considerable detail in the extended discussion of precedents concerning amendments (pages 24-125 of that volume). On the pages facing three of the four charts from *Riddick's Senate Procedure* are "figures" that depict precisely the same situations and possibilities, but in different ways. The discussion that follows in this section focuses on these figures as an alternative way of visualizing and understanding the amendment situations that can develop on the Senate floor. An understanding of the charts and figures will lead to the same practical conclusions. However, only the charts in *Riddick's Senate Procedure* have any standing as Senate precedents.

The amendment trees in the Senate generally reflect the meaning and principles of precedence among amendments. The three principles discussed in the previous section of this report are summary statements derived from an examination of Senate precedents under which certain amendments have been offered under various conditions. However, the Senate does not permit every amendment to be offered, under all circumstances, that might seem to be in order under the logic of these principles. The principles of precedence are sufficient to account for the order in which the Senate acts on amendments that have been offered.

The amendments that are in order at any one time depend on the form and scope of the first amendment to be proposed, and then on the form, scope, and degree of subsequent amendments. Thus, depending on the form and scope of the first amendment to be offered, as few as two or as many as ten other amendments may be offered before the Senate must vote on any one of them. But whether all of these amendments actually will be pending depends on what amendments Senators wish to offer and the order in which they are recognized to do so.

With An Amendment to Insert Pending

An amendment to insert additional matter in a measure is a first degree perfecting amendment. While such an amendment to the text of the measure is pending, no other first degree amendments may be offered (because no other first degree amendment has precedence over such a perfecting amendment to a measure). However, the amendment to insert, as a first degree amendment, is open to an amendment in the second degree, which may be either a perfecting amendment or a substitute amendment.

If a second degree perfecting amendment is offered—that is, an amendment to alter or perfect the matter proposed to be inserted—no further amendments are in order until the second degree amendment is disposed of. The second degree perfecting amendment may propose to delete, insert, or replace matter in the first degree amendment. Once the second degree amendment is disposed of, another perfecting or substitute amendment may be proposed to the pending first degree amendment, so long as a subsequent second degree amendment does not propose only to amend matter in the first degree amendment that already has been amended. The process of offering and disposing of second degree amendments may continue until no further second degree amendments are proposed or until the entire text of the first degree amendment has been amended. After acting on all second degree amendments, the Senate proceeds to vote on the first degree amendment, if and as amended.

An additional possibility becomes available if the first amendment in the second degree to be offered is a substitute rather than a perfecting amendment, or more generally, if a second degree substitute is offered when a second degree perfecting amendment is not already pending. In such a case, while the second degree substitute is pending to the first degree perfecting amendment, it also is in order for a Senator to offer a second degree perfecting amendment to the first degree amendment. (See Chart 1 and Figure 1.) The order in which the second degree amendments are offered is decisive. Because a perfecting amendment has precedence over a substitute amendment directed to the same text (in this case, the text being the first degree amendment), a second degree perfecting amendment may be offered before the Senate votes on a pending second degree substitute. The converse, however, is not true: a second substitute is not in order while a second degree perfecting amendment is pending.

If second degree perfecting and substitute amendments are pending at the same time to a first degree amendment to insert, the Senate acts first on the second degree perfecting amendment and then on the second degree substitute amendment; after disposing of both second degree amendments, the Senate then acts on the first degree amendment, if and as amended. This voting order also reflects the principles of precedence: the perfecting amendment has precedence over the substitute amendment directed to the same text, and both second degree amendments have precedence over the first degree amendment.

Figure 1.

With an amendment to insert pending

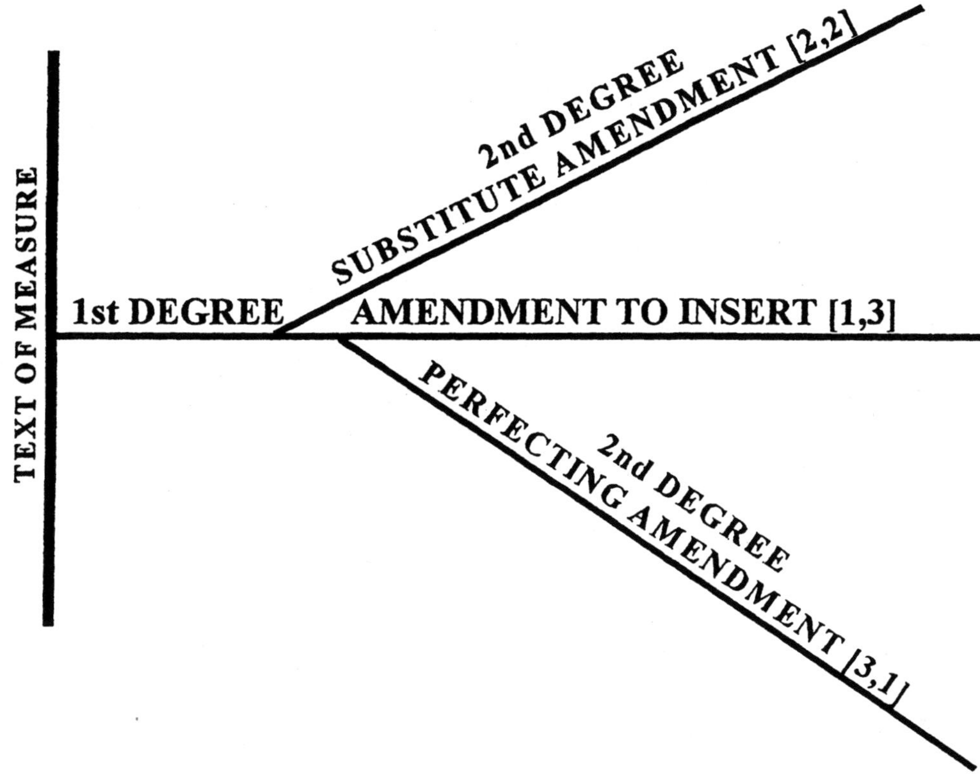

(x,y) = order of offering, order of voting

Chart 1: AMENDMENT TO INSERT

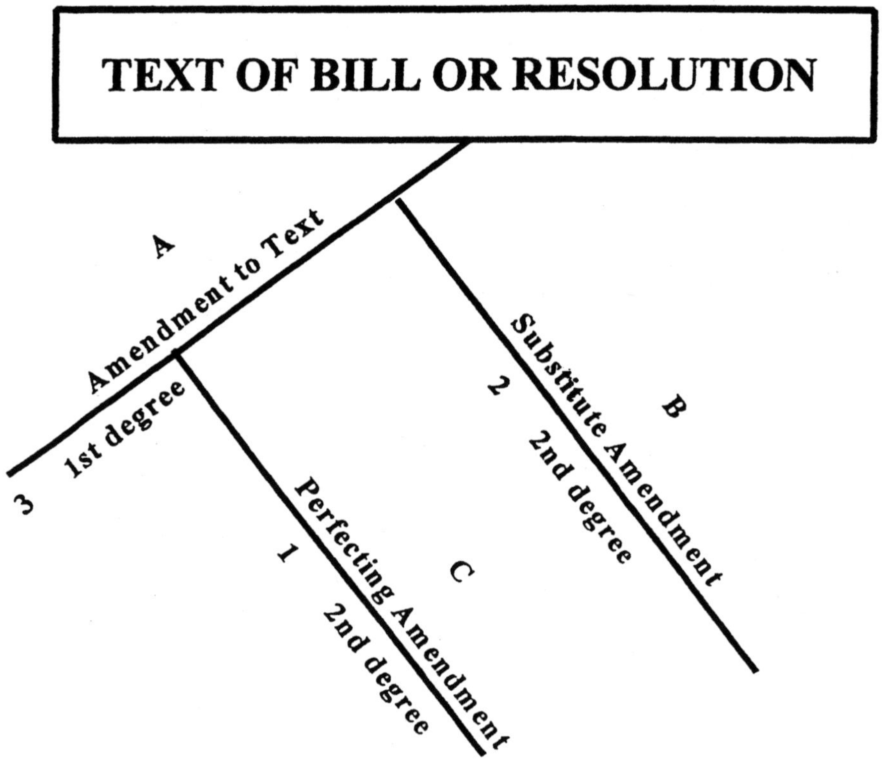

A through C = order of offering
1 through 3 = order of voting

Thus, there may be three amendments pending at the same time: the first degree perfecting amendment to insert additional matter, a second degree perfecting amendment to that amendment, and a second degree substitute amendment. After the Senate acts on the second degree perfecting amendment, Senators may offer other such amendments, one at a time, and the Senate acts on each of them before acting on the second degree substitute. By the same token, if the second degree substitute is rejected or tabled, another such substitute may be proposed and, while it is pending, additional second degree perfecting amendments may be offered. Neither of the second degree amendments is open to amendment because third degree amendments are prohibited.

In general, then, while there is pending a first degree amendment to insert additional matter, (1) a second degree substitute for that amendment is in order unless a second degree perfecting amendment already is pending, and (2) one or more second degree perfecting amendments may be offered and must be disposed of, one at a time, before the Senate acts on a pending second degree substitute.

With An Amendment To Strike Out And Insert Pending

If a Senator offers a first degree perfecting amendment that proposes to insert additional matter in a measure, no more than two additional amendments (both in the second degree) may be offered and pending at the same time. If, however, a Senator proposes a first degree amendment in the form of a motion to strike out and insert and does so when no other such amendment is pending, that motion to strike out and insert is considered to be a substitute amendment for part of the measure, and as many as four other amendments may be pending simultaneously, but only if the amendments are offered in a particular order. (See Chart 3 and Figure 2.)

Like a first degree perfecting amendment, a first degree substitute for part of the measure is open to an amendment in the second degree, and the second degree amendment may be either a perfecting amendment or a substitute amendment. If a second degree perfecting amendment is offered, no additional amendments to the first degree substitute are in order until the Senate acts on the second degree amendment. At that time, a second degree substitute amendment or another second degree perfecting amendment may be offered while the first degree substitute remains pending.

However, if a Senator offers a second degree substitute amendment for the pending first degree substitute, a second degree perfecting amendment also may be offered while the first and second degree substitute amendments are pending. This situation may arise if the second degree substitute is offered (1) before any second degree perfecting amendment has been offered, or (2) after one or more second degree perfecting amendments already have been offered and acted on. With a second degree substitute amendment pending, the Senate may consider and act on a series of second degree perfecting amendments before it votes the second degree substitute. Should the second degree substitute be rejected or tabled, another such substitute may be offered and, while it is pending, additional second degree perfecting amendments may be offered to the first degree substitute amendment.

To this extent, the same number and types of amendments may be offered if the first degree amendment that is pending is a perfecting amendment in the form of a motion to insert or if it is a substitute amendment for part of the measure in the form of a motion to strike out and insert. However, additional amendments may be offered when a substitute amendment for part of the measure is the only first degree amendment pending—amendments that are not in order when a first degree perfecting amendment to insert has been offered.

A perfecting amendment has precedence over a substitute amendment that is directed to the same text, and the perfecting amendment also has precedence over an amendment to the substitute. As a result, while a substitute amendment for part of the measure is pending, and while a second degree perfecting amendment or a second degree substitute amendment, or both, is pending to the first degree substitute, it is also in order for a Senator to offer a perfecting amendment to the part of the measure that the first degree substitute would strike out and replace. Thus, first degree perfecting and substitute amendments may be pending to the same part of the measure at the same time. The perfecting amendment may take the form of an amendment to insert, to strike out, or to strike out and insert. Moreover, because the perfecting amendment to the measure is a first degree amendment, it is open to an amendment in the second degree.

With a substitute amendment pending for part of the measure, therefore, as many as four additional amendments may be pending simultaneously: (1) a second degree substitute amendment for the first degree substitute, (2) a second degree perfecting amendment to the first degree substitute, (3) a first degree perfecting amendment directed to the same part of the measure that the first degree substitute would strike out and replace, and (4) a second degree perfecting or substitute amendment directed to the first degree perfecting amendment.

(The logic of precedence suggests that a sixth amendment also would be in order: that second degree perfecting and substitute amendments could be pending at the same time to the first degree perfecting amendment. Under Senate precedents, however, either a second degree perfecting amendment or a second degree substitute amendment may be offered to the pending first degree perfecting amendment, but both second degree amendments may not be pending simultaneously. Whenever there appears to be a discrepancy between the logic of precedence and the amendment charts depicted in *Riddick's Senate Procedure*, the charts are controlling.)

In this situation, the first degree perfecting amendment to the measure may be a motion to strike out and insert, but if so, it proposes to replace less of the measure than the initial motion to strike out and insert. This is one situation in which a first degree amendment is considered to be a perfecting amendment even though it might be treated as a substitute amendment under other circumstances. For example, if the first degree substitute amendment (the first motion to strike out and insert to be offered) proposes to replace a title of the measure, the first degree perfecting amendment may propose to replace an entire section of that title. This latter amendment would be considered a substitute if no other amendments already were pending, but it is treated as a perfecting amendment if it is offered while a substitute amendment for a larger part of the measure is pending.

Figure 2.

With an amendment to strike out and insert pending

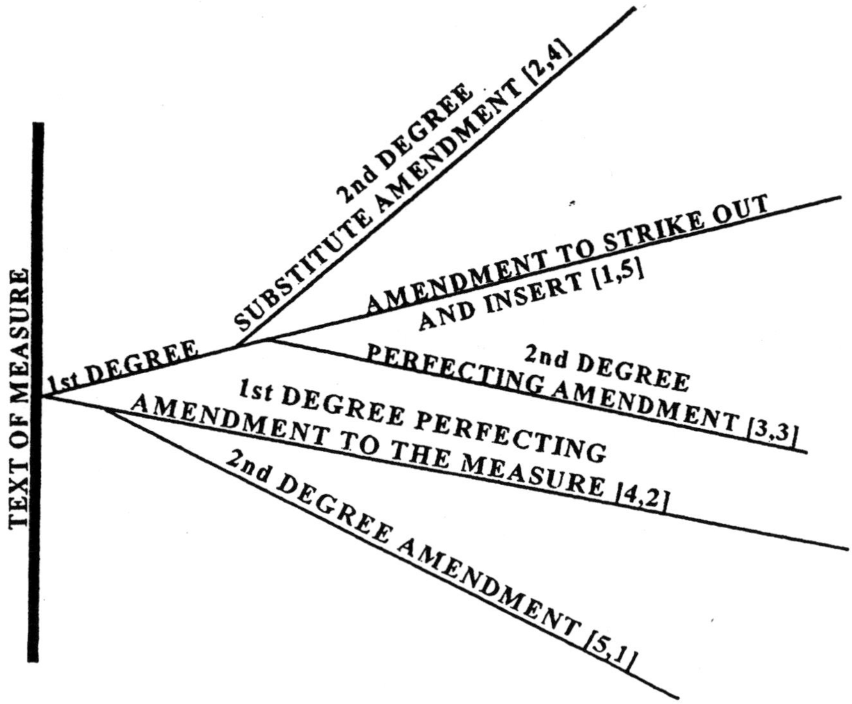

(x,y) = order of offering, order of voting

Chart 3: AMENDMENT TO STRIKE AND INSERT (SUBSTITUTE FOR SECTION OF A BILL)

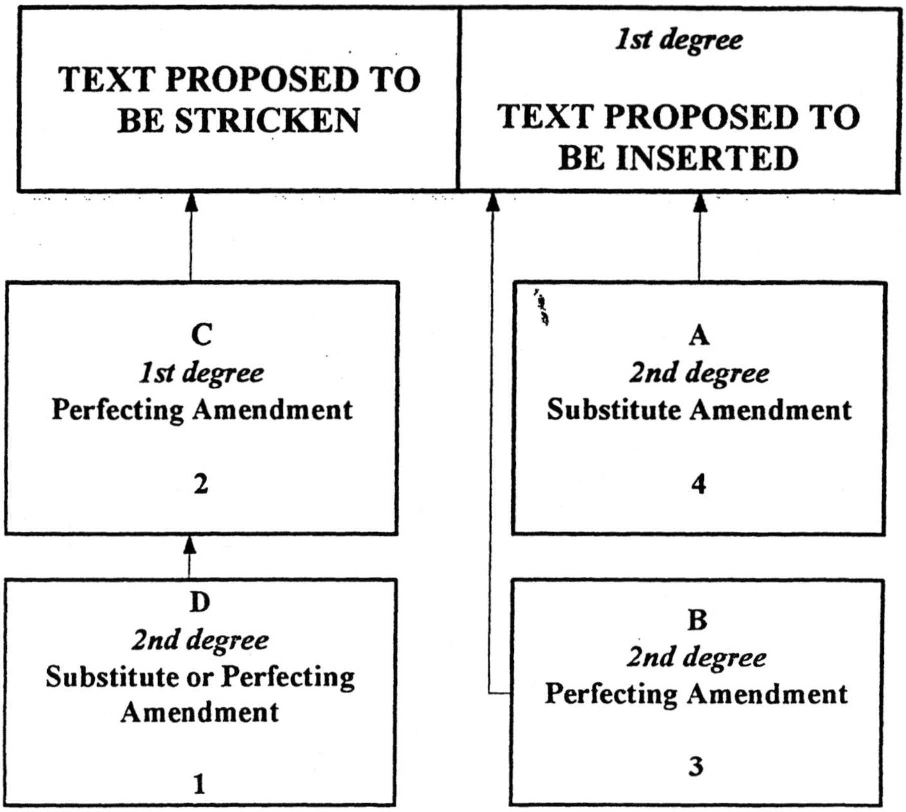

A through D = order of offering to get all the above amendments before the Senate

1 through 4 = order of voting

For all five amendments to be pending simultaneously, they must be offered in exactly the order in which they were listed earlier. Because a perfecting amendment to a measure has precedence over a substitute for part or all of the measure, and over second degree amendments to such a substitute, the first degree substitute and amendments to it must be offered before the first degree perfecting amendment (and any amendment to it). If the first two amendments offered were, in order, the first degree substitute amendment for part of the measure and then the first degree perfecting amendment to that same part of the measure, no second degree amendments could be offered to the substitute until after Senate action on the first degree perfecting amendment.

Of the possible amendments to the first degree substitute amendment, the second degree substitute must be offered before the second degree perfecting amendment if both are to be pending simultaneously. Naturally, second degree perfecting amendments may only be offered to first degree amendments that already are pending.

If the various amendments are not proposed in the specific order noted in Figure 2 and Chart 3, only part of the five-branched tree may develop.

If part or all of this tree does develop, the amendments are disposed of in accordance with the same principles of precedence. The Senate acts first on perfecting amendments to the measure; the first vote occurs on the second degree amendment (or on a tabling motion), after which the Senate disposes of the first degree perfecting amendment to the measure (as amended, if amended). The Senate then acts, in order, on the second degree perfecting amendment to the first degree substitute, the second substitute for the first degree substitute, and, finally, the first degree substitute (as amended, if amended). This order of voting is the reverse of the order in which the amendments are offered.

The five amendments may not be disposed of in any other order (except by unanimous consent), but the Senate may consider and act on several amendments on one branch of the amendment tree before it turns to the amendment on the next branch in order. For example, if all five amendments have been offered, and the Senate has acted on the first and second degree perfecting amendments to the measure, Senators may offer additional such amendments, and they must be acted on before the Senate acts on the second degree amendments to the first degree substitute. Similarly, once the text of the measure has been perfected, a succession of second degree perfecting amendments to the first degree substitute may be proposed and acted on before a vote occurs on the second degree substitute. If the first degree substitute (as amended, if amended) finally is rejected by the Senate, another first degree substitute may be offered and this amendment tree may develop once again.

With An Amendment to Strike Out Pending

An amendment (or motion) to strike out is not amendable. However, the precedence among amendments permits Senators to offer amendments to the part of the measure that is proposed to be stricken. A motion to insert has precedence over a motion to strike out; therefore, an amendment may be offered to insert new matter in the text against which a motion to strike out is pending. By the same token, a motion to strike out and insert has precedence over a motion to strike out; while a motion is pending to strike out matter from a bill, therefore, amendments may be offered to replace some or all of that matter.

Finally, a perfecting amendment has precedence over a substitute amendment directed to the same text. Therefore, after one Senator has moved to strike out some matter from a measure, it also would be in order for another Senator to move to strike out only part of that matter. Under these circumstances, one may think of the first motion to strike out as akin to a substitute amendment—in that it proposes to substitute nothing for something—and the second motion to strike out as a perfecting amendment—proposing to strike out less than the first motion.

Senate precedents permit variations of the amendment trees in Figures 1 and 2 (Charts 1 and 3) to develop after a motion to strike out has been offered and before the Senate votes on it. Which of these amendments (and how many of them) may be offered while a motion to strike out is pending depends first on the next amendment that is called up—that is, whether or not it is an amendment to strike out and insert that would replace all of the text proposed to be stricken—and then on the other amendments that Senators seek recognition to offer.

The maximum number of amendments that Senators can offer with a motion to strike out pending is depicted in Chart 2 of *Riddick's Senate Procedure*. These five amendments to the text proposed to be stricken are the same five amendments shown in Figure 2. In other words, the amendment tree in Figure 2 may develop while a motion to strike out is pending if the first amendment offered after the motion to strike out is a complete substitute for the text proposed to be stricken. That motion to strike out and insert is amendable by a perfecting amendment or a substitute amendment or both, and, while any or all of these amendments are pending, Senators may propose perfecting amendments in two degrees to the text that is proposed to be stricken or entirely replaced.

On the other hand, the motion to strike out may be followed by an amendment that is either (1) a motion to insert or (2) a motion to strike out and insert that would replace only part of the text proposed to be stricken. Either amendment is considered to be a perfecting amendment and it may be amended in the second degree. However, only one second degree amendment may be pending at a time; Senators may not offer both the second degree perfecting amendment and the second degree substitute amendment depicted in Figure 1 before either is voted on. Finally, if the motion to strike out is followed by a motion to strike out less of the text that is at issue, neither motion to strike out is amendable.

Since Figure 2 may develop with a motion to strike out pending, there can be as many as three amendments offered to change a section (or any part) of a measure before the Senate must act on any one of them—a motion to strike out the section, an amendment to strike out and insert that constitutes a complete substitute for the section, and an amendment to perfect the section (by inserting, striking out, or striking out and inserting).

Chart 2: AMENDMENT TO STRIKE

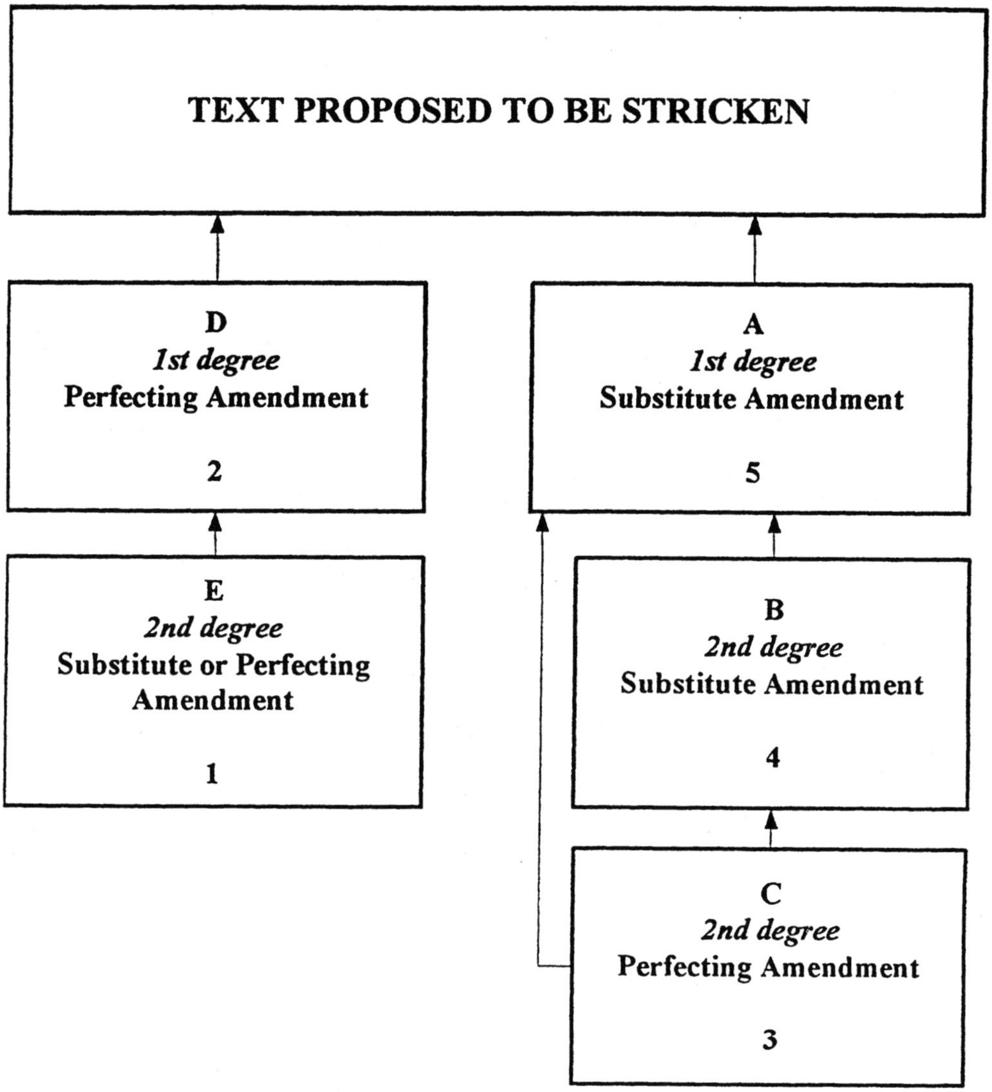

A through **E** = order of offering to get all of the above amendments before the Senate

1 through **5** = order of voting

The Senate acts on any and all of the amendments that "come behind" a motion to strike out before it then acts on that motion to strike out. If a Senator offers an amendment to perfect the text proposed to be stricken, the Senate votes on that amendment (as and if amended) and then it proceeds to vote on the motion to strike out. If that motion is agreed to, the effect is to remove the text at issue, as it has been perfected. On the other hand, if the Senate agrees to a complete substitute for the text proposed to be stricken, the motion to strike out falls automatically without being voted on. The entire text in question having been amended, the motion to strike out would constitute an attempt to re-amend that text and, therefore, is no longer in order.

It should be noted that it would be highly unusual for all of the amendments depicted in Figure 2 to be proposed after an amendment to strike out is offered. Also, the opportunity to perfect or substitute for the text that a motion to strike out proposes to eliminate is only available when the motion to strike out is directed to a part of the text of a measure or to a part of a complete substitute for the text of the measure (which is treated as an original question for purposes of amendment). If a Senator offers a second degree perfecting amendment that proposes to strike out part of a first degree amendment, that part of the first degree amendment may not be perfected while the motion to strike out is pending.

With An Amendment in the Nature of A Substitute Pending

The most complex amendment tree may develop when a Senator or Senate committee proposes an amendment in the nature of a substitute for the full text of the measure—that is, a complete substitute that proposes to strike out all after the enacting (or resolving) clause of the measure and replace it with a completely different text. Individual Senators do not offer such amendments very often, but it is a common practice for Senate committees to report a House or Senate measure with an amendment in the nature of a substitute that preserves the original number of the bill or resolution while proposing to replace its entire text.

Under the precedents of the Senate, such an amendment is treated as an original question for purposes of amendment under either of two circumstances: (1) when it is a reported committee amendment that becomes pending automatically when the measure itself is called up, or (2) when an individual Senator offers it at a time that no other amendment of any kind is pending. As an original question for purposes of amendment, such a complete substitute is not considered to be a first degree amendment that may only be amended in one further degree. Instead, both the amendment in the nature of a substitute and the text of the measure itself may be amended in two degrees, creating the possibility of seven or even eleven amendments pending simultaneously. (See Figure 3 and Chart 4.)

To repeat, when an amendment in the nature of a substitute is considered as an original question, it is amendable in two degrees. A Senator may propose a first degree amendment that is a substitute for the amendment in the nature of the substitute for the measure; the effect of such an amendment is to propose a third version of the text of the bill or resolution. If so, it is then in order also to offer a first degree perfecting amendment to the text of the substitute for the measure that the first degree substitute would replace. Furthermore, both the first degree substitute amendment and the first degree perfecting amendment are open to amendments in the second degree.

This much is in accordance with the principles of precedence, in that a perfecting amendment (and an amendment to it) has precedence over a substitute amendment that is directed to the same text (and an amendment to that substitute). However, only one second degree amendment may be pending at a time to each of the first degree amendments. Second degree perfecting and substitute amendments may not be pending at the same time to either the first degree perfecting amendment or the first degree substitute amendment.

Although any or all of these amendments are pending to the amendment in the nature of a substitute, the text of the measure itself is amendable in two degrees. Any first degree amendment to the measure is considered to be a perfecting amendment, even though it might be a substitute under other circumstances, because it must affect less of the measure than the pending amendment in the nature of a substitute. Furthermore, this perfecting amendment to the text of the measure may be amended by either a perfecting amendment or a substitute amendment in the second degree, but second degree perfecting and substitute amendments may not both be pending simultaneously.

Once a perfecting amendment is offered to the text of the measure, no further amendments are in order to the amendment in the nature of a substitute until the Senate disposes of that perfecting amendment and any amendment proposed to it.

Thus, as many as seven amendments may be pending at the same time, but only if offered in the following order:

1) the amendment in the nature of a substitute, considered to be an original question for purposes of amendment;
2) the first degree substitute for the text of the amendment in the nature of a substitute;
3) the second degree perfecting or substitute amendment directed in the first degree substitute;
4) the first degree perfecting amendment to the amendment in the nature of a substitute;
5) the second degree perfecting or substitute amendment directed to the perfecting amendment to the amendment in the nature of a substitute;
6) the first degree perfecting amendment to the text of the measure; and
7) the second degree perfecting or substitute amendment directed to the first degree perfecting amendment to the measure.

The order in which these amendments must be offered if they are all to be pending is dictated by their relative precedence, and primarily by the principle that a perfecting amendment (and an amendment to it) has precedence over a substitute amendment (and an amendment to it). This principle applies to the amendments depicted in Figure 3, whether the substitute in question is the amendment in the nature of a substitute or the first degree substitute for that amendment.

Figure 3.

With an amendment in the nature of a substitute pending

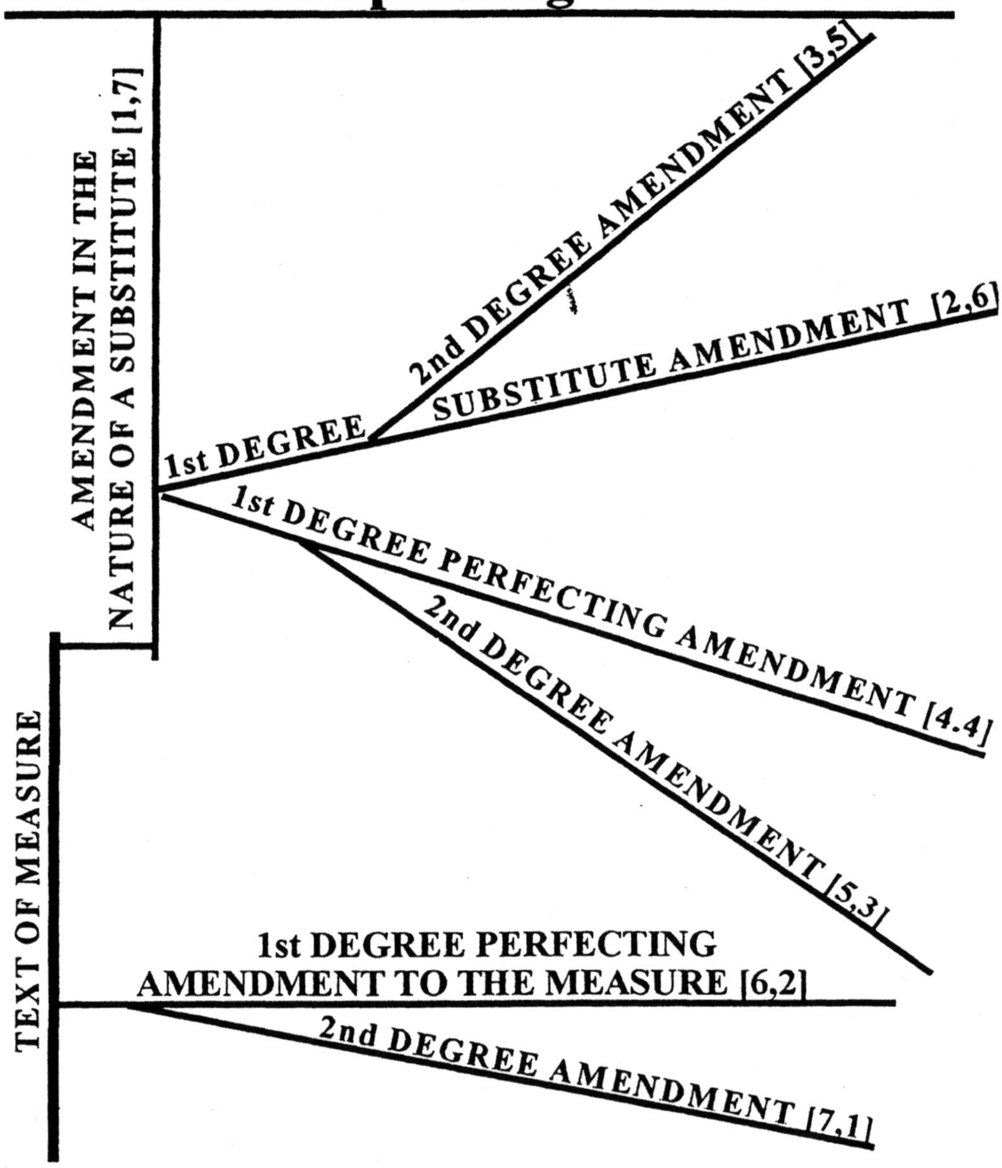

(x,y) = order of offering, order of voting

Chart 4:

AMENDMENT TO STRIKE AND INSERT (SUBSTITUTE FOR BILL)

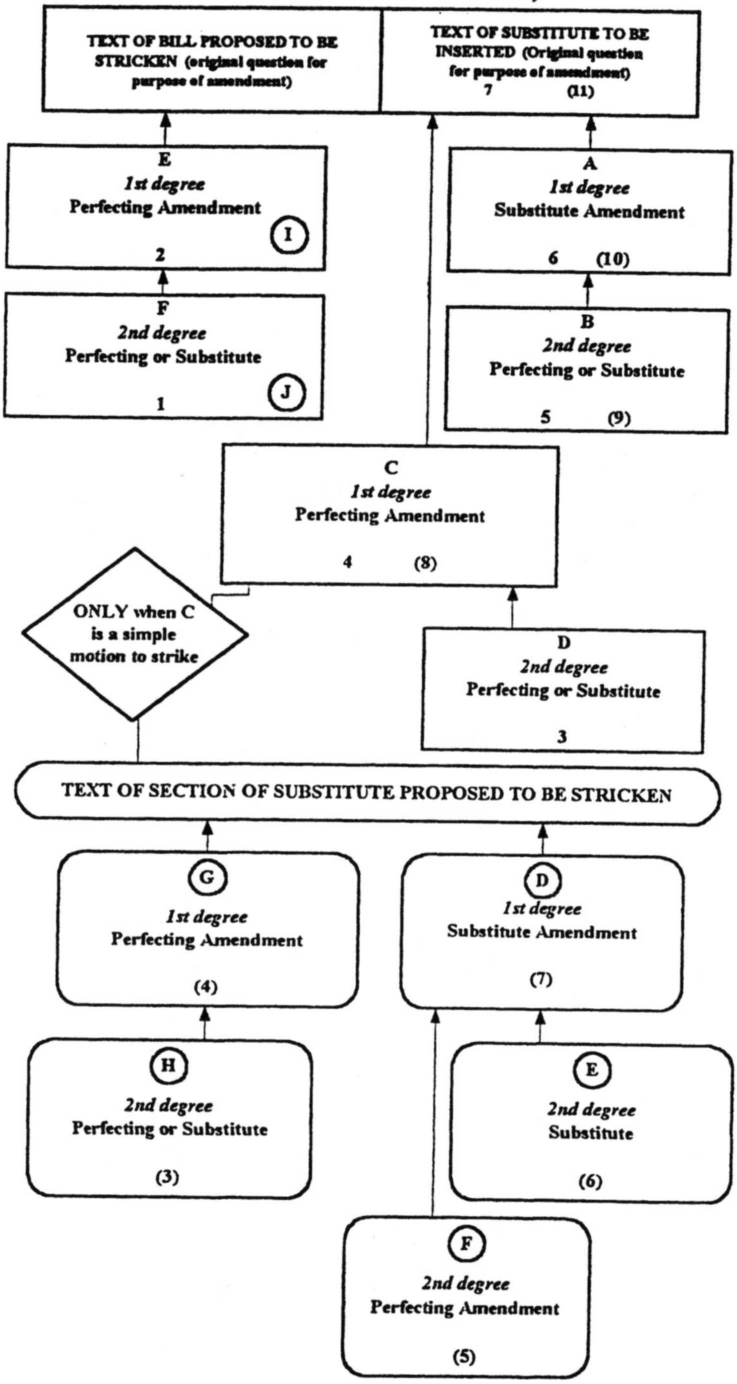

A through J = order of offering to have all amendments pending at the same time
1 through 11 = order of voting
Circled and parenthetical material apply only when C is a motion to strike

Should all seven amendments be pending simultaneously, the order for acting on them is the reverse of the order for offering them. First, the Senate perfects the original text of the measure, considering and acting on any second degree amendments, one at a time, before acting on the first degree amendment, if and as amended. Other perfecting amendments to the measure then may be offered, amended, and acted on. Second, the Senate disposes of the perfecting amendments (and amendments to them) to the amendment in the nature of a substitute. Third, the Senate turns to the amendment to the first degree substitute, and then to the first degree substitute as it may have been amended.

Restrictions on Amendments

In General

In addition to the limitations on the amending process that already have been noted—for example, the general prohibition against third degree amendments—the Senate imposes a number of other restrictions on the amendments that its members may offer. Several of these restrictions are a matter of precedent and apply to all amendments. It is not in order, for instance, to offer an amendment that is substantially the same as an amendment that already has been offered and disposed of unfavorably (for example, an amendment that has been tabled). However, a Senator may offer part of a previously rejected or tabled amendment as a separate amendment, and an amendment that has been rejected or tabled may be re-offered as part of a later amendment that proposes other changes as well. An amendment that has been offered and withdrawn may be offered again without being substantially changed, except under cloture (see "Modification, Withdrawal and Division of Amendments").

Under some circumstances, the substance of an amendment that has been offered and agreed to may be proposed a second time. For example, if the Senate has agreed to an amendment to a substitute for part or all of the measure, an amendment with the same effect also may be proposed to the text of the measure that the substitute would replace. In this way, the effect of the amendment is certain to survive, regardless of the fate of the substitute.

Once the text of a measure or first degree amendment has been amended, it is not in order to propose an amendment that simply would re-amend the text already amended (with certain limited exceptions made by the Budget Act). However, a Senator may offer a second amendment that takes a "bigger bite" out of the measure or first degree amendment—that is, an amendment that re-amends text that already has been amended, but does so in the process of proposing a substantive change in a larger part of the text. For example, after the Senate has adopted an amendment that changes provisions within a section of a measure, a substitute for the whole section is in order. Similarly, after substitutes have been adopted for several sections of a title, a Senator may move to strike out the entire title. But once the Senate agrees to an amendment for the entire text of a measure (or first degree amendment), no further amendments to that text are in order because there is no part of the measure (or first degree amendment) that has not already been amended.

An amendment that would amend a measure in several different places is actually a series of amendments that may be considered *en bloc* without objection or by unanimous consent.

A second degree amendment should affect the same portion of the measure as the first degree amendment to which it is offered. By the same token, while a substitute is pending for part of a measure, any perfecting amendment to the measure should deal with the same part of the measure that the substitute would replace.

In the House, Representatives frequently offer "*pro forma*" amendments, proposing to strike out "the last word" or "the requisite number of words," in order to secure time for debate. Because debate on amendments in the Senate is limited only by unanimous consent, cloture, or a successful motion to table, *pro forma* amendments are neither permitted nor necessary in the Senate.

Germaneness and Relevancy

The Standing Rules of the Senate require that first degree amendments be germane only when offered (1) to general appropriations measures or (2) under cloture. Rule-making statutes also may impose a germaneness requirement—for example, Section 305(b) of the Congressional Budget Act prohibits non-germane amendments to concurrent budget resolutions. Amendments to budget reconciliation bills also must be germane. Under all other circumstances, there is no rule limiting the subjects of amendments.

However, Senators often impose a germaneness requirement on themselves as part of unanimous consent agreements. An agreement that limits and divides control of the time for debating a measure and all amendments thereto may include an additional provision that "no amendment that is not germane to the provisions of the said bill shall be received." This germaneness requirement is included routinely whenever the Senate accepts a unanimous consent agreement "in the usual form." Senators who wish to protect their right to offer non-germane amendments may object to the inclusion of the germaneness provision or request that their proposed amendments be specifically exempted under the terms of the agreement.

Alternatively, the Senate sometimes includes in unanimous consent agreements the requirement that amendments to a specific bill must be relevant. To be relevant, an amendment must not introduce a subject that the bill does not already address. It is possible for an amendment to be relevant but not germane--for example, if the amendment were to expand the applicability of the bill or the authority it grants. The parliamentarian advises the presiding officer and other Senators as to whether amendments qualify as germane or relevant.

In contrast to the Senate, the rules of the House require that all amendments be germane. This difference has been the cause of occasional controversy between the two chambers, and it should be noted that House rules also permit a separate vote on the House floor on a Senate amendment or conference report provision that would have been ruled non-germane if it had been offered as a floor amendment to the measure in the House.

On General Appropriations Measures

The Senate imposes certain special restrictions on the amendments that may be offered to *general* appropriations measures. In contrast to *special* appropriations bills, a general appropriations bill is a measure that appropriates funds for more than a single, specific purpose or program. In addition to the regular annual appropriations bills, some supplemental and deficiency appropriations bills and joint resolutions making continuing appropriations have been held by the Senate to be general appropriations bills, depending on their scope.

Rule XVI of the Senate is devoted to the subject of appropriations measures and amendments to them. Because of the longstanding practice that general appropriations are enacted into law as House bills, much of this rule concerns Senate amendments to House-passed appropriations bills. Recently, however, the Senate has considered more appropriations in the form of Senate bills. The text of a Senate appropriations bill that the Senate has debated and amended ultimately is adopted as an amendment in the nature of a substitute for the text of the companion House bill when the Senate receives it.

Paragraph 8 of Rule XVI states that no general appropriations bill, or amendment to such a bill, shall be considered if it would reappropriate unexpended balances of appropriations—that is, if it would continue the availability of appropriations that otherwise would lapse—unless "in continuation of appropriations for public works on which work has commenced." The rationale underlying this prohibition is that money should be appropriated anew each year, so that Congress can accurately gauge the annual costs of federal activities. Paragraph 5 of the same rule prohibits amendments to general appropriations bills that would provide funds for a private claim unless the proposed amendment would carry out the provisions of some existing law or treaty.

Generally, the provisions of Rule XVI are designed to preserve a separation between the process of appropriating funds and the process of enacting substantive legislation, including authorizations and re-authorizations. However, each of the restrictions in the rule is modified by exceptions, derived either from the rule itself or from precedents. In some respects, these exceptions are so major that the Senate cannot be said to enforce a strict separation between appropriations on the one hand and authorizations and other substantive legislation on the other. Certainly the restrictions on amendments to general appropriations measures are not nearly as severe in the Senate as they are in the House.

Paragraphs 1, 3, and 7 of Rule XVI address the relationship between authorizations and appropriations. Paragraph 2, 4, and 6 restrict the inclusion of other legislative provisions in general appropriations measures.

Paragraph 1 deals with appropriations amendments, whether recommended by a Senate committee or offered by a Senator in his or her individual capacity. Under the terms of this paragraph, no amendment may propose to add or increase an item of appropriation unless it meets one of four conditions. Such an amendment is in order (1) if it already has been authorized by law or treaty, (2) if it would carry out the provisions of a bill or joint resolution already passed by the Senate during that session, even if the measure has not yet been enacted into law, (3) if it is recommended by the Appropriations Committee or a Senate committee with legislative jurisdiction over the subject of the amendment, or (4) if the appropriation amendment is "proposed in pursuance of an estimate submitted in accordance with law."

The rules of the House impose a flat prohibition on unauthorized appropriations except for public works already in progress (although this prohibition may be waived). By contrast, the requirements of Senate Rule XVI are far less demanding. The Senate may consider an amendment making an unauthorized appropriation if the authorization has passed the Senate alone or if the appropriation is recommended by the Committee on Appropriations. The Appropriations Committee is free to propose any appropriation it wishes, whether authorized or not. The existence of a statutory authorization is merely one of the conditions, and not a necessary one, by which an appropriation amendment is eligible for consideration in the Senate.

Paragraph 3 requires that, when an amendment to add or increase an appropriation is offered at the direction of any other Senate committee, the amendment is to be referred to the Appropriations Committee at least one day before it is offered on the floor. This procedure, which very rarely is invoked, is designed to give the Appropriations Committee an opportunity to examine the proposed amendment but not to prevent the Senate from considering it. Paragraph 3 also provides that the appropriation proposed in any such amendment may not be increased by a further amendment on the Senate floor.

Paragraph 7 of the rule requires that the reports of the Appropriations Committee on general appropriations bills must indicate all amendments it is proposing for appropriations that do not have prior Senate or statutory authorization.

Other provisions of Rule XVI address the inclusion of legislative amendments in general appropriations measures. Paragraph 2 deals with amendments recommended by the Appropriations Committee; legislative amendments proposed by other committees or individual Senators are the subject of paragraph 4. Although these provisions of the rule remain in force, a 1995 decision by the Senate casts doubt as to whether, or the degree to which, they now are enforceable.[3]

Paragraph 2 prohibits the Appropriations Committee from reporting an appropriations measure "containing amendments proposing new or general legislation." However, the rule implicitly acknowledges that legislative amendments are in order in the form of limitations—amendments that impose some restrictions on how appropriations may be expended without, for example, repealing or amending existing statutory authorities. No such limitation amendment is in order under paragraph 2 if its effect is dependent on some contingency, such as the subsequent enactment of an unrelated measure.

---

[3] See the CRS memorandum on the "1995 Senate Decision Concerning Legislating on Appropriations Bills," October 16, 1996, by Stanley Bach.

Paragraph 4 imposes similar restrictions on amendments to general appropriations bills other than those recommended by the Appropriations Committee. No such amendment may propose general legislation except in the form of a limitation, and no limitation may be tied to the occurrence of a contingency. In addition, this paragraph imposes a germaneness requirement on all amendments to general appropriations bills, even amendments recommended by the Appropriations Committee.

Although the precedents cited in *Riddick's Senate Procedure* do not provide clear and explicit criteria for determining in all cases whether a particular limitation amendment is in order, paragraph 6 of Rule XVI directs that points of order against questionable limitations should be sustained. However, the Senate enjoys somewhat greater discretion when it amends a limitation that already has been passed by the House. If the House includes a limitation (or some other legislative provision) in a general appropriations bill, the limitation is subject to germane amendments in the Senate, even if the amendments would have the effect of changing existing law. If the House of Representatives "opens the door" by incorporating legislation in a general appropriations bill, the Senate allows itself the opportunity to walk through that door and perfect or replace the House's language.

The Senate's germaneness requirement and the prohibition against legislative amendments apply only to general appropriations measures. Amendments to special appropriations bills need not be germane and may be legislative in character and effect. Moreover, Senate rules and precedents do not prohibit legislative measures from including appropriations, but this asymmetry is more apparent than real because the House may well refuse to consider an appropriation originating in the Senate.

Points of Order Against Amendments

Under regular Senate procedure, a Senator who has the floor can make a point of order against an amendment at any time after the amendment is offered but before the Senate begins to act on it. However, when an amendment is being considered under a unanimous consent agreement limiting debate, no point of order may be made against the amendment until at least all of the proponent's time for debating it has expired or has been yielded back. In either case, a point of order may not be made against only part of an amendment; if a point of order is sustained against any portion of an amendment, the entire amendment is tainted and is out of order. However, the Senator offering an amendment may modify it even while a point of order is pending against it, so long as the Senate has not already taken some action on the amendment (see "Modification, Withdrawal and Division of Amendments").

Rule XX provides that most questions of order are to be decided by the Presiding Officer, but he or she may submit any question of order directly to the Senate instead. Some questions of order must be decided by a vote of the Senate itself, not by the presiding officer; for example, only the Senate as a whole may decide whether a measure or amendment is out of order on the ground that it is unconstitutional. Similarly, Rule XVI requires that questions of germaneness raised against proposed amendments to general appropriations bills shall be submitted directly to the Senate and decided without debate.

When a point of order is to be decided by the presiding officer, Senators have no right to debate it, although the chair may entertain as much or as little debate as he or she chooses. Points of order to be decided by the Senate generally are debatable unless a rule provides otherwise, as in the case of questions of germaneness on general appropriations bills. Time agreements on measures usually limit debate relating to points of order, and questions of order are not debatable when the Senate is operating under cloture.

In most cases, a proposed amendment may be ruled out of order without affecting the status of the measure to which it is offered. For example, if an amendment to add or increase appropriations on a general appropriations bill is ruled out of order, the Senate proceeds to consider other amendments to the bill. However, if the Appropriations Committee proposes an amendment to add new or general legislation to such a measure, a point of order may be made against the bill itself; if the point of order is sustained, the bill is recommitted to the committee. If a point of order is made against any amendment to a general appropriations bill on the ground that it is legislative in character, a Senator may raise the question of germaneness before the point of order is decided. If the Senate votes that the amendment is germane, the point of order falls automatically; the presiding officer does not rule on it.

The most frequent bases for points of order against amendments are those already mentioned: the germaneness or relevancy requirement when in force, and the restrictions on amendments to general appropriations bills under Rule XVI. In addition, points of order may be made against amendments for violating one of several provisions of the Congressional Budget Act of 1974, as amended. The points of order that can be made in the Senate under these increasingly complex procedures are identified and described in a separate CRS report by James V. Saturno on *Points of Order in the Congressional Budget Process* (Report 97-865; October 1, 1997).

If the measure itself would violate a provision of the Budget Act, the Senate may adopt a resolution waiving that provision. Such a resolution protects consideration of the measure, but it does not protect amendments, including committee amendments, that may be offered to it. Under Section 904(b) of the Budget Act, an amendment (or provision of a measure) can be protected against certain point of orders if a majority of the Senate agrees to a motion to waive the applicable provision of the Act. Section 904(c) requires a vote of three-fifths of the entire Senate (not just the Senators present and voting) to waive other Budget Act and related statutory provisions.

Possible points of order against amendments also may be waived by unanimous consent agreements. If an agreement under which a measure is considered provides for a specific amendment, that amendment is protected against the general requirement imposed by the agreement that all amendments to the measure must be germane or relevant.

Any Senator may appeal the ruling of the presiding officer on a point of order, and such appeals are not unusual in the Senate. When a ruling is appealed, the Senate votes on whether it will sustain the ruling of the chair. There are no constraints, of course, on the criteria that Senators may apply in deciding how to vote on appeals.

Modification, Withdrawal, and Division of Amendments

Modification of Amendments

Under certain conditions, an amendment may be modified—that is, its text may be changed without the Senate acting on a second degree amendment to it.

Except under cloture, a Senator who has offered an amendment may modify it, without unanimous consent, at any time before the Senate takes some action on the amendment. Under Senate precedents, the Senate has taken action for this purpose if (1) the yeas and nays have been ordered on the amendment, (2) the Senate has entered into a unanimous consent agreement limiting debate on that specific amendment, (3) the Senate has amended the amendment, or (4) the amendment itself has been agreed to, rejected, or tabled. An amendment may be modified even while a tabling motion or a point of order against the amendment is pending.

After the Senate has taken some action on an amendment, it may be modified only by unanimous consent. However, a Senator who has lost the right to modify his or her own amendment has another recourse; that Senator may offer an amendment to his or her own amendment instead. This is the only condition under which a Senator may propose to amend his or her own amendment.

One Senator may modify an amendment offered by another Senator only by unanimous consent, and committee amendments may be modified only at the direction of the committee or by unanimous consent.

Withdrawal of Amendments

Even under cloture, a Senator who has offered an amendment may withdraw it from consideration, without unanimous consent, unless the Senate already has taken some action on it in one of the four ways listed above. The amendment may be withdrawn even while a point of order is pending against it. But after the Senate has taken some action on an amendment, it may be withdrawn only by unanimous consent. Withdrawing a first degree amendment also eliminates any second degree amendment that may be pending to it, even if the yeas and nays have been ordered on the second degree amendment. An amendment that has been withdrawn may be re-offered at a later time, except under cloture.

One Senator may withdraw another Senator's amendment only by unanimous consent, and committee amendments may be withdrawn only by unanimous consent or at the direction of the committee.

Division of Amendments

Rule XV permits any Senator to demand that an amendment containing several propositions be divided into its component parts. The presiding officer determines, subject to appeal to the Senate, whether an amendment is susceptible to division—that is, whether its parts can stand independently. When an amendment is divided, each part is considered as if it were a separate amendment. After the Senate disposes of one part (division), the next division is placed automatically before the Senate for consideration.

An amendment may be divided even after the yeas and nays have been ordered on it. In such a case, a rollcall vote occurs on each part unless the order for the yeas and nays is vitiated by unanimous consent. Amendments considered *en bloc* may be divided only by unanimous consent.

Rule XVIII also includes an important exception: motions to strike out and insert are not divisible. Consequently, the only amendments that typically are subject to demands for division are amendments to add new provisions to a measure or pending amendment.

Voting on Amendments

The Senate may act on an amendment either by voting on it directly or by voting on a motion to table the amendment. If an amendment is tabled, it is disposed of adversely and permanently (unless the Senate reconsiders the vote on the tabling motion). Tabling an amendment does not affect the status of the measure to which it was offered. Except under cloture or the provisions of certain rule-making statutes or by unanimous consent, the Senate may not vote on an amendment if there are Senators seeking recognition to debate it further (subject to the two-speech limit of Rule XIX). Under these circumstances, the motion to table offers two advantages: it may be offered by a Senator who has the floor at any time after debate on the amendment has begun, and the motion is not debatable. So a tabling motion can be used to end debate on an amendment, but only if the Senate is prepared to reject the amendment. If a tabling motion is made and defeated, debate on the amendment may resume. Another motion to table the same amendment may not be made unless the amendment has been changed significantly or a substantial period of time has elapsed (normally three days in practice).

Under a unanimous consent agreement that limits and divides control of the time for debating an amendment, a motion to table is not in order until at least all the proponent's time on the amendment has expired or has been yielded back, at which point the Senate may be ready to vote on the amendment itself. As a result, tabling motions are somewhat less frequent and useful when amendments are being considered under the terms of unanimous consent agreements.

In practice, the Senate usually votes on amendments and motions to table amendments either by voice vote or by rollcall vote. Division votes occur infrequently. The Constitution provides that a rollcall vote may be demanded by one-fifth of the Senators present, a quorum being present. Since a quorum of the Senate is 51 Senators, the minimum number required for demanding a rollcall is 11 (unless the number of Senators actually present was ascertained shortly before the demand).

The yeas and nays may be demanded on an amendment at any time that it is pending before the Senate, but not before it is offered nor while an amendment that has precedence is pending (except by unanimous consent). A rollcall vote may be demanded even after a voice or division vote has occurred, but before the result has been announced. In practice, however, rollcall votes normally are ordered while debate on the amendment is still in progress. The yeas and nays must be ordered separately on a tabling motion, even if a rollcall already has been ordered on the amendment proposed to be tabled. The yeas and nays on a measure may be ordered at any time it is before the Senate, even while an amendment to the measure is pending.

The Senate acts on all amendments and tabling motions by majority vote of the Senators present and voting, even if offered during consideration of a measure or matter such as a constitutional amendment that requires a two-thirds vote for final action. The Constitution requires that a quorum (a majority of all Senators) must be present for the Senate to conduct business. But the Senate assumes that a quorum always is present unless a majority of Senators fail to respond to a quorum call or fail to participate in a rollcall vote. Consequently, a voice or division vote in which only a few Senators participate is still valid unless challenged.

Amendments Under Cloture

A decision by the Senate to invoke cloture, under the terms of Rule XXII, affects the amending process in a number of important respects.

First, the cloture rule imposes a time limit on the amending process. After the Senate has considered a matter under cloture for a total of thirty hours, no further amendments may be called up for consideration and the Senate proceeds to vote on any pending amendments and then on the matter on which cloture was invoked. (The thirty hours for consideration may be increased by a three-fifths vote of all Senators.)

Second, no Senator may offer more than two amendments until every other Senator has had an opportunity to offer two amendments. This provision is intended to give every Senator a chance to offer some amendments during the thirty hours of consideration under cloture.

Third, to be in order under cloture, amendments must be submitted in writing to the Journal clerk by certain deadlines before the Senate votes on the cloture motion. Specifically, any first degree amendment must be submitted by 1:00 P.M. on the day after the cloture motion is filed; any second degree amendment must be received at least one hour before the Senate begins to vote on the cloture motion. The difference between these two deadlines is designed to give all Senators roughly one day to examine the first degree amendments that may be proposed and to frame any second degree amendments they may wish to offer.

Fourth, after cloture is invoked, all amendments must be germane to the matter under consideration. The presiding officer also is empowered in extreme circumstances to rule amendments out of order as being dilatory.

Fifth, the reading of an amendment is dispensed with automatically, not by unanimous consent, if it has been reproduced and available for at least 24 hours.

Sixth, unanimous consent is required to modify amendments, except for changes in page and line numbers that may be required if the matter under consideration is reprinted after cloture is invoked.

Finally, once an amendment has been submitted in writing, it may be called up by any Senator. Thus, any Senator may call up any amendment that is eligible for consideration under cloture. But once an amendment has been withdrawn under cloture, it may not be re-offered. Consequently, if one Senator offers and withdraws an amendment, another Senator may not bring the same amendment back before the Senate for a vote unless he or she also had submitted it in writing before cloture was invoked.

Congress of the United States:
Powers,Structure, and Procedures

FILIBUSTERS AND CLOTURE IN THE SENATE

Stanley Bach

Summary

The right of Senators to speak on the floor at great length—and so to filibuster—is the single most defining characteristic of the Senate as a legislative body. The possibility of filibusters derives from the absence of any effective Senate rules that limit the number or length of floor speeches.

The Senate's rules provide that, in most cases, a Senator who seeks recognition has a right to the floor if no other Senator is speaking, and that Senator then may speak for as long as he or she wishes. There is no motion by which a simple majority of the Senate can stop a debate and allow the Senate to vote in favor of an amendment, a bill or resolution, or any other debatable question. Almost every bill actually is subject to two potential filibusters before the Senate votes on whether to pass it: first, a filibuster on a motion to proceed to the bill's consideration; and second, after the Senate agrees to this motion, a filibuster on the bill itself.

Senate Rule XXII enables Senators to end a filibuster by invoking cloture on whatever debatable matter it is considering. Sixteen Senators initiate this process by presenting a motion to end the debate. The Senate does not vote on this cloture motion until the second day after the day on which the motion is made. Then it usually requires the votes of at least three-fifths of all Senators, or at least 60 votes, to invoke cloture. Invoking cloture on a proposal to amend the Senate's standing rules requires the support of two-thirds of the Senators present and voting.

The primary effect of invoking cloture on a question is to impose a maximum of 30 additional hours for considering that question. This 30-hour period for consideration encompasses all time consumed by rollcall votes, quorum calls, and other actions, as well as the time used for debate. During this 30-hour period, each Senator may speak for no more than one hour apiece (although several Senators can have additional time yielded to them). Under cloture, the only amendments that Senators can offer are amendments that are germane and that were submitted in writing before the cloture vote took place. The presiding officer also enjoys certain additional powers under cloture: for example, to count to determine whether a quorum is present, and to rule amendments, motions, and other actions out of order on the grounds that they are dilatory.

The ability of Senators to engage in filibusters has a profound and pervasive effect on how the Senate conducts its business on the floor. In the face of a threatened filibuster, for example, the majority leader may decide not to call a bill up for floor consideration, or to defer calling it up if there are other, equally important bills that the Senate can consider and pass without undue delay. Similarly, the prospect of a filibuster can persuade a bill's proponents to accept changes in the bill that they do not support but that are necessary to prevent the threat of a filibuster from becoming a reality.

The right of Senators to speak on the floor at great length—and so to filibuster—is the single most defining characteristic of the Senate as a legislative body. This report discusses filibusters and the Senate's cloture rule for ending them. The report begins with a discussion of the Senate rules that make filibusters possible, and the rules and precedents that affect the conduct of filibusters. Next the report discusses provisions of the Senate's cloture rule, how cloture is invoked, and what effect cloture has on the process of floor debate and amendment. The report concludes with comments on the effects of filibusters, and the threat of filibusters, on how the Senate conducts its legislative business, and on recent developments affecting the use of both filibusters and cloture.

This report discusses the major aspects of the Senate's filibuster- and cloture-related procedures. However, it does not encompass every relevant precedent and every possible contingency and nuance. Authoritative information on cloture procedure can be found under that heading in *Riddick's Senate Procedure*.[1] Senators and staff also may consult the Senate parliamentarian on any question concerning the Senate's procedural rules, precedents, and practices.

The Right to Debate

The core rule of the Senate governing floor debate is paragraph 1(a) of Rule XIX, which states that:

> When a Senator desires to speak, he shall rise and address the Presiding Officer, and shall not proceed until he is recognized, and the Presiding Officer shall recognize the Senator who shall first address him. No Senator shall interrupt another Senator in debate without his consent, and to obtain such consent he shall first address the Presiding Officer, and no Senator shall speak more than twice upon any one question in debate on the same legislative day without leave of the Senate, which shall be determined without debate.

This is essentially all that the Senate's rules have to say about the right to speak on the floor, so the rule is just as important for what it *does not* say as for what it *does* say.

The Right to Recognition.

Several provisions of this paragraph combine to create the possibility of filibusters. First, "the presiding officer shall recognize the Senator who shall first address him." The presiding officer has no choice and no discretion. As a general

---

[1]U.S. Senate. *Riddick's Senate Procedure*. Senate Document No. 101-28. 101st Congress, 2nd Session, 1992; pp. 282-334.

rule, if a Senator seeks recognition when no other Senator has the floor, the presiding officer must recognize that Senator. The presiding officer may not decline to recognize the Senator, whether for reasons of personal preference or partisan advantage, or simply to enable the Senate to reach a vote on whatever question it has been debating.

Rule XIX directs the presiding officer to recognize whichever Senator is the first to seek recognition. By well-established precedent and practice, however, the Senate does not comply strictly with this provision of the rule. All Senators accept that the majority leader and then the minority leader should receive preference in recognition. This means that, if two Senators are seeking recognition at more or less the same time, and one of them is the majority or the minority leader, the Presiding officer recognizes the leader (and the majority leader in preference to the minority leader). The majority and minority floor managers of legislation the Senate is debating also generally are accorded preference in recognition after the two party leaders.

In this respect, Senators give up their equal rights to recognition under Rule XIX. They do so because they all appreciate that the party leaders must be able to secure recognition if they are to do some of the things the Senate expects them to do: to arrange the Senate's daily agenda and weekly schedule, and to make the motions and propound the unanimous consent agreements that are necessary for the relatively orderly conduct of business on the Senate floor. Bill managers also receive preference in recognition because they presumably are among the best-informed (and most influential) Senators on the pending legislation, so all Senators can benefit from hearing their opinions and considering their amendments and other motions.

The result is that, during debate on a bill, a Senator who does not hold one of these leadership positions cannot be sure that he or she will be recognized *promptly*, but each Senator can be sure that he or she will be recognized *eventually*. Because the presiding officer cannot refuse to recognize a Senator who seeks the floor, the Senate cannot vote on whatever debatable question is pending so long as any Senator wants to be recognized to debate it (barring a unanimous consent agreement to the contrary or a tabling motion, as discussed below).

The Right to Speak at Length and the Two-Speech Rule.

Once a Senator has been recognized, that Senator may speak for as long as he or she wishes (again, except when the Senate has agreed to limit debate, usually by unanimous consent). The record for the longest single speech remains the speech made by Senator Thurmond (R, SC) on August 28-29, 1957, which consumed 24 hours and 18 minutes.[2] A Senator who is speaking usually cannot be interrupted without his or her consent. (There are some exceptions: for example, a Senator can be interrupted if he or she is violating the Senate's standards of decorum in debate or, what is more relevant for our purposes, if another Senator wishes to present a cloture motion.)

---

[2]U.S. Senate. Committee on Rules and Administration. *Senate Cloture Rule*. Committee Print. S. Prt. 99-95. 99th Congress, 1st Session; 1985; p 40.

Although there is no limit on the length of individual speeches or on the number of Senators who may speak on whatever question is pending, Senate debate is governed by the provision of Rule XIX, quoted above, that is commonly called the *two-speech rule*. To reiterate, paragraph 1(a) of that rule states that "no Senator shall speak more than twice upon any one question in debate on the same legislative day without leave of the Senate, which shall be determined without debate." Therefore, each Senator is limited to making two speeches per day, however long each speech may be, on each debatable question that the Senate considers. Furthermore, a Senator can make no more than two speeches on that question during the same *legislative* day, even though that legislative day may extend over several or many calendar days.

Senators rarely invoke this rule because they generally do not believe that there is any need to do so. During filibusters, however, Senators may insist that the rule be enforced, in which case its effect can be stricter than some Senators may expect. A Senator does not have to speak for very long at all before that statement will be counted under the two-speech rule. According to the Senate's precedents, the Senate has rejected the position "that recognition for any purpose constituted a speech," and that "certain procedural motions and requests were examples of actions that did not constitute speeches for purposes of the two speech rule." These matters include such things as making a parliamentary inquiry and suggesting the absence of a quorum.[3] On the other hand, a substantive comment, however brief, on the pending question, may count as a speech.

Senators often can circumvent the two-speech rule by making a motion or offering an amendment that constitutes a new and different debatable question. For example, each Senator can make two speeches on each bill and on each first-degree amendment to the bill, but also on each second-degree amendment to each of those amendments.

The Motion to Table.

There is one way in which the Senate can, and often does, end debate on an amendment (or any other question) even though there may be Senators who still might want to speak on it. During the debate, any Senator who has been recognized may move to table the amendment, unless there is a unanimous consent agreement limiting the time for debate.[4] That motion is not debatable and requires only a simple majority vote to be adopted. In the Senate, to table something is to kill it. So when the Senate votes to table an amendment (more formally, to lay the amendment on the table), the Senate disposes of the amendment permanently and adversely. Then it can go on to consider another amendment or to continue debate on the underlying bill.

By this means, the Senate can prevent a debate from continuing indefinitely if a majority of Senators are prepared to reject the amendment, motion, or bill that is being debated. On the other hand, if the Senate votes against the tabling motion, the pending question remains before the Senate, and Senators can resume debating it.

---

[3] "Therefore, the two speech rule requires not a mechanical test, but the application of the rule of reason." *Riddick's Senate Procedure*, pp. 782-783.

[4] When one Senator is debating a question, for however long, another Senator cannot interrupt to move to table that question.

The Senate frequently disposes of amendments by voting to table them, rather than by taking what often are called "up or down" votes to agree to (or not agree to) the amendment itself.

Thus, the opponents of a question can prevail more or less at a time of their choosing by moving and voting to table the question. However, if the opponents constitute less than a majority of the Senate,[5] they may decide to extend the debate by conducting what supporters of the measure might well characterize as a filibuster.

The Conduct of Filibusters

Conducting a filibuster is simple, though it can be physically demanding. A Senator seeks recognition and, once recognized, speaks at length. When that first Senator concludes and yields the floor, another Senator seeks recognition and continues the debate. The debate can proceed in this way until all the participating Senators have made their two speeches on the pending question. Then it usually is possible to make a motion or offer an amendment in order to create a new debatable question on which the same Senators can make two more speeches.

There is no need for the participating Senators to monopolize the debate. What is important is that someone speak, not that it be someone on their side of the question. Although one purpose of a filibuster is to try to change the minds of Senators who support the question being debated, the purpose of delay is served by Senators speaking, no matter which side of the question they take.

The Germaneness of Debate.

More often than not, there is no need for the debate to be germane to the question being considered, with one important exception. Paragraph 1(b) of Rule XIX (often called the "Pastore rule" in recognition of former Senator John Pastore of Rhode Island) requires that debate be germane each calendar day during the first three hours after the Senate begins to consider its unfinished or pending legislative business. In other words, the time consumed by the majority and minority leaders, and any speeches during "routine morning business," at the beginning of a daily session is not included in this three-hour period. The Senate can waive this germaneness requirement by unanimous consent or by agreeing to a non-debatable motion for that purpose.

Like the two-speech rule, the Pastore rule usually is not enforced because Senators do not see the need to enforce it. During filibusters, however, Senators may be called upon to comply with the germaneness requirement on debate when it is in effect. In practice, this does not put much of an extra burden on participating Senators, because most speeches made during filibusters today tend to be germane anyway. In earlier times, filibustering Senators were known to speak about virtually anything. In his 1940 study of filibusters, Franklin Burdette reported that Senator Huey Long of Louisiana "would dictate for the benefit of the Congressional Record

---

[5]Or, more accurately, less than a majority of the Senators who would be voting on the question, those Senators constituting a quorum.

recipes for cooking upon which his authoritative advice had been regularly in demand in Washington social circles....He then proceeded to tell the Senate at great length and in meticulous detail how to fry oysters. Nor did he omit a rambling discourse on the subject of 'potlikker.'"[6]

Although Senator Long's discourse was unusual during the 1930s, it would be even more unexpected in the Senate today, when Senators generally do not stray very far in their speeches from the subject at hand. It bears repeating, however, that the requirement for germane debate is in effect for only three hours on each calendar day.

Yielding the Floor and Yielding for Questions.

A Senator who has the floor for purposes of debate must remain standing and must speak more or less continuously.[7] Complying with these requirements obviously becomes more of a strain as time passes. However, Senators must be careful when they try to give some relief to their colleagues who are speaking. Senate precedents prohibit Senators from yielding the floor to each other. To gain the floor, a Senator must seek recognition from the presiding officer. Thus, if a Senator simply yields to a colleague, he or she has yielded (relinquished) the floor, however inadvertently. This is another one of those Senate procedures that often is not observed during the normal conduct of business on the floor. But during filibusters, Senators are much more likely to insist on it being observed.

A Senator may yield to a colleague without losing the floor only if the Senator yields for a question.[8] With this in mind, a colleague of a filibustering Senator may give that Senator some relief by asking him or her to yield for a question. The Senator who retains control of the floor must remain standing while the question is being asked. The peculiar advantage of this tactic is that it sometimes takes Senators quite some time to ask their question, and the presiding officer is reluctant to force them to state their question before they are ready to do so. In this way, participating Senators can extend the debate through an exchange of what sometimes are long questions followed by short answers, rather than by relying exclusively on a series of long, uninterrupted speeches.

Quorums and Quorum Calls.

There are ways other than debate by which Senators can delay and sometimes even prevent the Senate from voting on a question that it is considering. For example, each amendment that is offered on the Senate floor must be read in full before debate on it can begin, although the Senate usually agrees by unanimous consent to waive the reading. In addition, quorum calls can be demanded not for the purpose of confirming or securing the presence of a quorum, but in order to consume time.

---

[6]Franklin Burdette, *Filibustering in the Senate*. New York: Russell & Russell, 1965 (reprint of 1940 Princeton University Press edition), p. 4.

[7]*Riddick's Senate Procedure*, p. 755.

[8]Senators sometimes ask unanimous consent to yield to a colleague for something other than a question without losing their right to the floor. Any Senator can object to this request.

A Senator who has been recognized can "suggest the absence of a quorum," asking in effect whether the Senate is complying with the constitutional requirement that a quorum—a majority of all Senators—be present for the Senate to conduct business. The presiding officer normally does not have the authority to count to determine whether a quorum actually is present (which is rarely the case), and so directs the clerk to call the roll.

Senators usually use quorum calls to suspend the Senate's floor proceedings temporarily, perhaps to discuss a procedural or policy problem or to await the arrival of a certain Senator. In those cases, the clerk calls the roll very slowly and, before the call of the roll is completed, the Senate agrees by unanimous consent to call off the quorum call (to "dispense with further proceedings under the quorum call"). Because the absence of a quorum has not actually been demonstrated, the Senate can resume its business. Such quorum calls can be time-consuming and so can serve the interests of filibustering Senators.

During a filibuster, however, the clerk may be directed to call the roll more rapidly, as if a rollcall vote were in progress. Doing so reduces the time that the quorum call consumes, but it also creates the real possibility that the quorum call may demonstrate that a quorum in fact is not present. In that case, the Senate has only two options: to adjourn, or to take steps necessary to secure the presence of enough absent Senators to create a quorum. Typically, the majority leader or the majority floor manager opts for the latter course, and makes a motion that the sergeant at arms secure the attendance of absent Senators, and then asks for a rollcall vote on that motion. Senators who did not respond to the quorum call are likely to come to the floor for the rollcall vote on this motion. Almost always, therefore, the vote establishes that a quorum is present, so the Senate can resume its business without the sergeant at arms actually having to execute the Senate's directive.

This process also can be time-consuming because of the time required to conduct the rollcall vote just discussed. Nonetheless, the proponents of the bill (or other matter) being filibustered may prefer that the roll be called quickly because it requires unanimous consent to call off a routine quorum call, in which the clerk calls the roll very slowly, before it is completed. A filibustering Senator has only to suggest the absence of a quorum and then object to calling off the quorum call in order to provoke a motion to secure the attendance of absentees and (with the support of at least 10 other Senators) a rollcall vote on that motion.[9] If this motion is likely to be necessary, one way or the other, it is usually in the interests of the bill's proponents to have the motion made (and agreed to) as soon as possible.

---

[9]However, when a Senator suggests the absence of a quorum, he or she loses the floor. Also, "[i]t is not in order for a Senator to demand a quorum call if no business has intervened since the last call; business must intervene before a second quorum call or between calls if the question is raised or a point of order made." *Riddick's Senate Procedure*, p. 1053. On what constitutes intervening business, see pp. 1042-1046.

Rollcall Voting.

As the preceding discussion indicates, rollcall votes are another source of delay. Any question put to the Senate for its decision requires a vote, and a minimum of 11 Senators can require that it be a rollcall vote. Each such vote consumes at least 15 minutes unless the Senate agrees in advance to reduce the time for voting.[10]

The Constitution provides that the "yeas and nays" shall be ordered "at the desire of one-fifth of those present" (Article I, Section 5). Because a quorum is presumed to be present, the Senate requires at least 11 Senators (one-fifth of the minimal quorum of 51) to request a rollcall vote on the pending question.

When a Senator wants a rollcall vote, other Senators frequently support the request as a courtesy to a colleague. During a filibuster, however, the supporters of the bill or amendment sometimes try to discourage other Senators from supporting requests for time-consuming rollcall votes. Also, the proponents sometimes can make it more difficult for their opponents to secure a rollcall vote. When the request for a rollcall vote is made immediately after a quorum call or another rollcall vote, Senators can insist that the request be supported by one-fifth of however many Senators answered that call or cast their votes.[11] Since this is almost certainly more than 51 and, in practice, is much closer to 100, the number of Senators required to secure a rollcall can increase to a maximum of 20.

The time allowed for Senators to cast rollcall votes is a minimum of 15 minutes, unless the Senate agrees, before the vote begins, to a reduced time. When the 15 minutes expire, the vote usually is left open for some additional time in order to accommodate other Senators who are thought to be en route to the floor to vote. Thus, the actual time for a rollcall vote can extend to 20 minutes or more. During filibusters, however, a call for the regular order can lead the presiding officer to announce the result of a rollcall vote soon after the 15 minutes allotted for it.

Senators usually can secure two votes in connection with the disposition of bills, amendments, motions, and other questions. The first is the vote on the question itself or on a motion to table it. The second is the vote on a motion to *reconsider* the vote by which the first question was decided (or on a motion to table the motion to reconsider). With sufficient support, rollcall votes can be ordered on each motion. so that completing action on both of them consumes at least 30 minutes.

---

[10]The Senate, unlike the House, does not use an electronic voting system.

[11]"[T] sufficiency of the number of Senators demanding a rollcall is based on the last preceding rollcall. The Chair, noting that 81 Senators had just voted, denied the yeas and nays when only 16 Senators responded to a request for a sufficient second. A demand for the yeas and nays immediately following a call of the Senate is seconded by one-fifth of those answering such call, or immediately following a yea and nay vote, seconded by one-fifth of those voting." *Riddick's Senate Procedure*, p. 1417.

Scheduling Filibusters.

Contemporary filibusters usually are fairly courteous affairs. The Senate's daily schedule normally is arranged so that filibusters are not unduly disruptive or inconvenient to Senators. One way to make conducting a filibuster more costly and difficult is to keep the Senate in session until late at night, or even all night, requiring the participating Senators to speak or otherwise consume the Senate's time. During some contentious filibusters of the 1950s, cots were brought into the Senate's anterooms for Senators to use during around-the-clock sessions.

Today, all-night sessions are very unusual. The Senate may not even convene earlier or remain in session later when a filibuster is in progress than it does on other days. One reason may be that filibusters are not the extraordinary and unusual occurrences that they once were. Another may be that Senators are less willing to endure the inconvenience and discomfort of prolonged sessions. The latter point is important because late-night or all-night sessions put as much or more of a burden on the proponents of the question being debated than on its opponents.

The Senators participating in the filibuster need only ensure that at least one of their number always is present on the floor to speak. The proponents of the question, however, need to ensure that a majority of the Senate is present or at least available to respond to a quorum call or rollcall vote. If, late in the evening or in the middle of the night, a Senator suggests the absence of a quorum and a quorum does not appear, the Senate must adjourn or at least suspend its proceedings until a quorum is established. This works to the advantage of the filibustering Senators, so the burden rests on their opponents to ensure that the constitutional quorum requirement always can be met.

Invoking Cloture

The procedures for invoking cloture are governed by paragraph 2 of Rule XXII (which also governs procedures under cloture, as discussed later in this report).

The process begins when a Senator presents a cloture motion that is signed by 16 Senators, proposing "to bring to a close the debate upon [the pending question]." The motion is presented to the Senate while it is in session. When one Senator is speaking, another Senator may interrupt for purposes of presenting this motion. It is read to the Senate, but the Senate then returns to whatever business it had been transacting. The Senate does not act on the cloture motion in any way on the day on which it is submitted, or on the following day.

The Senate acts on the cloture motion "on the following calendar day but one"—that is, on the second day after it is presented. So if the motion is presented on a Monday, the Senate acts on it on Wednesday. During the intervening time, the Senate does not have to continue debating the question on which cloture has been proposed. When the time arrives for voting on the cloture motion, the presiding officer presents it to the Senate for a vote, regardless of what the Senate may be considering at that time.

One hour after the Senate convenes on the day the cloture motion has "ripened" or "matured," the presiding officer is required to direct that an actual (or "live") quorum call take place. (The Senate often waives this quorum call by unanimous consent.) When the presence of a quorum is established, the Senate proceeds, without debate, to a rollcall vote on the motion: "the Presiding Officer shall, without debate, submit to the Senate by a yea-and-nay vote the question: 'Is it the sense of the Senate that the debate shall be brought to a close?'"[12] Notice that the rule requires there to be a rollcall vote on the motion.

Invoking cloture usually requires a three-fifths vote of the entire Senate—"three-fifths of the Senators duly chosen and sworn." If there are no vacancies, therefore, 60 Senators must vote to invoke cloture. In contrast, most other votes require only a simple majority (that is, 51 percent) of the Senators present and voting, assuming that those Senators constitute a quorum. In the case of a cloture vote, the key is the number of Senators voting for cloture, not the number voting against. Failing to vote on a cloture motion has the same effect as voting against the motion: it deprives the motion of one of the 60 votes needed to agree to it.

If the Senate does vote to invoke cloture, that vote may not be reconsidered. On the other hand, it is in order to reconsider the vote by which the Senate voted against invoking cloture.

There is an important exception to the three-fifths requirement to invoke cloture. Under Rule XXII, an affirmative vote of two-thirds of the Senators present and voting is required to invoke cloture on a measure or motion to amend the Senate rules. This exception has its origin in the recent history of the cloture rule.

The majority needed to invoke cloture has changed from time to time. Before 1975, two-thirds of the Senators present and voting (a quorum being present) was required for cloture on all matters. In early 1975, at the beginning of the 94th Congress, Senators sought to amend the rule to make it somewhat easier to invoke cloture. However, some Senators feared that if this effort succeeded, that would only make it easier to amend the rule again, making cloture still easier to invoke. As a compromise, the Senate agreed to move from a maximum of 67 votes (two-thirds of the Senators present and voting) to a minimum of 60 votes (three-fifths of the Senators duly chosen and sworn) on all matters except future rules changes, including changes in the cloture rule itself.[13]

Matters on Which Cloture May be Invoked.

There usually can be at least two filibusters on bills and resolutions that the Senate considers: first, a filibuster on the motion to proceed to the measure's consideration; and second, after the Senate agrees to this motion, a filibuster on the measure itself. If the Senate cannot agree to take up a measure by unanimous consent, the majority leader's recourse is to make a motion that the Senate proceed

---

[12]Rule XXII, paragraph 2. The Senate sometimes agrees by unanimous consent to change the date or time (or both) for conducting a cloture vote.

[13]U.S. Senate. Committee on Rules and Administration. *Senate Cloture Rule,* pp. 119-121.

to its consideration. This *motion to proceed*, as it is called, usually is debatable and, consequently, subject to a filibuster. Therefore, the Senate may have to invoke cloture on this motion before being able to vote on it. Once the Senate votes in favor of the motion and begins consideration of the measure itself, a filibuster on the measure then may begin. Threatened filibusters on motions to proceed once were rare, but have become somewhat more common in recent years. Conference reports are not subject to such a double filibuster because they are privileged matters, so motions to proceed to their consideration are not debatable.[14]

A cloture motion can be filed on a question only when it is pending before the Senate. For example, it is not in order for a Senator to present a motion to invoke cloture on a bill that the Senate has not yet agreed to consider or on an amendment that has not yet been offered. On the other hand, it is not necessary for the Senate to continue debating a question between the time a motion to invoke cloture on it is presented and the time the Senate votes on the motion. During this period, the Senate can turn to other business because, when the time comes for voting on the motion, the presiding officer interrupts the proceedings for purposes of the mandatory quorum call and the rollcall vote on the cloture motion.

Any debatable question that the Senate considers can be filibustered and, therefore, may be the subject of a cloture motion, unless the time for debate is limited by the Senate's rules, by law, or by a unanimous consent agreement. Consequently, Senators may present cloture motions to end debate on bills, resolutions, amendments, conference reports, and various debatable motions. Sometimes, in fact, it can be necessary to invoke cloture on an amendment to a bill and then to invoke cloture again on the bill itself. The reason lies in the fact that amendments that the Senate considers under cloture must be germane (as discussed in the section of this report on the effects of invoking cloture).

Filing Successive Cloture Motions.

There often has been more than one cloture vote on the same question. If and when the Senate rejects a cloture motion, a Senator then can file a second motion to invoke cloture on that question. In some cases, Senators even have anticipated that a cloture motion may fail, so they have filed a second motion before the Senate has voted on the first one. For example, one cloture motion may be presented on Monday and another on Tuesday. If the Senate rejects the first motion when it matures on Wednesday, the second motion will ripen for a vote on Thursday. (If the Senate agrees to the first motion, there is no need, of course, for it to act on the second.) There have been instances in which there have been even more cloture votes on the same question. During the 100th Congress (1987-1988), for example, there were eight cloture votes, all unsuccessful, in connection with a campaign finance reform bill.

---

[14]A nomination also is subject to only one filibuster, because no debate is allowed on a motion that the Senate go into executive session to consider a particular nomination.

The Effects of Invoking Cloture

Invoking cloture on a bill (or on any other question) does not produce an immediate vote on it. The effect of invoking cloture is only to guarantee that a vote will take place eventually.

The Time for Post-Cloture Consideration and Debate.

Rule XXII imposes a cap of no more than 30 additional hours for the Senate to consider a question after invoking cloture on it. This 30-hour cap is a ceiling on the time available for post-cloture *consideration*, not just for *debate*. The time used in debate is counted against the 30 hours, but so too is the time consumed by quorum calls, rollcall votes, parliamentary inquiries, and all other proceedings that occur while the Senate is operating under cloture. The 30-hour period can be increased if the Senate agrees to a non-debatable motion for that purpose. Adopting this motion also requires a three-fifths vote of the Senators duly chosen and sworn.

During the period for post-cloture consideration, each Senator is entitled to *speak* for a total of not more than one hour. Senators may yield part or all of their time to any of four others: the majority or minority leaders or the majority or minority floor managers. None of these Senators can accumulate more than two hours of additional time for debate; but, in turn, they can yield some or all of their time to others.[15]

Note that there is insufficient time for each Senator to use his or her hour for debate within the 30-hour cap for post-cloture consideration. This disparity results from a recent amendment to the cloture rule. Before 1979, there was no cap at all on post-cloture consideration; the only restriction in Rule XXII was the limit of one hour per Senator for debate. The time consumed by reading amendments and conducting rollcall votes and quorum calls was not deducted from anyone's hour. As a result, Senators could (and did) engage in what became known as post-cloture filibusters. By offering one amendment after another, for example, and demanding rollcall votes to dispose of them, Senators could consume hours of the Senate's time while consuming little if any of their allotted hour for debate. In reaction, the Senate amended Rule XXII in 1979 to impose a 100-hour cap on post-cloture consideration. In theory, at least, this time period could accommodate the one hour of debate per Senator (but only if Senators used all of the 100 hours only for debate). Then, in 1985, the Senate agreed, without significant dissent, to reduce the 100 hours to 30 hours, while leaving unchanged the allocation of one hour for each Senator to debate.

---

[15]Hypothetically, therefore, one Senator could control a maximum of 13 hours for debate. This would require eight Senators to yield all of their time to the four designated party leaders and floor managers (two Senators yielding their time to one of the four), giving each party leader and floor manager control of three hours apiece. If the four designated Senators then yielded all of their combined 12 hours to a fifth Senator, who controls one hour in his or her own right, that Senator would control 13 hours.

The result is that there is not enough time available under cloture for each Senator to speak for an hour.[16] In principle, 30 Senators speaking for one hour each could consume all the time for post-cloture consideration. However, Rule XXII does provide a limited protection for all Senators by providing that, when the 30 hours expire, "any Senator who has not used or yielded at least ten minutes, is, if he seeks recognition, guaranteed up to ten minutes, inclusive, to speak only."[17]

There is one other notable difference in the Senate's debate rules before and after cloture is invoked. As discussed above, Senate floor debate normally does not have to be germane, except when the Pastore rule applies. Under cloture, debate must be germane. This requirement derives from the language of Rule XXII that allows each Senator to speak for no more than one hour "on the measure, motion, or other matter pending before the Senate...." Senate precedents make clear that Senators should not expect the presiding officer to insist on germane debate at his or her initiative. Senators wishing to enforce the requirement that debate be germane can do so by making points of order from the floor.

Offering Amendments and Motions Under Cloture.

There are four key restrictions governing the amendments that Senators can propose under cloture that do not apply to Senate floor amendments under most other circumstances. The last of these restrictions also applies to other motions that Senators may offer under cloture.

Germane Amendments Only. First, only germane amendments are eligible for floor consideration under cloture.[18] This germaneness requirement applies to the amendments that Senators offer after cloture is invoked, and the requirement applies as well to any amendments that were pending (that is, amendments that were offered but not yet disposed of) at the time that the Senate votes for cloture. Thus, immediately after a successful cloture vote, the presiding officer may announce at his own initiative that one or more amendments that were pending when the vote began now must "fall" because they are not germane to the matter on which the Senate just invoked cloture.

Because of this germaneness requirement, the Senate could have to invoke cloture on an amendment to a bill, and then invoke cloture again on the bill itself. It is quite common for a Senate committee to report a bill back to the Senate with an amendment in the nature of a substitute—a complete alternative for the text of the bill as introduced. The Senate almost always adopts this substitute immediately before voting to pass the bill as amended by the substitute. However, it also is not unusual for the committee substitute to be nongermane to the bill in some respect. Thus, if

---

[16]When one Senator yields to another for a question, the time required to ask the question comes out of the hour controlled by the Senator who yielded.

[17]When a Senator has consumed all of his or her hour for debate, that Senator may continue to offer amendments, but has no time to explain them. At the end of the 30 hours for post-cloture consideration, no further amendments may be offered.

[18]On what constitutes a germane amendment, see *Riddick's Senate Procedure*, pp. 291-294.

the Senate invokes cloture on the bill before it votes on the committee substitute, the substitute falls as nongermane, so the Senate cannot agree to it. To protect the committee substitute (or any other nongermane amendment that the Senate is considering), the Senate can invoke cloture on the amendment. Doing so limits further consideration of the amendment to no more than 30 more hours. After the Senate votes for the committee substitute, cloture no longer is in effect, so Senators can filibuster the bill as amended unless they again vote to invoke cloture, this time on the bill as amended.

With respect to amendments offered after the cloture vote, the presiding officer may wait for a Senator to make a point of order against an amendment before ruling that it is not germane. Sometimes, however, the presiding officer has taken the initiative to rule amendments out of order as nongermane. In fact, "when obviously nongermane the Chair may rule the amendment out of order even before it has been read or stated by the clerk."[19] (Similarly, presiding officers have taken the initiative to rule amendments out of order—sometimes even before they were read—because the amendments sought to change a bill in two or more noncontiguous places.)

Any Senator can appeal the chair's ruling that a certain amendment is nongermane, allowing the Senate to overturn that ruling by simple majority vote. However, the Senate is unlikely to take this action because doing so could fundamentally undermine the integrity and utility of the cloture procedure. In a sense, the decision to invoke cloture constitutes a kind of treaty by which Senators relinquish their right to filibuster in exchange for a guarantee that no nongermane amendments will be offered under cloture that some of those Senators would want to filibuster. Unless a Senator could be confident that, under cloture, his colleagues could not offer amendments on unrelated subjects that the Senator would insist on filibustering, that Senator would have serious qualms about ever again voting for cloture.

Although there are some Senate rules that Senators sometimes choose not to enforce when enforcing them would be inconvenient, the requirement for germane amendments under cloture is not one of them. On some occasions when a Senator did appeal a ruling of the chair under cloture that an amendment was not germane, Senators who may have supported the amendment on its merits nonetheless voted to sustain the ruling of the chair with the long-term viability of the cloture procedure in mind.

Amendments Submitted in Writing. Second, to be in order under cloture, amendments must be submitted in writing (and for printing in the *Congressional Record*) before the cloture vote takes place.[20] There are different requirements for first-degree amendments (amendments to change the text of a bill or resolution) and second-degree amendments (amendments to change the text of a pending first-degree amendment). Under Rule XXII,

---

[19]*Riddick's Senate Procedure*, p. 291.

[20]A Senator can call up an amendment that another Senator had submitted in writing, though Senators rarely do so. Also, a Senator may recall amendments that he or she submitted in writing before a cloture vote. By recalling an amendment, the Senator removes it from potential consideration under cloture.

> Except by unanimous consent, no amendment shall be proposed after the vote to bring the debate to a close, unless it had been submitted in writing to the Journal Clerk by 1 o'clock p.m. on the day following the filing of the cloture motion if an amendment in the first degree, and unless it had been so submitted at least one hour prior to the beginning of the cloture vote if an amendment in the second degree.

Senators sometimes submit a large number of amendments to a bill for printing in the *Congressional Record* even before a cloture motion is presented. This often is intended and understood to be a clear signal that the Senators who submitted the amendments for printing are contemplating a filibuster.

In practice, the deadline in Rule XXII usually gives Senators most or all of a day after cloture is proposed to draft germane amendments to the bill. Senators then usually have most or all of the next day to review those first-degree amendments and to decide what second-degree amendments, if any, they might offer to them. In this way, Senators can be fully aware of all the amendments they may encounter under cloture before they vote on whether or not to invoke cloture. (Submitting an amendment in writing does not exempt that amendment from the restriction that only germane amendments are in order under cloture.)

One result of these requirements is that Senators and their staffs must decide whether they need to prepare amendments whenever cloture is proposed. When the Senate has voted to invoke cloture on a bill, it is too late for a Senator then to think about what amendments to the bill he or she might want to propose. When a cloture motion is filed, Senators often conclude that they need to proceed with drafting whatever amendments they might want to offer on the assumption that the Senate will approve the motion two days later. One result is that there often are more amendments submitted for printing in the *Record* than Senators actually offer after cloture is invoked.

Under cloture, a Senator may not modify an amendment that he or she has offered. Permitting modifications would be inconsistent with the principle implicit in the cloture rule that Senators should be able to know what amendments may be offered under cloture before the Senate decides if it will invoke cloture. Rule XXII permits only one limited circumstance in which Senators are allowed to change the amendments they offer under cloture. If a measure or other matter is reprinted for some reason after the Senate has invoked cloture on it and if the reprinting changes page and line numbers, amendments that otherwise are in order will remain in order and can be reprinted to make conforming changes in page and line numbering.

Multiple Amendments. Third, Rule XXII states that "[n]o Senator shall call up more than two amendments until every other Senator shall have had the opportunity to do likewise." The evident purpose of this provision is to prevent some Senators from dominating the Senate's proceedings under cloture. This restriction, which Senators have rarely if ever chosen to enforce, does not create a significant problem for those wishing to consume the time available for post-cloture consideration. From their perspective, what is most important is that amendments be offered. not who offers them.

Dilatory Amendments and Motions. Fourth, and finally, Rule XXII provides that no dilatory motion or amendment is in order under cloture. Furthermore, the Senate has established precedents that empower the presiding officer to rule motions and amendments out of order as dilatory without Senators first making points of order to that effect from the floor. Presiding officers rarely have exercised this authority. On occasion, however, and whether at their own initiative or in response to points of order, presiding officers have ruled amendments and various kinds of motions to be dilatory and, therefore, not in order.[21] For example, motions to adjourn, postpone, recess, and reconsider have been held to be dilatory. There also is precedent supporting the authority of the presiding officer to rule that a quorum call is dilatory. In extraordinary circumstances, even appeals from rulings of the chair have been ruled out of order as dilatory.[22]

The Authority of the Presiding Officer.

It bears emphasizing that the Senate's presiding officer has powers when the Senate is operating under cloture that he or she does not have under the Senate's regular procedures. As already noted, the presiding officer may rule amendments and motions out of order at his or her own initiative, without waiting for Senators to make points of order from the floor, and even without waiting for the amendments to be read. Under the Senate's precedents, "[o]nce cloture has been invoked, the Chair is required to take the initiative to rule out of order dilatory amendments, and the Chair makes the determination regarding dilatory intent." Also "under cloture, the Chair has taken the initiative to rule out of order amendments that were dilatory, nongermane or improperly drafted as each was called up and before the amendment could be reported."[23]

There is one other potentially important authority that the presiding officer exercises after the Senate votes to invoke cloture. Under normal Senate procedure, the chair is not empowered to count whether a quorum is present on the floor. When a Senator suggests the absence of a quorum, the chair's only response is to direct the clerk to call the roll. Under cloture, however, the presiding officer can count to ascertain the presence of a quorum.

Other Procedural Changes Under Cloture.

Three other noteworthy changes in Senate floor procedure are triggered when the Senate votes to invoke cloture:

---

[21] Amendments that only express the sense of the Senate or the sense of Congress (and, therefore, would not have the force of law if enacted) have been considered dilatory *per se* under cloture. No other type of amendment has been held to be dilatory *per se* under cloture.

[22] In 1982, the presiding officer stated that "the right to appeal is a basic right of each Senator and would be held dilatory only in the most extraordinary circumstances." *Riddick's Senate Procedure*, p. 312.

[23] *Riddick's Senate Procedure*, p. 287.

- Under normal Senate procedure, each amendment that is offered must be read before debate on it may begin, unless the reading is waived by unanimous consent, as it usually is. Under Rule XXII, however, the reading of any amendment automatically is waived if it "has been available in printed form at the desk of the Members for not less than twenty-four hours." This requirement usually is satisfied because amendments considered under cloture must have been submitted for printing before the cloture vote.

- Under normal Senate procedure, any Senator can demand that an amendment be divided into two or more component parts if each part could stand as an independent proposition (but amendments in the form of motions to strike out and insert are not divisible). Under cloture, however, a Senator cannot demand as a matter of right that an amendment be divided.[24]

- Under normal Senate procedures, appeals from rulings of the chair usually are debatable (though they also are subject to tabling motions). Under cloture, however, appeals are not debatable.

The Impact of Filibusters

Obviously, a filibuster has the greatest impact on the Senate when a 60-vote majority cannot be assembled to invoke cloture. In that case, the measure or other matter that is being filibustered is doomed unless its opponents relent and allow the Senate to vote on it. Even if cloture is invoked, however, a filibuster can significantly affect how, when, and even whether the Senate conducts its legislative and executive business. In fact, it is not an exaggeration to say that filibusters and the prospect of filibusters shape much of the way in which the Senate does its work on the floor.

Impact on the Time for Consideration.

In principle, a truly determined minority of Senators usually can delay for as much as two weeks the time at which the Senate finally votes to pass a bill that most Senators support.

Assume, for example, that a motion to proceed to the bill's consideration is made on a Monday (Day 1). If a filibuster on that motion is begun or is anticipated, proponents of the motion and the bill can present a cloture motion on the same day. However, under Rule XXII, the cloture vote on the motion to proceed does not take place until Wednesday (Day 3). Assuming the Senate invokes cloture on Wednesday, there then begins the 30-hour period for post-cloture consideration of the motion. If the Senate is in session for eight hours per day, Monday through Friday, the 30-hour period, if fully consumed, would extend over almost four full days of session, or at least until the end of the Senate's session on the following Monday (Day 6). If, at that time, the Senate votes for the motion to proceed, the bill's opponents then may begin to filibuster the bill itself, requiring another cloture motion, another successful cloture vote (on Day 8), and the expiration of another 30-hour period for post-cloture

---

[24]An amendment that was offered and divided before the cloture vote continues to be considered as divided after cloture is invoked.

consideration. Rule XXII would require that the vote on final passage occur on what would be the 11th day of consideration, or the 15th calendar day after the motion to proceed was made.

To summarize this hypothetical example:

SENATE ACTION	*NUMBER OF DAYS CONSUMED*	
	Days of Session	Calendar Days
Motion to proceed made	1	1
Cloture motion filed on motion	1	1
Vote on invoking cloture on motion	3	3
Vote on motion to proceed	6	8
Cloture motion filed on measure	6	8
Vote on invoking cloture on measure	8	10
Vote on final passage of measure	11	15

There are many factors that can shorten or extend this hypothetical timetable. Is cloture proposed as soon as the motion to proceed is made, and then again as soon as the Senate takes up the bill (after having agreed to the motion to proceed)? Can the bill's supporters secure the 60 votes needed to agree to the first cloture motion on the motion to proceed, or is more than one attempt necessary before the Senate votes for cloture on the motion? Similarly, does the Senate adopt the first cloture motion on the bill itself, or is cloture invoked on the bill only on the second or third or fourth attempt? Can the Senate agree by unanimous consent to expedite the process by providing for votes on cloture before the time specified in Rule XXII? Are the bill's opponents willing and able to consume the entire 30-hour period for post-cloture consideration of the motion to proceed, and also the same amount of time for post-cloture consideration of the bill? After the Senate invokes cloture, for how many days, and for how many hours per day, is the Senate in session to consider the bill? Does the Senate meet late into the evening, or all night, or on the weekend, in order to consume both 30-hour periods more quickly than it otherwise would?

The answers to questions such as these affect how long a filibuster can delay final Senate action, even when there are 60-vote majorities to invoke cloture. Although the actual time consumed varies from case to case, clearly filibusters can create significant delays. How much delay the Senate experiences depends in part on how much time the Senate, and especially its majority party leadership, is prepared to devote to the bill in question. If the bill is particularly important to the nation and to the majority party's legislative agenda, for example, the majority leader may be willing to invest the days or even weeks that can be necessary to withstand and ultimately end a filibuster.

Another consideration is the point in the annual session and in the biennial life of a Congress at which a filibuster takes place. In the first months of the first session, for example, there may be relatively little business that is ready for Senate floor consideration. In that case, the Senate may be able to endure an extended filibuster without sacrificing its ability to act in a timely way on other legislation. Toward the end of each session, however, and especially as the Senate approaches *sine die* adjournment at the end of the second session, time becomes increasingly scarce and precious. Every hour and every day of floor time that one bill consumes is time that is not available for the Senate to act on other measures that will die if not enacted into law before the end of the Congress. Therefore, the costs of filibusters increase because the damage they do to the legislative prospects of other bills becomes greater and greater.

Even at early stages of a Congress, 30 hours for post-cloture consideration is a long time for the Senate to devote to any single matter. In fact, the Senate never has actually consumed the entire 30-hour period for considering any measure or motion under cloture. As noted earlier, the Senate voted in 1985 to reduce from 100 to 30 hours the time permitted for considering a matter on which cloture has been invoked. This change in Rule XXII provoked little if any controversy, probably because the Senate had never even come very close to consuming the entire 100 hours. Cutting that time by more than two-thirds was not expected to have much practical effect on the ability of Senators to delay final floor votes.

There is one other provision of Rule XXII that affects the consequences of a filibuster for other legislative and executive business that the Senate could conduct. The cloture rule provides that once the Senate invokes cloture, "then said measure, motion or other matter pending before the Senate, or the unfinished business, shall be the unfinished business to the exclusion of all other business until disposed of." In other words, if the Senate invokes cloture on a bill, the Senate must continue to consider that bill until it completes action on it. It requires unanimous consent for the Senate to set the bill aside, even temporarily, in order to consider other matters, even if those other matters are of an emergency nature and are far less contentious.

Thus, a filibuster can affect not only the fate of the matter that provokes it, but also other matters that the Senate may not be able to consider (or at least not as soon as it would like) because of the filibuster.

The Prospect of a Filibuster.

However much effect filibusters have on the operations of the Senate, perhaps a more pervasive effect is attributable to filibusters that have not taken place—at least not yet. The prospect of a filibuster often affects when or if the Senate will consider a measure on the floor, and how the Senate will consider it.

Holds. Fundamentally, for example, when a Senator places a *hold* on a bill or resolution, the Senator is implicitly registering his or her intention to object to any unanimous consent request for the measure's consideration, and then perhaps to begin a filibuster on the measure itself. The Senator also is requesting that the majority leader not even try to call up the measure for consideration, at least not without giving advance notice to the Senator who has placed the hold.

A Senator who does not want the Senate to take up a certain measure, whether temporarily or permanently, can monitor the Senate floor and then object if and when the majority leader proposes to call up the bill for consideration. However, the practice of placing holds on measures has developed informally as a way for Senators to interpose such an objection in advance and without having to do so in person on the floor. In turn, the majority leader and the measure's prospective floor manager understand that a Senator who objects to allowing the bill or resolution to be called up by unanimous consent is threatening to filibuster a motion to proceed to its consideration. So recent majority leaders have tended to honor holds both as a courtesy to their colleagues and in recognition that if they choose not to do so, they may well confront filibusters that they prefer to avoid.

In this way, the threat of a filibuster often is sufficient to prevent a bill from coming to the Senate floor. At a minimum, the bill's supporters may discuss with the Senators making the threat (frequently but not necessarily by placing a hold on it) whether the bill can be amended in a way that satisfies their concerns and removes any danger of a filibuster. Even if the bill's proponents are satisfied that they could invoke cloture on the bill, they still may be willing to accept unwelcome amendments to the bill in order to avoid a protracted process of floor consideration. In fact, depending on the importance of the bill and the other measures that await floor action, the majority leader may be reluctant to schedule the bill unless he is assured that the Senate can complete action on it without undue delay.

Leverage. As noted above, sometimes a filibuster or the threat of a filibuster can affect the prospects of other bills simply by compelling the Senate to devote so much time to the filibustered bill that there is insufficient time available to take up all the other measures that it otherwise would consider and pass. Senators also have been known to use their rights under Rule XXII to delay action on one bill as leverage to secure the action (or inaction) they want on another, unrelated measure.

Suppose, for example, that a Senator opposes S. 1, but knows that he or she lacks the support to filibuster against it effectively. A Senator in this situation may not have enough leverage to prevent Senate floor consideration of S. 1 or to secure satisfactory changes in the bill. So the Senator may seek to increase his or her leverage by delaying, or threatening to delay, the Senate's consideration of other bills that are scheduled for floor action before S.1. By threatening to filibuster S. 2, S. 3, and S. 4, for example, or by actually delaying their consideration, the Senator may strengthen his or her bargaining position by making it clear that more is at stake than the prospects and provisions of S. 1. In this way, Senators' opposition to one bill can affect the Senate's floor agenda in unexpected and unpredictable ways.

Consensus. More generally, the possibility of filibusters creates a powerful incentive for Senators to strive for legislative consensus. The votes of only 51 Senators are needed to pass a bill on the floor. However, it can require the votes of 60 Senators to invoke cloture on the bill in order to overcome a filibuster and enable the Senate to reach that vote on final passage. Knowing this, a bill's supporters have good reason to write it in a way that will attract the support of at least three-fifths of all Senators. Since 1980, neither party has ever held 60 percent of all the seats in the Senate. Thus, as long as this situation persists, every bill that the Senate passes must enjoy at least a minimal degree of bipartisan support.

What is more, there often are more bills that are ready to be considered on the Senate floor than there is time available for acting on them. Under these circumstances, the majority leader may be reluctant, especially toward the end of a Congress, even to call up a bill unless he can be assured that it will not be filibustered at all. As detailed earlier, even an unsuccessful filibuster can consume most of two weeks of the Senate's time, if the bill's opponents are numerous and determined. So the threat of a filibuster may be enough to convince the majority leader to devote the Senate's time to other matters instead, even if all concerned agree that the filibuster ultimately would not succeed in preventing the Senate from passing the bill.

In such a case, a bill's supporters may not be content with securing the support of even 60 Senators. In the hope of eliminating the threat of a filibuster, the proponents may try to accommodate the interests of all Senators, or at least to convince them that a good faith effort has been made to assuage their concerns. At best, opponents can become supporters. At worst, opponents may remain opposed, but may decide against expressing their opposition through a filibuster. While true consensus on major legislative issues may be impossible, the dynamics of the Senate's legislative process do promote efforts to come as close to consensus as the strongly held beliefs of Senators permit.

Recent Developments

Since 1917, when the Senate first adopted a cloture rule, that rule has been the single most controversial element of the Senate's legislative procedures. Until recent decades, however, cloture was not sought very often and rarely was invoked. From 1919 through 1960, there were a total of 23 cloture votes on the Senate floor, of which five were successful. In at least 24 of those years, there were no cloture votes at all, and the Senate did not invoke cloture even once throughout the 1950s.[25] More recently, cloture votes have become a much more common phenomenon in the Senate. During the 105th Congress (1997-1998) alone, the Senate voted on 53 cloture motions and invoked cloture 18 times.[26]

Filibustering often is associated with the intense and sometimes dramatic debates over civil rights legislation during the 1950s, in large part because the issues at stake were so important and because the tactics employed were so unusual. In the contemporary Senate, by contrast, there is widespread agreement that threatened and actual filibusters, as well as cloture votes, have become much more commonplace. Senators today are thought to be more likely than their predecessors to filibuster or threaten to filibuster, and to do so on a wider range of issues, not all of which have been of the greatest national importance. One consequence has been the increase, cited above, in the number of attempts to invoke cloture. There is less agreement, however, as to whether the increase in cloture votes has been an appropriate and proportional response to the increase in filibusters.

In the view of some Senators, the Senate has become a more partisan institution in which less effort is made to accommodate the interests and opinions of Senators with differing views on major legislation. In this view, it is only natural that Senators have resorted to extended debates as the best means available to them to influence the

---

[25]Norman Ornstein, *et. al.* (eds.), *Vital Statistics on Congress*. Washington: Congressional Quarterly, Inc., 1998, p. 171. Rule XXII made it somewhat more difficult to invoke cloture during the 1950s than it is today.

[26]*Congressional Quarterly Almanacs* for 1997 (p. 1-5) and 1998 (p. 1-4). Washington: Congressional Quarterly, Inc., 1998 and 1999.

Senate's decisions. In the view of others, the filibuster has become trivialized. Instead of reserving filibusters as the tactic of last resort, Senators have become more prone to engage in deliberate delay on almost any legislation with which they disagree, regardless of its importance. Both Senators and observers of the Senate have asserted that it now requires 60 votes (the majority required for cloture) for the Senate to pass almost any significant legislation.

While this may be an exaggeration, it certainly is true that the threat of filibusters seems more pervasive than it ever has been before. One prominent manifestation of this change is the increasing number of cloture motions filed on motions to proceed. Seventeen cloture motions were filed on such motions during the Congresses of the 1970s (1971-1980), compared with 47 during the five Congresses of the 1980s (1981-1990). By comparison, Senators filed 44 cloture motions on motions to proceed during only the first two Congresses of the 1990s. Not only were more bills on a wider array of issues becoming the subject of cloture motions, so too were motions to begin consideration of those bills.

These data may be misleading, however. Some Senators, especially those in the majority, argue that the increasing number of cloture motions and votes is a necessary response to the increasing number of filibusters. Other Senators, however, and especially those in the minority, respond that cloture motions have been filed prematurely and sometimes unnecessarily. When filibusters were much less frequent than they have become, the general practice of the Senate was to allow the debate to proceed for a considerable period of time, perhaps several days or longer, before a cloture motion was presented. As filibusters and the threat of filibusters have become more common, Senators now are not waiting as long before filing cloture motions. In fact, it no longer is unusual for a bill's proponents to file a cloture motion as soon as the Senate begins considering the bill—before a filibuster has begun, but in anticipation of a filibuster that the proponents believe will ensue.

Critics of this tendency argue that it sometimes seeks to solve a problem that does yet not exist and that may not arise. These Senators argue that, in view of the central importance of the right to debate in the Senate, Senators should at least demonstrate their intent to debate at length before the effort begins to invoke Rule XXII against them. Furthermore, the cloture procedure sometimes has been used in recent years not to end a filibuster, but to prevent Senators from securing rollcall votes on nongermane amendments.

Suppose that a majority of the Senate is prepared to pass a bill that the majority party leadership is reluctant to schedule for floor consideration. Perhaps the best option available to the bill's proponents is to offer the text of that bill as a nongermane amendment to another bill that the majority party leadership is anxious to bring up and pass. If this nongermane amendment is offered, its opponents can decide to file a cloture motion on the bill and then prolong the debate on the bill and the pending nongermane amendment until the time comes for voting on the cloture motion. If the Senate votes to invoke cloture, the presiding officer announces that the nongermane amendment falls. In this way, its opponents can dispose of it adversely without ever having to vote on it, or even on a motion to table it—but only, of course, if they can mobilize three-fifths of the Senate to vote for cloture.

This possibility, which is more than hypothetical, illustrates that not every cloture vote takes place to break a filibuster that is in progress. Some cloture votes are intended to preempt filibusters that only are anticipated, and still others are primarily for the purpose of triggering the requirement that only germane amendments are in order under cloture, not the debate limits that invoking cloture imposes.

The number of cloture votes exaggerates the number of filibusters that Senators have begun, and even the number of filibusters that Senators have threatened to begin. What some might call filibusters have been described by participating Senators with characterizations such as educational debates; the difference is in the eye of the beholder. For these and other reasons, it is exceedingly difficult to measure the frequency of filibusters in ways that all observers would accept. However, these difficulties do not affect the more general and ultimately more important conclusion that both actual and threatened filibusters, and the cloture procedure for responding to them, are at least as central to the life and work of the Senate today as they have been at any other period of its history.

COMMITTEES OF THE UNITED STATES HOUSE OF REPRESENTATIVES

Carol Hardy Vincent

SUMMARY

This report presents a profile of each House committee. For each committee, the information includes a jurisdictional summary, a list of subcommittees, the number of members of each party on the committee, and a brief historical review.

At the organization of the 105th Congress, there were 20 full House committees—19 standing committees and the Permanent Select Committee on Intelligence. In addition, there were 86 House subcommittees. These numbers are unchanged from the 104th Congress.

Introduction

This report presents selected information for each House committee—information on its jurisdiction, subcommittees, current membership, and history. House Rule X, clause 1, identifies the 19 House standing committees and their legislative jurisdictions, while clauses 2 and 3 identify the general and special oversight responsibilities of committees. For each standing committee, this report lists the topics of legislative jurisdiction and the oversight duties as stated in House Rule X. The House also has one select committee, the Permanent Select Committee on Intelligence, which has functions similar to the standing committees except that its jurisdiction is somewhat narrower. For the jurisdiction and other duties of the Committee on Intelligence, this report draws on House Rule XLVIII, clauses 2 and 3.

This report states committee jurisdictions essentially verbatim from House rules, although some terms may be imprecise or outdated. Moreover, the jurisdictional statements do not necessarily reflect all issues handled by each committee, because some issues are not stated explicitly and factors such as patterns of previous bill referrals affect committee jurisdictions. Finally, House rules, not this report, are the authorities for statements of committee legislative and oversight jurisdiction.

The names of subcommittees and current membership figures are drawn from the *Congressional Quarterly Weekly Report* (March 22, 1997, vol. 55, supplement to no. 12). In general, the history section for each committee notes its date of creation. This section also may include the names of other panels that were merged with the committee and the merger dates, as well as issues acquired (principally from other committees) after the codification of standing committee jurisdictions in 1946.

The jurisdictional histories presented for each committee indicate areas acquired by committees as their jurisdictions are currently constituted. They do not indicate the previous jurisdictional assignments of areas that were transferred. The histories use the following three expressions to characterize changes in a committee's responsibility:

1. "Added jurisdiction," for new responsibility for the committee;

2. "Gained formal responsibility," for areas where a committee appears to have had jurisdiction, but for which House rules did not explicitly assign jurisdiction; and

3. "Enhanced jurisdiction," for areas where a committee's responsibility was expanded.

Finally, in cases where a committee is known to have published a history, a bibliographic citation is provided. This report does not identify committee documents with historical material where the primary focus is not committee evolution, such as activity reports and calendars. Similarly, it does not cite historical information in the committee profiles on the World Wide Web.

Committee on Agriculture

Jurisdiction:

Adulteration of seeds, insect pests, and protection of birds and animals in forest reserves; agriculture generally; agricultural and industrial chemistry; agricultural colleges and experiment stations; agricultural economics and research; agricultural education extension services; agricultural production and marketing, stabilization of prices of agricultural products, and commodities (not including distribution outside of the United States); animal industry and diseases of animals; commodities exchanges; crop insurance and soil conservation; dairy industry; entomology and plant quarantine; extension of farm credit and farm security; forestry in general, and forest reserves other than those created from the public domain; human nutrition and home economics; inspection of livestock, poultry, meat products, and seafood and seafood products; plant industry, soils, and agricultural engineering; rural electrification; rural development; and water conservation related to activities of the Department of Agriculture.

Subcommittees:

1. Department Operations, Nutrition, and Foreign Agriculture
2. Forestry, Resource Conservation, and Research
3. General Farm Commodities
4. Livestock, Dairy, and Poultry
5. Risk Management and Specialty Crops

Membership:

Majority:	27
Minority:	23
Total:	50

History:

Created in 1820

Added jurisdiction over agricultural commodities, including the Commodity Credit Corporation, effective 1975

Added jurisdiction over inspection of poultry and seafood and seafood products, and water conservation related to the Department of Agriculture, in 1995

Printed History:

U.S. Congress, House Committee on Agriculture, *Committee on Agriculture, 150th Anniversary*, H. Doc. 91-350, 91st Cong., 2nd sess. (Washington: GPO, 1970), 32 p.

Committee on Appropriations

Jurisdiction:

Appropriation of revenue for the support of the government; rescissions of appropriations contained in appropriations acts; transfers of unexpended balances; the amount of new spending authority (as described in the Congressional Budget Act of 1974) which is to be effective for a fiscal year, including bills and resolutions (reported by other committees) which provide new spending authority and are referred to the committee under House Rule X, clause 4(a).

General oversight responsibility with respect to the organization and operation of executive departments and other executive agencies (including any agency the majority of the stock of which is owned by the government of the United States) as it deems necessary for determining matters within its jurisdiction.

Subcommittees:

1. Agriculture, Rural Development, Food and Drug Administration, and Related Agencies
2. Commerce, Justice, State, and Judiciary
3. District of Columbia
4. Energy and Water Development
5. Foreign Operations, Export Financing, and Related Programs
6. Interior
7. Labor, Health and Human Services, and Education
8. Legislative Branch
9. Military Construction
10. National Security
11. Transportation
12. Treasury, Postal Service, and General Government
13. Veterans Affairs, Housing and Urban Development, and Independent Agencies

Membership:

Majority:	34
Minority:	26
Total:	60

History:

Created in 1865

Added jurisdiction over certain special presidential messages on rescissions and deferrals of budget authority and certain rescission bills and impoundment resolutions under the Congressional Budget and Impoundment Control Act of 1974, in 1974

Added jurisdiction over rescissions of appropriations, transfers of unexpended balances, and the amount of new spending authority effective for a fiscal year in 1974 (as perfected by H.Res. 988, effective 1975)

Printed History:

U.S. Congress, House Committee on Appropriations, *A History of the Committee on Appropriations, House of Representatives*, H. Doc. 77-299, 77th Cong., 1st sess. (Washington: GPO, 1941), 88 p.

Committee on Banking and Financial Services

Jurisdiction:

Banks and banking, including deposit insurance and federal monetary policy; bank capital markets activities generally; depository institution securities activities generally, including the activities of any affiliates, except for functional regulation under applicable securities laws not involving safety and soundness; economic stabilization, defense production, renegotiation, and control of the price of commodities, rents, and services; financial aid to commerce and industry (other than transportation); international finance; international financial and monetary organizations; money and credit, including currency and the issuance of notes and redemption thereof; gold and silver, including the coinage thereof; valuation and revaluation of the dollar; public and private housing; urban development.

Subcommittees:

1. Capital Markets, Securities, and Government-Sponsored Enterprises
2. Domestic and International Monetary Policy
3. Financial Institutions and Consumer Credit
4. General Oversight and Investigations
5. Housing and Community Opportunity

Membership:

Majority:	29
Minority:	24
Other:	1
Total:	54

History:

Created in 1865 as the Committee on Banking and Currency

Added jurisdiction of the Committee on Coinage, Weights, and Measures (created 1864) by the Legislative Reorganization Act of 1946 (except for standardization of weights and measures and metric system)

Renamed Committee on Banking, Currency, and Housing effective 1975, and Committee on Banking, Finance, and Urban Affairs in 1977

Added jurisdiction over international financial and monetary organizations, and renegotiation effective 1975

Gained formal responsibility for bank capital markets activities generally, and depository institution securities activities generally in 1995

Acquired current name in 1995

Printed History:

None

Committee on the Budget

Jurisdiction:

All concurrent resolutions on the budget (as defined in section 3 of the Congressional Budget Act of 1974), other matters required to be referred under titles III and IV of that act,[1] and other measures setting forth appropriate levels of budget totals for the United States Government.

Measures relating to the budget process generally.

Measures relating to the establishment, extension, and enforcement of special controls over the federal budget, including the budgetary treatment of off-budget federal agencies and measures providing exemption from reduction under any order issued under part C of the Balanced Budget and Emergency Deficit Control Act of 1985.

In addition, the committee is to (1) report the required matters under titles III and IV of the Congressional Budget Act of 1974;[2] and (2) review, on a continuing basis, the conduct by the Congressional Budget Office of its functions and duties.

Special oversight responsibility to (1) make continuing studies of the effect on budget outlays of relevant existing and proposed legislation, and report the results of such studies to the House on a recurring basis; and (2) request and evaluate continuing studies of tax expenditures; devise methods of coordinating tax expenditures, policies, and programs with direct budget outlays; and report the results of such studies to the House on a recurring basis.

Subcommittees:

None

Membership:

Majority:	24
Minority:	19
Total:	43

History:

Created in 1974 by the Congressional Budget Act of 1974

Added jurisdiction over the congressional budget process generally; the establishment, extension, and enforcement of special controls over the federal budget; and enhanced jurisdiction over measures setting forth appropriate levels of budget totals for the United States government, in 1995

Enhanced jurisdiction over the budget process generally in 1997

Printed History:

None

Committee on Commerce

Jurisdiction:

Biomedical research and development; consumer affairs and consumer protection; health and health facilities, except health care supported by payroll deductions; interstate energy compacts; interstate and foreign commerce generally; the exploration, production, storage, supply, marketing, pricing, and regulation of energy resources, including all fossil fuels, solar energy, and other unconventional or renewable energy resources; the conservation of energy resources; energy information generally; the generation and marketing of power (except by federally chartered or federal regional power marketing authorities), the reliability and interstate transmission of, and ratemaking for, all power, and the siting of generation facilities, except the installation of interconnections between government waterpower projects; general management of the Department of Energy, and the management and all functions of the Federal Energy Regulatory Commission; national energy policy generally; public health and quarantine; regulation of the domestic nuclear energy industry, including regulation of research and development reactors and nuclear regulatory research; regulation of interstate and foreign communications; securities and exchanges; travel and tourism.

The committee has the same jurisdiction with respect to regulation of nuclear facilities and of use of nuclear energy as it has with respect to regulation of nonnuclear facilities and of use of nonnuclear energy.

Special oversight responsibility with respect to nuclear and other energy, and nonmilitary nuclear energy and research and development including the disposal of nuclear waste.

Subcommittees:

1. Energy and Power
2. Finance and Hazardous Materials
3. Health and Environment
4. Oversight and Investigations
5. Telecommunications, Trade, and Consumer Protection

Membership:

Majority:	28
Minority:	23
Total:	51

History:

Created in 1795 as the Committee on Commerce and Manufactures

Separate Committees on Commerce and on Manufactures established in 1819

Committee on Commerce renamed Committee on Interstate and Foreign Commerce in 1892

Added jurisdiction over health and health facilities (except health care supported by payroll deductions) effective 1975

Added jurisdiction over use of nuclear energy and regulation facilities in 1977

Renamed Committee on Energy and Commerce, and enhanced energy jurisdiction effective 1981

Acquired current name and added jurisdiction over regulation of the domestic nuclear energy industry in 1995

Printed History:

U.S. Congress, House Committee on Interstate and Foreign Commerce, *180 Years of Service: A Brief History of the Committee on Interstate and Foreign Commerce*, committee print, 94th Cong., 1st sess. (Washington: GPO, 1976), 102 p.

Committee on Education and the Workforce

Jurisdiction:

Child labor; Columbia Institution for the Deaf, Dumb, and Blind;[3] Howard University; Freedmen's Hospital;[4] convict labor and the entry of goods made by convicts into interstate commerce; food programs for children in schools; labor standards and statistics; education or labor generally; mediation and arbitration of labor disputes; regulation or prevention of importation of foreign laborers under contract; United States Employees' Compensation Commission;[5] vocational rehabilitation; wages and hours of labor; welfare of miners; and work incentive programs.

Special oversight responsibility with respect to domestic educational programs and institutions, and programs of student assistance which are within the jurisdiction of other committees.

Subcommittees:

1. Early Childhood, Youth, and Families
2. Employer-Employee Relations
3. Oversight and Investigations
4. Postsecondary Education, Training, and Life-Long Learning
5. Workforce Protections

Membership:

Majority:	25
Minority:	20
Total:	45

History:

Created as the Committee on Education and Labor by the Legislative Reorganization Act of 1946, merging the Committees on Education (created 1867) and Labor (created 1883)

Added jurisdiction over Indian education and work incentive programs effective 1975

Renamed Committee on Economic and Educational Opportunities in 1995

Acquired current name in 1997

Printed History:

None

Committee on Government Reform and Oversight

Jurisdiction:

The federal civil service, including intergovernmental personnel; the status and officers of employees of the United States, including their compensation, classification, and retirement; municipal affairs of the District of Columbia in general, other than appropriations; federal paperwork reduction; government management and accounting measures generally; holidays and celebrations; the overall economy, efficiency, and management of government operations and activities, including federal procurement; national archives; population and demography generally, including the census; postal service generally, including transportation of the mails; public information and records; relationship of the federal government to the states and municipalities generally; reorganizations in the executive branch of the government.

General oversight responsibility with respect to the operation of government activities at all levels, to determine their economy and efficiency.

Subcommittees:

1. Civil Service
2. District of Columbia
3. Government Management, Information, and Technology
4. Human Resources
5. National Economic Growth, Natural Resources, and Regulatory Affairs
6. National Security, International Affairs, and Criminal Justice
7. Postal Service

Membership:

Majority:	24
Minority:	19
Other:	1
Total:	44

History:

Created in 1927 as the Committee on Expenditures in the Executive Departments, when 11 separate Expenditure Committees were combined

Renamed Committee on Government Operations in 1952

Added jurisdiction over general revenue sharing and over the National Archives effective 1975

Acquired current name; gained formal responsibility over public information and records, and federal paperwork reduction; and added jurisdiction of the Committees on the District of Columbia (created 1808) and Post Office and Civil Service (created 1947) (except Franking Commission) in 1995

Gained formal responsibility over government management and accounting measures generally in 1997

Printed History:

None

Committee on House Oversight

Jurisdiction:

Appropriations from accounts for committee salaries and expenses (except for the Committee on Appropriations), House information systems, and allowances and expenses of Members, House officers, and administrative offices of the House; auditing and settling of all accounts described above; employment of persons by the House, including clerks for Members and committees, and reporters of debates; the Library of Congress (including its management) and the House library,[6] the Smithsonian Institution and the incorporation of similar institutions, and the Botanic Gardens,[7] except measures relating to the construction or reconstruction, maintenance, and care of the buildings and grounds of the Botanic Gardens,[7] the Library of Congress, and the Smithsonian Institution; statuary and pictures; acceptance or purchase of works of art for the Capitol; purchase of books and manuscripts; expenditure of accounts described above; Franking Commission; printing and correction of the *Congressional Record*; accounts of the House generally; assignment of office space for Members and committees; disposition of useless executive papers; election of the President, Vice President, or Members of Congress; corrupt practices; contested elections; credentials and qualifications; federal elections generally; services to the House, including the House restaurant, parking facilities and administration of the House office buildings and the House wing of the Capitol; travel of Members of the House; raising, reporting, and use of campaign contributions for candidates for office of Representative in the House of Representatives, Delegate, and Resident Commissioner to the United States from Puerto Rico; compensation, retirement, and other benefits of the Members, officers, and employees of Congress.

Subcommittees:

None

Membership:

Majority:	5
Minority:	3
Total:	8

History:

Created as the Committee on House Administration by the Legislative Reorganization Act of 1946, merging Committees on Enrolled Bills (created 1789 as Joint Committee), Elections (created 1794), Accounts (created 1803), Printing (created 1846), Disposition of Executive Papers (created 1889), Memorials (created 1929), and some functions of the Joint Committee on the Library (created 1806 as Joint Committee)

[6]Now called Legislative Resource Center.

[7]U.S. Botanic Garden.

History: (Cont.)

Added jurisdiction over parking facilities of the House and over campaign contributions to House candidates effective 1975

Acquired current name, and added jurisdiction over the Franking Commission, in 1995

Printed History:

None

Committee on Intelligence, Permanent Select

Jurisdiction:

The Central Intelligence Agency and the director of central intelligence, and the national foreign intelligence program as defined in section 3(6) of the National Security Act of 1947; intelligence and intelligence-related activities of all other departments and agencies of the government, including, but not limited to, the tactical intelligence and intelligence-related activities of the Department of Defense; the organization or reorganization of any department or agency of the government to the extent that the organization or reorganization relates to a function or activity involving intelligence or intelligence-related activities; authorizations for appropriations, both direct and indirect, for the following: (1) Central Intelligence Agency, director of central intelligence, and the national foreign intelligence program as defined in section 3(6) of the National Security Act of 1947; (2) intelligence and intelligence-related activities of all other departments and agencies of the government, including, but not limited to, the tactical intelligence and intelligence-related activities of the Department of Defense; and (3) any department, agency, or subdivision, or program that is a successor to any agency or program named in (1) or (2).

Any legislation initially reported by the committee (except related to the Central Intelligence Agency, the director of central intelligence, and the national foreign intelligence program, including authorizations therefor) that contains matter within the jurisdiction of any standing committee shall, at the request of the chairman of such standing committee, be referred to the standing committee and reported to the House within the time prescribed by the Speaker. Any legislation reported by any other committee containing matter within the jurisdiction of Intelligence shall, at the request of the chair, be referred to Intelligence and reported to the House within the time prescribed by the Speaker.

The committee is to make regular and periodic reports to the House on the nature and extent of the intelligence and intelligence-related activities of the various departments and agencies of the United States. The Committee also is to call to the attention of the House or to any appropriate committee(s) any matters requiring their attention.

The Committee is to obtain an annual intelligence report from the Director of the Central Intelligence Agency, the Secretary of Defense, the Secretary of State, and the Director of the Federal Bureau of Investigation.

Subcommittees:

1. Human Intelligence, Analysis, and Counterintelligence
2. Technical and Tactical Intelligence

Membership:

Majority:	9
Minority:	7
Total:	16

History:

Created in 1977

Printed History:

None

Committee on International Relations

Jurisdiction:

Relations of the United States with foreign nations generally; acquisition of land and buildings for embassies and legations in foreign countries; establishment of boundary lines between the United States and foreign nations; export controls, including nonproliferation of nuclear technology and nuclear hardware; foreign loans; international commodity agreements (except sugar), including for cooperation in the export of nuclear technology and nuclear hardware; international conferences and congresses; international education; intervention abroad and declarations of war; the diplomatic service; fostering commercial intercourse with foreign nations and safeguarding American business interests abroad; international economic policy; neutrality; protection of American citizens abroad and expatriation; American National Red Cross; trading with the enemy; United Nations organizations.

Special oversight responsibility with respect to customs administration, intelligence activities relating to foreign policy, international financial and monetary organizations, and international fishing agreements.

Subcommittees:

1. Africa
2. Asia and the Pacific
3. International Economic Policy and Trade
4. International Operations and Human Rights
5. Western Hemisphere

Membership:

Majority:	26
Minority:	21
Total:	47

History:

Created in 1822 as the Committee on Foreign Affairs

Added jurisdiction over export controls, international commodity agreements (except sugar), international economic policy, trading with the enemy, and international education effective 1975

Renamed Committee on International Relations in 1975, Committee on Foreign Affairs in 1979, and back to Committee on International Relations in 1995

Printed History:

None

Committee on the Judiciary

Jurisdiction:

Judiciary and judicial proceedings, civil and criminal; administrative practice and procedure; apportionment of Representatives; bankruptcy, mutiny, espionage, and counterfeiting; civil liberties; constitutional amendments; federal courts and judges, and local courts in the territories and possessions; immigration and naturalization; interstate compacts generally; claims against the United States; meetings of Congress, attendance of Members and their acceptance of incompatible offices; national penitentiaries; patents, the Patent Office,[9] copyrights, and trademarks; presidential succession; protection of trade and commerce against unlawful restraints and monopolies; revision and codification of the Statutes of the United States; state and territorial boundaries; subversive activities affecting the internal security of the United States.

Subcommittees:

1. Commercial and Administrative Law
2. Constitution
3. Courts and Intellectual Property
4. Crime
5. Immigration and Claims

Membership:

Majority:	20
Minority:	15
Total:	35

History:

Created in 1813

Legislative Reorganization Act of 1946 added jurisdictions of Committees on Claims (created 1794), Patents (created 1837), Revision of the Laws (created 1868), War Claims (created 1883), and Immigration and Naturalization (created 1893)

Added jurisdiction over subversive activities affecting the internal security of the United States in 1975, upon the abolition of the Committee on Internal Security (as clarified in 1995)

Gained formal responsibility over administrative practice and procedure in 1995

Printed History:

U.S. Congress, House Committee on the Judiciary, *History of the Committee on the Judiciary*, committee print, 97th Cong., 2nd sess. (Washington: GPO, 1982), 235 p.

[9]Now called Patent and Trademark Office.

Committee on National Security

Jurisdiction:

Ammunition depots; forts; arsenals; army, navy, and air force reservations and establishments; common defense generally; conservation, development, and use of naval petroleum and oil shale reserves; the Department of Defense generally, including the Departments of the Army, Navy, and Air Force generally; interoceanic canals generally, including measures relating to the maintenance, operation, and administration of interoceanic canals; Merchant Marine Academy, and state maritime academies; military applications of nuclear energy; tactical intelligence and intelligence related activities of the Department of the Defense; national security aspects of merchant marine, including financial assistance for the construction and operation of vessels, the maintenance of the U.S. shipbuilding and ship repair industrial base, cabotage, cargo preference, and merchant marine officers and seamen as these matters relate to the national security; pay, promotion, retirement, and other benefits and privileges of members of the armed forces; scientific research and development in support of the armed services; selective service; size and composition of the Army, Navy, Marine Corps, and Air Force; soldiers' and sailors' homes; strategic and critical materials necessary for the common defense.

Special oversight responsibility with respect to international arms control and disarmament, and to the education of military dependents in schools.

Subcommittees:[10]

1. Military Installations and Facilities
2. Military Personnel
3. Military Procurement
4. Military Readiness
5. Military Research and Development

Membership:

Majority:	30
Minority:	25
Total:	55

History:

Committee on Military Affairs and Committee on Naval Affairs created in 1822

Committee on Militia (created 1835) dissolved and militia matters transferred to Committee on Military Affairs in 1911

Legislative Reorganization Act of 1946 created Committee on Armed Services by merging Committees on Military and Naval Affairs

[10]The Committee also has two panels: (1) Merchant Marine, and (2) Morale, Welfare, and Recreation.

History: (Cont.)

Gained formal responsibility over Department of Defense in 1953

Added jurisdiction over military application of nuclear energy in 1977

Acquired current name; gained formal responsibility over size and composition of the Marine Corps; and added jurisdiction over interoceanic canals generally, Merchant Marine Academy and state maritime academies, tactical intelligence and intelligence related activities of the Department of Defense, and national security aspects of merchant marine in 1995

Printed History:

None

Committee on Resources

Jurisdiction:

Fisheries and wildlife, including research, restoration, refuges, and conservation; forest reserves and national parks created from the public domain; forfeiture of land grants and alien ownership, including alien ownership of mineral lands; Geological Survey;[11] international fishing agreements; interstate compacts relating to apportionment of waters for irrigation purposes; irrigation and reclamation, including water supply for reclamation projects, easements on public lands for irrigation projects, and acquisition of private lands when necessary to complete irrigation projects; care and management of indians, including the care and allotment of Indian lands and general and special measures relating to claims paid out of Indian funds; insular possessions of the United States, except those affecting the revenue and appropriations; military parks and battlefields, national cemeteries administered by the Secretary of the Interior, parks within the District of Columbia, and the erection of monuments to the memory of individuals; mineral land laws and claims and entries thereunder; mineral resources of the public lands; mining interests generally; mining schools and experimental stations; marine affairs (including coastal zone management), except for measures relating to oil and other pollution of navigable waters; oceanography; petroleum conservation on the public lands and conservation of the radium supply in the United States; preservation of prehistoric ruins and objects of interest on the public domain; public lands generally, including entry, easements, and grazing thereon; relations of the United States with Indians and the Indian tribes; and Trans-Alaska Oil Pipeline (except ratemaking).

Special oversight responsibility with respect to Indians.

Subcommittees:

1. Energy and Mineral Resources
2. Fisheries Conservation, Wildlife, and Oceans
3. Forests and Forest Health
4. National Parks and Public Lands
5. Water and Power

Membership:

Majority:	27
Minority:	23
Total:	50

[11]United States Geological Survey.

History:

Created as the Committee on Public Lands by the Legislative Reorganization Act of 1946, merging the Committees on Public Lands (created 1805); Indian Affairs (created 1821); Territories (created 1825); Mines and Mining (created 1865) (except welfare of mine workers); Irrigation and Reclamation (created 1893); Insular Affairs (created 1899); and certain responsibilities of the Committee on Military Affairs (created 1822), including military parks, battlefields, and the national cemeteries

Renamed Committee on Interior and Insular Affairs in 1951

Added jurisdiction over parks within the District of Columbia effective 1975

Renamed Committee on Natural Resources in 1993 and acquired current name in 1995

Added jurisdiction over fisheries and wildlife; international fishing agreements; erection of monuments to the memory of individuals; marine affairs (including coastal zone management), except for measures relating to oil and other pollution of navigable waters; oceanography; and Trans-Alaska Oil pipeline (except ratemaking), in 1995

Printed History:

None

Committee on Rules

Jurisdiction:

The rules and joint rules (except relating to the code of official conduct), and order of business of the House; and recesses and final adjournments of Congress.

Special oversight responsibility with respect to the congressional budget process, and from time to time the Committee is to report its findings and recommendations to the House.

Subcommittees:

1. Legislative and Budget Process
2. Rules and Organization of the House

Membership:

Majority:	9
Minority:	4
Total:	13

History:

Created in 1880
Predecessor Select Committee on Rules (created 1789)
Added jurisdiction over emergency waivers of the required reporting date for measures authorizing new budget authority in 1974
Added jurisdiction over rules relating to financial disclosure in 1977

Printed History:

U.S. Congress, House Committee on Rules, *A History of the Committee on Rules*, committee print, 97th Cong., 2nd sess. (Washington: GPO, 1983), 298 p.

Committee on Science

Jurisdiction:

All energy research, development, and demonstration, and projects therefor, and all federally owned or operated nonmilitary energy laboratories; astronautical research and development, including resources, personnel, equipment, and facilities; civil aviation research and development; environmental research and development; marine research; commercial application of energy technology; National Institute of Standards and Technology, standardization of weights and measures, and the metric system; National Aeronautics and Space Administration; National Space Council;[12] National Science Foundation; National Weather Service; outer space, including exploration and control thereof; science scholarships; and scientific research, development, and demonstration, and projects therefor.

Special oversight responsibility with respect to nonmilitary research and development.

Subcommittees:

1. Basic Research
2. Energy and Environment
3. Space and Aeronautics
4. Technology

Membership:

Majority:	25
Minority:	21
Total:	46

History:

Created in 1958 as the Committee on Science and Astronautics

Enhanced jurisdiction over research and development issues, and added jurisdiction over the National Weather Service effective 1975

Added jurisdiction over nuclear research and development in 1977

Renamed Committee on Science and Technology effective 1975; Committee on Science, Space, and Technology in 1987; and acquired current name in 1995

Added jurisdiction over marine research, and the commercial application of energy technology in 1995

Printed History:

U.S. Congress, House Committee on Science and Technology, *Toward the Endless Frontier: History of the Committee on Science and Technology, 1959-1979*, committee print, 96th Cong., 1st sess. (Washington: GPO, 1980), 1073 p.

---

[12]Abolished, 1993. Functions now handled by Office of Science and Technology Policy, Executive Office of the President.

Committee on Small Business

Jurisdiction:

Assistance to and protection of small business, including financial aid, regulatory flexibility and paperwork reduction; and participation of small-business enterprises in federal procurement and government contracts.

Special oversight responsibility with respect to the problems of all types of small business.

Subcommittees:

1. Empowerment
2. Government Programs and Oversight
3. Regulatory Reform and Paperwork Reduction
4. Tax, Finance, and Exports

Membership:

Majority:	19
Minority:	16
Total:	35

History:

Created in 1975

Predecessor Select Committee on Small Business (created 1941)

Gained formal responsibility over regulatory flexibility and paperwork reduction in 1995

Printed History:

U.S. Congress, House Permanent Select Committee on Small Business, *A History and Accomplishments of the Permanent Select Committee on Small Business, House of Representatives of the United States: 77th to 92nd Congress, 1941-1972*, H. Doc. 93-197, 93rd Cong., 2nd sess. (Washington: GPO, 1974), 231 p.

Committee on Standards of Official Conduct

Jurisdiction:
Measures relating to the code of official conduct.

Subcommittees:
None

Membership:[13]
Majority: —
Minority: —
Total: —

History:
Created in 1967
Predecessor Select Committee on Standards (created 1966)
Designated committee to perform functions described in Title I of the Ethics in Government Act of 1978, effective 1979

Printed History:
None

[13]As of April 27, 1997, the membership of the Committee had not been elected.

Committee on Transportation and Infrastructure

Jurisdiction:

Coast Guard, including lifesaving service, lighthouses, lightships, ocean derelicts, and the Coast Guard Academy; federal management of emergencies and natural disasters; flood control and improvement of rivers and harbors; inland waterways; inspection of merchant marine vessels, lights and signals, lifesaving equipment, and fire protection on such vessels; navigation and the laws relating thereto, including pilotage; registering and licensing of vessels and small boats; rules and international arrangements to prevent collisions at sea; Capitol building and the Senate and House office buildings; construction or maintenance of roads and post roads, other than appropriations therefor, but no bill providing general legislation in relation to roads may contain any provision for any specific road, and no bill relating to a specific road may embrace a provision relating to any other specific road; construction or reconstruction, maintenance, and care of the buildings and grounds of the Botanic Gardens,[14] Library of Congress, and the Smithsonian Institution; merchant marine, except national security aspects; purchase of sites and construction of post offices, customhouses, federal courthouses, and government buildings within the District of Columbia; oil and other pollution of navigable water, including inland, coastal, and ocean waters; marine affairs (including coastal zone management) as they relate to oil and other pollution of navigable waters; public buildings and occupied or improved grounds of the United States generally; public works for the benefit of navigation, including bridges and dams (other than international bridges and dams); related transportation regulatory agencies; roads and the safety thereof; transportation, including civil aviation, railroads, water transportation, transportation safety (except automobile safety), transportation infrastructure, transportation labor, and railroad retirement and unemployment (except revenue measures related thereto); water power.

Subcommittees:

1. Aviation
2. Coast Guard and Maritime Transportation
3. Public Buildings and Economic Development
4. Railroads
5. Surface Transportation
6. Water Resources and Environment

Membership:

Majority:	40
Minority:	33
Total:	73

---

[14]U.S. Botanic Garden.

History:

Created as the Committee on Public Works by the Legislative Reorganization Act of 1946, merging Committees on Public Buildings and Grounds (created 1837), Rivers and Harbors (created 1883), Roads (created 1913), and Flood Control (created 1916)

Renamed Committee on Public Works and Transportation and added jurisdiction over most aspects of transportation effective 1975

Acquired current name, and enhanced jurisdiction over federal management of emergencies and natural disasters, oil and other pollution of navigable waters, and transportation, in 1995

Added jurisdiction over the coast guard and Coast Guard Academy, inland waterways, navigation and related laws, registering and licensing of vessels and small boats, prevention of collisions at sea, merchant marine issues (including inspection and fire protection but excluding national security aspects), and marine affairs relating to oil and other pollution of navigable waters, in 1995

Printed History:

None

Committee on Veterans' Affairs

Jurisdiction:

Veterans' measures generally; cemeteries of the United States in which veterans of any war or conflict are or may be buried, whether in the United States or abroad, except cemeteries administered by the Secretary of the Interior; compensation, vocational rehabilitation, and education of veterans; life insurance issued by the government on account of service in the armed forces; pensions of all wars of the United States, general and special; readjustment of servicemen to civil life; soldiers' and sailors' civil relief; and veterans' hospitals, medical care, and treatment of veterans.

Subcommittees:

1. Benefits
2. Health
3. Oversight and Investigations

Membership:

Majority:	16
Minority:	13
Total:	29

History:

Created by the Legislative Reorganization Act of 1946, merging Committees on Pensions (created 1825), Invalid Pensions (created 1831), and World War Veterans' Legislation (created 1924)

Added jurisdiction over veterans' cemeteries administered by the Department of Defense in 1967

Printed History:

U.S. Congress, House Committee on Veterans' Affairs, *History of House Committees Considering Veterans' Legislation*, committee print, 101st Cong., 2nd sess. (Washington: GPO, 1990), 41 p.

Committee on Ways and Means

Jurisdiction:

Customs, collection districts, and ports of entry and delivery; reciprocal trade agreements; revenue measures generally; revenue measures relating to the insular possessions; the bonded debt of the United States (subject to House Rule X, clause 4(g))[15]; the deposit of public moneys; transportation of dutiable goods; tax exempt foundations and charitable trusts; national social security, except (1) health care and facilities programs that are supported from general revenues as opposed to payroll deductions and (2) work incentive programs.

Subcommittees:

1. Health
2. Human Resources
3. Oversight
4. Social Security
5. Trade

Membership:

Majority:	23
Minority:	16
Total:	39

History:

Created in 1802

Predecessor Select Committee on Ways and Means (created 1789)

Added jurisdiction over tax exempt foundations and charitable trusts effective 1975

Printed History:

U.S. Congress, House Committee on Ways and Means, *The Committee on Ways and Means: A Bicentennial History, 1789-1989*, committee print, 101st Cong., 1st sess. (Washington: GPO, 1989), 526 p.

---

[15]Rule X, clause 4(g), in part requires each standing committee to submit annually its views and estimates on matters within its jurisdiction to be contained in the concurrent resolution on the budget. Those of the Committee on Ways and Means are to include a specific recommendation as to the level of public debt which should be set forth in the concurrent resolution on the budget, which level serves as the basis for an increase or decrease in the statutory debt limit.

Congress of the United States:
Powers,Structure, and Procedures

The Committee Markup Process in the House of Representatives

Stanley Bach

Summary

The process of marking up bills and resolutions in committees of the House of Representatives generally resembles, but does not perfectly replicate, the process of amending measures on the House floor.

At the beginning of a markup, committee members often make opening statements, usually not exceeding five minutes apiece. The first reading of the text of the bill to be marked up almost always is waived, either by unanimous consent or by adopting a nondebatable motion. The bill then is read for amendment, one section at a time, with committee members offering their amendments to each section after it is read but before the next section is read. By unanimous consent only, the committee may agree to dispense with the reading of each section, or to consider a bill for amendment by titles or chapters instead of by sections. Also by unanimous consent, the committee may consider the entire bill as having been read and open to amendment at any point.

Each amendment must be read in full unless the committee waives that reading by unanimous consent. Committees debate amendments under the five-minute rule. A committee can end the debate on an amendment by ordering the previous question on it, or by agreeing to a motion to close debate on it. A committee also can order the previous question or close debate on the entire bill, once it has been read or that reading has been waived by unanimous consent. However, the committee can only close debate, not order the previous question, on individual sections (titles, chapters) of the bill. The various kinds of amendments, as well as most of the other motions, that are in order on the House floor are in order in committee as well.

Committees do not actually change the texts of the bills they mark up. Instead, committees vote on amendments that their members want to recommend that the House adopt when it considers the bill on the floor. The committee concludes a markup not by voting on the bill as a whole, but by voting on a motion to order the bill reported to the House with whatever amendments the committee has approved. A majority of the committee must be present when this final vote occurs. For all other stages of markups, committees may set their own quorum requirements, so long as that quorum is at least one-third of the committee's membership.

Like the Speaker of the House, committee chairmen are responsible for maintaining order and for enforcing proper procedure, either at their own initiative or by ruling on points of order that other committee members make. Chairmen also frequently respond to questions about procedure in the form of parliamentary inquiries.

A committee may report a bill back to the House without amendment, with several amendments, or with an amendment in the nature of a substitute that proposes an entirely different text for the bill. Alternatively, a committee may report a new or "clean" bill on the same subject as the bill (or other text) that it has marked up.

Introduction

The primary legislative function of standing committees in the House of Representatives is to evaluate the thousands of bills and resolutions that Members introduce during each Congress. This evaluation process typically begins with an initial screening by which the majority party leaders and staff of each committee identify the relatively small percentage of measures referred to it that may merit more consideration. The committee or one of its subcommittees then usually conducts one or more days of public hearings to receive testimony about the issue and the merits of the legislation proposed to address it. If the committee decides that it may want to recommend that the House take legislative action, the hearings are followed by markup meetings at which committee members propose and vote on amendments to a bill (or the draft of a bill). These meetings are called *markups* because committee members mark up the legislation before them as they decide what amendments to propose to the House. Finally, the committee votes to order the bill reported back to the House for consideration on the floor.

This report focuses on the markup stage of the legislative process in committee. It discusses the selection of the text to be marked up, the procedures for proposing and debating amendments to that text, the voting and quorum procedures that govern markups, and the final stages of ordering the marked-up text reported to the House for its consideration. CRS reports that discuss other aspects of the legislative process in committee include *Hearings in the House of Representatives: A Guide for Preparation and Conduct* (Report 96-623, updated periodically), and *House Rules Affecting Committees* (Report 97-357, updated periodically).

Applicability of House Rules.

In general, the markup process in House committees reflects many of the rules and practices that govern the amending process on the House floor. Clause 1(a)(1)(A) of House Rule XI states in part that "the Rules of the House are the rules of its committees and subcommittees so far as applicable." As this report will discuss, this clause is somewhat ambiguous in application because there is more than one House rule governing some aspects of the floor amendment process, such as the devices available to terminate debate or to preclude additional amendments from being offered.

Clause 2(a)(1) of Rule XI also empowers each standing committee to supplement and implement clause 1(a)(1)(A) by adopting its own written rules, which each committee does at one of its first meetings at the beginning of each Congress. According to clause 2(a)(1), these committee rules "may not be inconsistent with the

Rules of the House or with those provisions of law having the force and effect of Rules of the House...." This statement also is ambiguous in that a committee rule governing debate on amendments, for example, may be consistent with one House rule but inconsistent with another. As this report also will discuss, the House parliamentarian has given committees some helpful guidance about how these provisions should be understood and applied during the conduct of markups and other committee meetings.

The combined effect of these two clauses, therefore, is to give the House's standing committees some clear direction about how to proceed during markups, but also to give them some discretion in setting their own committee rules, procedures, and customary practices.

Variations Among Committees.

Committee markups tend to be less formal than the corresponding amending process on the House floor. Committees are much smaller bodies, so they do not always need elaborate rules that are strictly enforced in order for them to conduct their business. In fact, a more informal process sometimes contributes to efficient and collegial decision-making in committee. Furthermore, most committee markups are somewhat less constrained by rules than House floor sessions because the House parliamentarian and his assistants do not attend committee markups to advise chairmen and other committee members on procedural questions. Although many committees designate a majority party staff member to provide procedural advice, committee chairmen tend to rely much more on their own knowledge and judgment in conducting committee meetings than do the Speaker and other Representatives who preside over House floor sessions.

In addition, of course, the House has 20 different committees that are empowered to mark up bills and resolutions that fall within their respective jurisdictions. The rules of the House give its committees some discretion in how each of them conducts its markup meetings, and committees exercise this discretion in somewhat different ways—both in the formal rules they adopt to govern their meetings, and even more in the informal (and unrecorded) practices that different committees typically follow.

This report concentrates on the markup procedures that House committees are expected to employ, although not all committees follow these procedures in all respects and at all times. The report also discusses some informal practices and certain tactical alternatives that committee chairmen and members sometimes employ. However, the discussion here could not possibly encompass every variation in markup procedure that may be observed in committee practices. Readers of this report should not be surprised if it does not accord in every respect with what they may have observed at certain markup meetings of the committees with which they are most familiar. References to committees in what follows should be understood to refer to subcommittees as well, unless the text specifically distinguishes between them.

Selecting the Text

A key initial decision that can shape the course and outcome of a markup is the selection of the text that the committee considers. Essentially, there are two choices. First, the committee may mark up the text of one of the bills that Members had introduced and that the House parliamentarian, acting for the Speaker, had referred to the committee.

Second, the committee may mark up the draft of a bill that has not yet been formally introduced and referred to the committee. The chairman can direct the committee's staff to prepare the draft of a bill, usually written with the assistance of attorneys in the House's Office of Legislative Counsel, that reflects the chairman's policy preferences. The committee then may mark up this draft bill which, in its printed form, may be called a "discussion draft" or a "staff draft." Such a draft often now is known informally as a "chairman's mark." This phrase originated in committee consideration of budget resolutions, but now is commonly used to denote any draft that constitutes the legislative starting-point from which a committee chairman thinks a markup should begin.

In either case, the text that a committee marks up already may have been marked up by one or more of the committee's subcommittees. If there has been a subcommittee markup, the subcommittee then makes its legislative recommendations to its parent committee. In turn, the committee most often uses the product of the subcommittee's markup as the starting point for its own markup.

The selection of the text—or the "base text" or the "vehicle", as Members sometimes call it—that the committee will mark up is important because it sets the framework within which the markup, and the policy debates it inspires, will take place. Each provision of the selected text will survive the markup and be recommended to the House for passage unless a committee member takes the initiative to propose an amendment to it that the committee adopts. The burden is on those who would change the provisions of the base text; it is up to them to devise alternatives to that text and convince a majority of their committee colleagues to vote for those alternatives. Clearly, then, it is advantageous to be able to select the vehicle from among the bills that were referred to the committee, or to devise the vehicle by drafting a new text that very well may draw on selected provisions of the introduced bills on which the committee held hearings.

The Chairman's Authority in Practice.

Almost invariably, it is the committee chairman who selects the text to be marked up. Yet there is nothing in the rules of the House that explicitly gives chairmen this authority. Instead, this power would seem to derive from the authority of committee chairmen to schedule committee meetings and set the agenda for them.

Clause 2(b) of House Rule XI directs each committee to establish regular monthly meeting days to conduct business, which can include marking up legislation. Committees interpret this rule as giving the chairman the authority to decide what, if anything, the committee should consider at each of its regular meetings. Many committees also exercise the authority derived from clause 2(b) to allow their chairmen to cancel regular meetings when the chairman considers it appropriate to do so.

Clause 2(c)(1) of the same rule authorizes each standing committee chairman to call "additional and special" committee meetings "for the consideration of a bill or resolution pending before the committee or for the conduct of other committee business, subject to such rules as the committee may adopt." Again, this clause is understood to allow the chairman to decide what measure or what other committee business will be on the agenda of each such meeting. A committee may adopt a rule that requires the chairman to give prior notice to, or even consult with, the ranking minority member before scheduling a meeting. A committee's rules also may require that the chairman give all committee members advance notice of when the committee will meet and what matters will be on its agenda for that meeting. Still, the authority to schedule committee meetings, including markups, and to select matters for consideration at those meetings, rests effectively with the committee chairman.

Recourse of Committee Members.

Committee members have two different mechanisms they can use when they disagree with their chairman's decisions about what legislation the committee will meet to mark up, and when. However, members very rarely resort to either of these devices.

If a committee member objects to the committee marking up a matter that the chairman has placed on the agenda for a regular or additional committee meeting, the member may ask the committee to vote on whether it wants to consider that matter. To secure this vote, a member raises what is known as *the question of consideration*. Under clause 3 of House Rule XVI (which Rule XI, clause 1(a)(1)(A), makes applicable to committees),

> When a motion or proposition is entertained, the question, "Will the House now consider it?" may not be put unless demanded by a Member, Delegate, or Resident Commissioner.

Put differently, whenever a bill or resolution, or the draft text of a measure, is called up for markup at a committee meeting (but before debate on it actually begins), any member may compel a vote on the question of consideration. If a majority of the committee votes "no" on this question of consideration, the committee does not proceed to act on the matter in question. In this way, a majority of a committee can prevent its chairman from compelling them to mark up legislation that they prefer not to consider, at least at that time. However, the question of consideration rarely is raised, and, if raised, it is very unlikely that the committee will block consideration of a measure that the chairman wishes the committee to mark up.

There are two primary, and related, reasons. First, in setting the committee's markup agenda, the chairman usually is acting in support of the majority party's policy and political interests. Except in the most unusual cases, therefore, the chairman's agenda decisions can be expected to enjoy the support of all, or almost all, of his or her fellow party members on the committee. Second, whether in committee or on the floor, control of the agenda is at the very heart of the powers and prerogatives of the majority party in the House. Therefore, majority party members in committee are inclined to (and normally are expected to) support their chairman on procedural votes, such as votes on questions of consideration, when control of the committee's agenda is at stake.

Committee members have a different recourse if a committee chairman fails to schedule a meeting to mark up legislation that a majority of the committee wants to consider. Under clause 2(c)(2) of Rule XI, any three committee members can request in writing that their chairman call a special meeting for a specific purpose, such as to mark up a measure that is identified in the written request. If the chairman fails to call the meeting within three days, and if the meeting does not take place within seven days, a majority of the committee may require that the committee meet for that purpose (and only that purpose) at a designated date and time.

In this way, a majority of committee members may take control of the agenda away from their chairman and require the committee to mark up a measure that the chairman has failed to schedule for consideration. However, this rule has rarely, if ever, been formally invoked since the House first adopted it as part of the Legislative Reorganization Act of 1970. The reasons are not surprising. In the contemporary House, we would rarely expect to encounter serious and open conflicts between a committee chairman and many committee members of his or her own party. Therefore, we would expect this rule to be invoked by the committee's minority, joined by at least a few majority party members of the committee, who would have to be willing to undermine their party's control over the committee's agenda. On the other hand, the threat of invoking the clause 2(c)(2) procedure for calling a special meeting may have convinced chairmen to schedule matters for markup that they would have preferred not to bring up, at least at that time.

The combined effect of these rules, and the political and institutional conditions affecting their use, generally is to give committee chairmen effective control over what matters their committees mark up, when these markups take place, and precisely what text the committee considers. However, chairmen exercise this control within limits imposed by their knowledge that a chairman's decisions can be overridden if he or she thwarts the will of the committee's majority party members, and that the continuance of each chairman in that office depends on retaining the support of the entire majority party's conference or caucus. In practice, the minority party members of a committee usually have little effective recourse when they object to what their chairman has or has not scheduled for the committee to mark up.

The Markup Process in General

A general discussion of the markup process in House committees will provide a context for subsequent sections of this report that discuss the individual stages of the process.

As mentioned above, the rules of the House of Representatives are ambiguous with respect to the procedures that standing committees are to follow at markup meetings. Clause 1(a)(1)(A) of Rule XI generally provides that "the Rules of the House are the rules of its committees and subcommittees *so far as applicable...*" (italics added). And clause 2(a)(1) of the same rule directs each standing committee to adopt written rules governing its procedures that "*may not be inconsistent* with the Rules of the House...." (italics added).

Two problems arise in interpreting these rules. First, they do not provide criteria to judge whether committee rules are *not inconsistent* with House rules. Second, they do not define *which* House rules are applicable to committees and subcommittees. The House's rules make available different sets of procedures that the House uses under different circumstances to consider various bills and resolutions on the floor. It would not be possible for all of these procedures to be applicable to committees at the same time. By the same token, it would not be possible for committees to adopt rules that avoid being inconsistent with *any* of these procedures.

The House parliamentarian provides important guidance when he notes in the commentary accompanying Sec. XXX of *Jefferson's Manual* that "[t]he procedures applicable in the House as in the Committee of the Whole generally apply to proceedings in committees of the House of Representatives." He also points out several exceptions to this general statement that are discussed below.

The phrase "the House as in Committee of the Whole" refers to a distinctive set of procedures that the House may, but rarely does, use to consider measures on the floor. These procedures are not stated in the House's standing rules, but they are a matter of well-established precedent. As its name suggests, the procedures applicable in the House as in Committee of the Whole combine elements of the procedures that apply in the House and those that are followed in Committee of the Whole.

To summarize what is discussed in more detail below, when a standing committee begins a markup, the text to be considered first is to be read in full, although this reading usually can be waived by majority vote. The text then is considered for amendment, section by section. Each section is read, unless the reading of one or all sections is waived by unanimous consent. Committee members may offer amendments to each section after it is read but before the next section is read. Each amendment must be in writing and is to be read before debate on it begins. An amendment may be withdrawn without the need for unanimous consent unless the committee has acted on it. Committee members may speak on the bill and amendments under a five-minute rule, meaning that each member may speak for five minutes on each amendment unless the committee votes to bring the debate to an end.

There are two motions available to end debate. Members may vote either to close the debate or to order the previous question on (1) a pending amendment or (2) the entire bill after the last section of the bill has been read or considered as read. However, members may move only to close the debate, not to order the previous question, on the pending section of the bill (and all amendments to it). Both motions are decided by simple majority vote. The difference lies in the fact that ordering the previous question ends the debate and precludes additional amendments, while the motion to close debate does only that—it ends the debate, but it does not prevent members from offering additional, nondebatable amendments that otherwise are in order.

It should be emphasized that the rules of the House do not specifically describe these procedures and require committees to follow them. However, the House's standing committees typically follow these procedures during markups, unless the committee agrees otherwise by unanimous consent.

Beginning the Markup

A committee markup meeting usually begins by the chairman calling the committee to order and announcing the matters that the committee is expected to consider at that meeting. The chairman also may announce that the requisite quorum of members is present. The chairman begins the markup itself by announcing that the committee will proceed to the consideration of the bill, resolution, or draft that is scheduled for consideration. The chairman also may note that whatever requirements for prior notification the committee's rules impose have been satisfied.

First Reading.

The committee clerk then is to read the entire text of the bill (or whatever text is being considered).[1] However, this reading usually is waived by unanimous consent when all committee members already have had an opportunity to become familiar with the text. If unanimous consent cannot be obtained, a committee member may move to waive the first reading of a bill or resolution. Clause 1(a)(1)(B) of House Rule XI provides for a privileged and nondebatable motion to waive this first reading in committee or subcommittee if printed copies of the measure are available.

Opening Statements.

Either before or after the chairman formally presents the bill to the committee for consideration, he or she may entertain opening statements on the bill and the issues it raises. The chairman typically makes the first statement and next recognizes the ranking minority party member. The chairman then recognizes other members to speak, alternating between the parties. Members usually are recognized in the order of their seniority on the committee (to the extent that the party ratio permits). However, chairmen sometimes recognize members in the order in which they arrived at the committee meeting, just as chairmen sometimes follow this practice in recognizing members to question witnesses at committee hearings.

Members normally are recognized for no more than five minutes each to make their opening statements, though chairmen may allot more time to themselves and to their ranking minority members. In principle, members who have been recognized may yield to colleagues or request unanimous consent for additional time, but they are much less likely to do so while making opening statements than when debating amendments.

House rules do not provide for opening statements (although they are somewhat akin to the period for general debate in Committee of the Whole on the House floor), nor do the rules of many House committees. In the absence of a committee rule guaranteeing members' rights to make opening statements, committee chairmen

---

[1]In what follows, "bill" is used to refer to whatever text the committee is marking up, until the discussion turns to the final stages of the markup and the committee's reporting options.

typically reserve the right to limit the number or length of these statements. In the interest of time, for example, it is not unusual for a chairman to recognize only himself or herself and the ranking minority member, and then to announce that other committee members may submit their opening statements in writing and have them included in the formal record of the committee's proceedings. If some members insist on actually making their opening statements, the chairman may accommodate them. Committees rarely publish the transcripts of their markup meetings, so opening statements that are simply submitted for the record may receive little or no attention.

The chairman's authority to permit or restrict opening statements is somewhat clearer when these statements take place before the chairman actually calls up the bill for consideration, which constitutes the formal beginning of the markup. Before the markup formally begins, there is no business that is before the committee at that meeting, so the chairman can justify exercising more discretion in recognizing members to speak. After the bill has been presented and its first reading has taken place or has been waived, opening statements can be construed to be debate on the bill under the five-minute rule, which the chairman is better situated to constrain if he does so with the implicit consent of the committee.

Offering and Debating Amendments

After opening statements and after the first reading of the bill has been completed or dispensed with, the committee begins the markup process *per se* by entertaining, debating, and voting on amendments. Throughout this process, committee members often talk about how the committee is or is not amending the bill. In fact, the committee is *not* amending the bill. Instead, it is voting on what amendments, if any, the committee will recommend that the House adopt when it considers the bill on the floor.[2] Only the House as a whole (meeting as the House, not in Committee of the Whole) actually has the authority to change the text of bills that Members have introduced.

Reading Bills for Amendment.

The process of offering and debating amendments in committee closely resembles the amending process in Committee of the Whole on the House floor. In committee, members offer their amendments to each section of the bill in sequence unless the committee agrees otherwise by unanimous consent. The chairman directs the clerk to read the first section of the bill. Members then may propose amendments to that section, but only to that section. After the committee has disposed of any and all amendments to the first section, or after it has been amended in its entirety, the chairman directs the clerk to read the second section, which then is open to amendment. This process is repeated until the committee has voted on the last amendment to be offered to the last section of the bill. (Some committees may agree to use an informal system of giving priority consideration to amendments submitted in advance.)

---

[2]When a committee marks up the text of what will become a clean bill, the committee can amend that text because it is not yet the text of a bill.

Except in the most contentious markups, committee members do not insist that the clerk actually read each section of the bill. When the chairman first calls up the bill for consideration, he or she often asks unanimous consent that each section of the bill be considered as having been read. There usually is no objection because committee members already have been provided with copies of the bill in accordance with whatever markup notice requirements are in the committee's rules. One reason for requiring that each section be read is to delay the proceedings.

It requires unanimous consent for a committee to do anything but have each section read for amendment in sequence. Longer and more complex bills often are divided into titles, and each title is subdivided into sections. The largest bills even may be divided into chapters that are subdivided into titles and then into sections. In such cases, the chairman may ask unanimous consent that the bill be open for amendment one title or one chapter at a time, so that members can propose amendments to any part of the title or chapter, not just to one section of it at a time. This arrangement normally saves some time, and also allows committee members to address at the same time all aspects of each title or chapter. If, for example, a committee member has an alternative for how a title of the bill deals with different dimensions of the same issue, the member may offer that alternative as a substitute for the entire title, rather than having to amend each section of the title as it is considered.

When the committee begins marking up a shorter bill, or one to which few amendments are expected, the chairman may ask unanimous consent that the entire text of the bill be considered as read and open to amendment at any point. In that case, members can offer their amendments to any part of the bill in any order. This could be confusing when members plan to offer many amendments to a long and complex bill. When there are few amendments to consider, however, opening the bill for amendment in this way can conserve time without causing confusion.

Committees normally agree to such unanimous consent requests, especially because they usually are made by the committee chairman. When any member objects, however, no motion is in order to open the bill for amendment by titles, chapters, or at any point. By the same token, it is not in order for a member to move to waive the reading of any section, title, or chapter of a bill, or to move that the entire bill be considered as having been read. As noted earlier, House rules do make in order a nondebatable motion in committee to dispense with the first reading of a bill at the very beginning of the markup. However, this rule does not make in order a motion to expedite or change the process of reading the bill for amendment.

Offering Amendments.

If a full committee is marking up a bill that one of its subcommittees already has marked up, the chairman is most likely to give priority consideration to any subcommittee-approved amendments to each section (or to whatever part of the text is open to amendment). To offer additional amendments to each section, the chairman usually first recognizes a senior member of his or her party. After the committee disposes of that amendment (and any amendments to it), the chairman normally recognizes a senior member of the minority party to offer another amendment to that section. Thereafter, the chairman typically recognizes other members to offer amendments to the section in order of their seniority, alternating between members of the two parties. However, there is nothing in House rules that requires chairmen to follow these recognition practices. Committee chairmen sometimes offer amendments themselves (unlike Members who preside over the House's floor sessions).

The amendments that members can offer in committee are subject to essentially the same requirements that apply to amendments offered on the House floor. Each amendment must be germane, for example, and it may not propose only to amend something that already has been amended. Amendments also must meet certain other requirements, including those of the congressional budget process. The House's rules do not explicitly prohibit members from offering amendments on matters that are not within the committee's jurisdiction. However, such amendments are quite likely to violate the germaneness requirement, and chairmen have refused to entertain amendments to portions of bills that were not referred to their committees. The process by which members can make points of order against amendments is discussed below.

The four kinds of amendments that House Rule XVI, clause 6, make in order on the floor also may be offered in committee. These are: (1) a first-degree amendment that proposes to change the text that is being marked up; (2) a second-degree perfecting amendment to that amendment; (3) a substitute that proposes to replace the entire text of the first-degree amendment; and (4) an amendment to the substitute. The same House rule also specifies the order in which members are to vote on these amendments, if two or more of them have been offered. (For an explanation of these kinds of amendments and the "amendment tree," see CRS Report 98-995, *The Amending Process in the House of Representatives*, by Stanley Bach.)

An amendment in the nature of a substitute—that is, an amendment that proposes to replace the entire text of the bill or resolution—is in order only at the beginning or the end of the amending process. Sometimes the chairman, or a member acting at his behest, offers such a complete substitute immediately after the first section of the bill has been opened for amendment. The reason, which is discussed in the next section, often is tactical, and has to do with the majority's ability to conclude the markup process when it chooses to do so.

Each amendment must be in writing, with enough copies for all committee members (and often for committee staff, reporters, and other interested observers). Members usually draft their amendments in advance with the assistance of the House's Office of Legislative Counsel. They are not required to do so, however, and members sometimes write amendments in long-hand as the markup progresses. Committee staff usually have blank amendment forms available, but members need not use them. Chairmen and committee staff much prefer (and sometimes request) that members provide copies of their amendments before the markup begins. However, members sometimes decide that it is in their interests not to do so.

As soon as any amendment is offered, the clerk must read it before debate on the amendment may begin. Typically, the sponsor of the amendment asks unanimous consent that this reading be dispensed with. If there is an objection, the amendment must be read in full. No motion is in order for the committee to dispense with the reading of an amendment. Members may insist that an amendment be read if they are unfamiliar with it or if they simply want to protract the proceedings. In the case of an amendment in the nature of a substitute, the reading can be time-consuming. However, the chairman may entertain a point of order against an amendment even before the amendment has been read in full.

Debating Amendments.

Each amendment is debated under the five-minute rule, much as members debate amendments on the floor in Committee of the Whole. The chairman first recognizes the amendment's sponsor for five minutes to explain and justify the amendment. Then the chairman recognizes a member who opposes the amendment to speak for five minutes. Thereafter, each committee member may be recognized to speak for five minutes (unless the committee votes to stop the debate, as discussed below). Members who seek recognition sometimes will "move to strike the last word" (a *pro forma* amendment), as they do on the floor. In committee markups, however, it usually is sufficient for a member to attract the chairman's attention and announce that he or she wishes to speak for or against the pending amendment (or even just to speak on the amendment). In principle, no member is to be recognized to speak more than once on the same amendment. After the initial 10 minutes of debate on an amendment, a member may seek recognition to offer an amendment to the pending amendment.

In recognizing members to debate amendments, chairmen normally follow the conventional recognition practices: alternating between majority and minority party members, and giving preference to members in the order of their seniority on the committee. Sometimes, however, chairmen depart from these practices in favor of giving junior members equitable opportunities to participate.

In most committees, there are green, yellow, and red lights at the staff table facing the members to indicate whether the member speaking has time remaining. The member who has been recognized for five minutes may ask unanimous consent to continue for additional time. While a member is speaking, another member may ask that member to yield. If the member who controls the time agrees, his or her time continues to run while the other member is speaking. For example, if Rep. White has been recognized, Rep. Black may interrupt him and ask, "Will the gentleman yield?" (Notice that the same rules of decorum in debate apply in committee as on the floor. All statements and questions are to be addressed to the chairman, not directly to other committee members.)

Rep. White is not required to yield, and may decide not to do so if, for example, he has much to say, or he does not expect to agree with what Rep. Black would say, or if he thinks that Rep. Black's request is disruptive or distracting. If Rep. White does agree to yield to Rep. Black, Rep. Black then speaks on Rep. White's time. Rep. White may not yield to his colleague for a specific period of time; he only has the choice of yielding or declining to do so. If Rep. White does yield to a colleague, however, he may reclaim his time whenever he wants. If Rep. Black is speaking or if the two members are engaged in an exchange when the chairman announces that Rep. White's five minutes have expired, Rep. Black may ask unanimous consent that Rep. White be granted an additional few minutes.

Committees sometimes permit questions to be addressed to committee staff or executive branch officials during debates on amendments.

The sponsor of an amendment may withdraw it without the need for unanimous consent, unless the committee already has amended or agreed to it. On the other hand, it requires unanimous consent to modify the text of a pending amendment.

Two Motions to Conclude a Debate

During committee markups, chairmen and amendment sponsors sometimes signal, by their words or demeanor, that they believe the committee should be ready to vote on the pending amendment or other question. If such signals prove ineffective, there are two different nondebatable motions that members can offer to conclude debates during markup. These are (1) the motion to order the previous question, and (2) the motion to close debate. The two motions are not in order under all circumstances, and they have somewhat different effects if adopted.

Ordering the Previous Question.

The *motion to order the previous question* proposes to stop the debate and block amendments. During debate on an amendment, for example, a member may seek recognition to move the previous question on that amendment. The committee immediately votes on the motion and, if it is agreed to by majority vote, the committee proceeds to vote on the amendment. No further debate on the amendment is in order, nor can members offer any amendments to it. If the committee orders the previous question on an amendment while an amendment to it already is pending, the committee first votes on the amendment to the amendment, and then on the first-degree amendment.

The previous question may be moved on a pending amendment (and amendments to it), or it may be moved on the entire bill if the last section of the bill has been read or if the reading of the bill has been waived by unanimous consent so that the bill is open to amendment at any point. A member may not move the previous question on the section (title, chapter) of the bill that is open for amendment. This protects the rights of committee members, especially minority party members, to offer their amendments to each part of the bill when it becomes subject to amendment.

Thus, the majority cannot necessarily control the length of a markup by ordering the previous question on the bill as a whole at whatever time it chooses. If the committee agrees to a unanimous consent request that the bill be considered as read and open to amendment at any point, a majority can expedite completion of the markup by agreeing to order the previous question on the bill and any pending amendments thereto. If there is no such unanimous consent agreement, however, the previous question can be used only to force votes on each amendment that is offered, until the clerk has read the last section of the bill.

Moving to Close the Debate.

The *motion to close debate* is in order under more circumstances, but its effect is more limited. A member may move to close the debate (1) on the pending amendment (and any pending amendments to it), or (2) on the section, title, or chapter (and any pending amendments to it) that is open for amendment, or (3) on the entire text of the bill (and any pending amendments to it), but only if the reading of the bill has been completed or dispensed with. So one difference between the two motions is that the committee can vote to close the debate on the pending section of the bill, but it may not order the previous question on it.

The other difference is in the effect of the two motions. The motion to close debate does only that: it brings a debate to an end. Unlike the previous question, the motion to close debate does not affect the rights of members to offer additional amendments. The motion to close debate may take one of three forms: it may propose to close the debate immediately, or at a certain time, or after a certain period of time for additional debate. When a committee uses this motion to close debate immediately on a section, for example, no more debate is in order on the section or on amendments to it. Members can continue to offer additional amendments to the section, and request rollcall votes on them, but they may not take any time at all to explain their amendments (except by unanimous consent, of course).

Because of its dual effect, committee members tend to move the previous question more often than they move to close debate when both motions are in order. Thus, members are most likely to move the previous question on a pending amendment or on the bill after it has been read in full or its reading has been dispensed with. On the other hand, members move to close the debate on a pending section of the bill because a motion to order the previous question on the section is not in order.

Majority Powers and Minority Rights.

The limitations on the use of these motions put the majority party in committee at a disadvantage that the majority party can avoid on the floor. The House frequently considers major bills on the floor under the terms of special rules recommended by the Rules Committee that restrict the floor amendments that members are allowed to offer. By this use of special rules, the majority can limit the number of amendments that members can offer on the floor, and permit some specific amendments to be offered while blocking consideration of others. In the process, the majority party can use special rules to control how long members can spend offering and debating amendments to bills in Committee of the Whole.

During committee markups, on the other hand, there is no equivalent to the Rules Committee or to special rules. There is no procedural device by which a committee majority can vote to preclude consideration of certain amendments that comply with House rules. By the same token, there is no motion by which a committee majority can vote to conclude a markup until the committee has completed the process of reading the bill for amendment.

To put it differently, the minority members of a committee can insist that a bill be marked up one section at a time and that each section be read. Then they can continue to offer their amendments to each section, and request rollcall votes on the amendments. The committee majority may vote to close the debate on each section after it is read, but doing so does not block the minority from offering more amendments to the section. The motion only precludes debate on amendments after debate on the section has been closed.

One way in which the majority can gain more control over how long a markup lasts is through the use of an amendment in the nature of a substitute. The committee's chairman (or another majority party member acting for the chairman) sometimes offers an amendment in the nature of a substitute as soon as the first section of the bill has been read. This complete substitute represents the majority's preferred version of the bill. While this substitute is pending, members may not offer amendments to the bill itself, except to the first section. This effectively blocks the minority from insisting that the bill be read for amendment by sections and from offering amendments to each section as it is read.[3]

After the substitute has been read and debate on it has begun, the majority can order the previous question on the substitute whenever it decides to do so. If the previous question is ordered on the complete substitute, the committee then votes on agreeing to it without further debate or amendment. Because the substitute was offered by or for the chairman, the committee is likely to agree to it, and that vote effectively ends the amending process. By agreeing to the substitute, the committee thereby amends the entire text of the bill. No more amendments to the bill are in order, therefore, because any further amendments would be subject to points of order for proposing to amend something that already has been amended.

In this way, the majority can use an amendment in the nature of a substitute to give it more control over the length of a markup. However, there are two potential disadvantages to this approach. First, any member can insist that the complete substitute be read in full, and this can be a time-consuming process. The majority cannot waive this reading by motion. Second, the majority's ability to use the amendment process to its advantage is limited. The majority's amendment in the nature of a substitute is a first-degree amendment to which the minority can offer second-degree perfecting amendments. When a minority party member offers a first-degree amendment that the majority opposes, the majority can respond by defeating it or, if that seems unlikely, by amending it in order to make it more palatable. However, when the minority offers unwelcome second-degree perfecting amendments to the majority's complete substitute, the majority can only attempt to defeat each minority amendment because second-degree amendments cannot be amended. If the committee agrees to consider an amendment in the nature of a substitute as "original text" or as "an original question for purpose of amendment," then committee members can offer amendments to it in two degrees. However, it requires unanimous consent to treat a complete substitute in this way.

---

[3]In the unlikely event that the committee eventually rejects the chairman's complete substitute, the clerk would be directed to read the second section of the bill and the normal amending process would resume.

Motions, Quorums, and Votes

Motions.

In addition to offering amendments, members may propose various other motions during markups. The House parliamentarian has stated in his commentary on Rule XI, clause 2(a), in the *House Rules and Manual* that committees "may employ the ordinary motions which are in order in the House," such as motions to adjourn, table, postpone to a day certain, postpone indefinitely, and reconsider. Chairmen also regularly assert the right to declare committee meetings in recess—for example, for lunch breaks and to permit Members to reach the floor in time to be recorded on quorum calls and to participate in electronically recorded votes.

The motions to table and reconsider deserve some comment. The *motion to table* rarely is made to dispose of amendments during committee markups because the effect of tabling an amendment is to table (or kill) the bill to which the amendment was offered. The *motion to reconsider* is offered from time to time, especially when members who are losing a rollcall vote (on an amendment, for example) believe that they are going to lose that vote only because one or more committee members are absent. In that case, a member who would prefer to vote on the losing side votes instead on the winning side. Doing so qualifies that member to move to reconsider the vote at some time before the markup ends. If a majority votes for the motion to reconsider, the committee then votes anew on the amendment and may reverse the outcome. Alternatively, the committee may vote to dispose of a motion to reconsider by voting to table it.

In principle, each motion, like each amendment, must be in writing. Members usually do not enforce this requirement, especially in the case of routine motions, such as motions to adjourn. In the case of a procedurally important motion, however, such as a motion to reconsider the vote by which the committee narrowly agreed to an amendment, a member opposed to the motion may insist that it be presented in written form.

Quorums.

There are two different quorum requirements governing committee markups. Clause 2(h)(1) of House Rule XI requires that a majority of the committee's membership must actually be present when the committee votes to order a measure reported. To facilitate the conduct of committee markups and other meetings, however, House rules do not insist that a majority be present for other purposes. For all other votes and for other proceedings during a markup, most committees may set their own quorum requirement in their committee rules, so long as that quorum is not less than one-third of the committee's members (Rule XI, clause 2(h)(3)). Most committees adopt a one-third quorum requirement as part of their rules.

It is much easier in committee than on the House floor for members to insist that a quorum be present. On the floor, a member rarely can demand the presence of a quorum unless a vote is taking place. In committee, on the other hand, any member whom the chairman has recognized can make a point of order that a quorum is not present. When a member makes this point of order, the chairman counts to determine whether in fact a quorum is present. The chairman's count is not subject to challenge or appeal. If a quorum is present, the chairman announces that fact and business resumes. If a quorum is not present, however, the chairman must initiate a quorum call and the necessary quorum of members must register their presence before business can resume.

Voting.

During committee meetings, like during House floor sessions, questions can be decided by voice, division, or record votes. Committees, like the House, first take a voice vote on each question. The chairman asks those favoring the question to call out "Aye," and then asks those opposed to call out "No." Based on what the chairman hears, he or she announces that the ayes or the noes appear to have it. At that point, any member who disagrees with the chair's announcement can demand a division vote. In that case, the chairman asks those in favor to raise their hands until counted, followed by those opposed.

Before the chairman announces the final result of either a voice vote or a division vote, any member may request that the question be decided by a call of the roll. The request for a rollcall vote must be supported by at least one-fifth of the members present, although some committees adopt rules that make it even easier to obtain rollcalls. In fact, a chairman may order a rollcall vote on a question as a courtesy to any member who requests it, or even in anticipation that members will request it.

When a rollcall vote is ordered, the chairman directs the clerk to call the roll. The clerk first calls the names of the majority party members, followed by the names of the minority party members. The chairman may direct the clerk to call his or her name either first or last. After the clerk completes calling the roll, the chairman normally directs the clerk to call the names of the members who failed to vote when their names were first called. The clerk then is to tally the vote and, at the chairman's direction, report the number of members voting aye and no.

Sometimes, however, the chairman delays asking the clerk to report the tally in order to allow absent members to reach the committee room and cast their votes. Members sometimes have two or more committee or subcommittee meetings at the same time, requiring them to leave one meeting in order to come to the other when a vote is taking place. Chairmen know that their committee members want to be recorded as having voted whenever possible, so they may delay announcing the result of a vote when they are informed that an absent member is on his or her way to the committee room to vote. When the outcome of an important vote hangs in the balance, a chairman may leave a vote open for even longer periods of time, if that is likely to allow the chairman's position to prevail.

Although committees typically require only a one-third quorum for all but the final vote in markup, committee staff do their best to make sure that all the members of their party are present to be recorded on each rollcall vote. The reason lies in the House's ban on proxy voting in committee. Before 1995, members could leave their proxies with one of their committee colleagues to cast for them. This often enabled a committee chairman, if he or she held enough proxies, to win a rollcall vote even when the chairman's position was opposed by a majority of the members who actually were present.

Proxy voting was prohibited in 1995. The result has been to put more of a premium on maximizing attendance, especially when the majority party holds only a few more committee seats than the minority. In those circumstances, the absence of only one or two majority-party members can enable the minority party to prevail on a party-line vote if all the minority party members are present. It is very important, therefore, for as many members as possible to attend markups, and for the committee staff of each party to know how to contact their absent members as soon as a rollcall vote begins (if not before). Committee staffs may devise systems to keep track of where their party's members are, and may rely on members' legislative assistants to ensure that those members are present when they are needed to make a quorum or to cast their votes.

Points of Order and Parliamentary Inquiries

In presiding over a markup, the chairman participates freely in the debate, unlike the Speaker and other members who preside over floor sessions of the House. Like the Speaker, however, the chairman is responsible for maintaining order, insisting on proper decorum, and enforcing applicable procedures. Committee chairmen are somewhat more likely than the Speaker to take the initiative in declining to recognize members who are about to say or do something in violation of proper procedure. In general, though, it is the responsibility of committee members to protect their rights by making points of order whenever they believe that appropriate procedures are being violated to their detriment.

Points of Order and Appeals.

To make a point of order, a committee member addresses the chairman at the appropriate time, and announces that he or she wishes to make a point of order. The chairman recognizes the member to make and explain the point of order, indicating precisely what procedural requirement or prohibition is being violated. The member whose action is being challenged by the point of order then is recognized to reply, after which the chairman may recognize other members to argue for or against the point of order. However, the chairman entertains all debate on a point of order at his or her discretion; members have no right to debate points of order.

Whenever the chairman has heard sufficient debate, he or she rules on the point of order, either sustaining or overruling it. The chairman bases the ruling on his or her understanding of proper procedure, perhaps with the advice of senior committee staff and with the benefit of whatever debate on the point of order has just taken place. The House parliamentarian and his assistants do not attend committee meetings to provide authoritative procedural guidance. However, committee staff may seek guidance from the Office of the Parliamentarian in advance of a committee meeting, or even by telephone during the course of the meeting.[4]

---

[4]Committees sometimes have requested CRS staff to attend committee meetings to offer (continued...)

Any committee member who disagrees with the chairman's ruling may challenge it by addressing the chair and appealing his or her ruling. The committee acts on the appeal by voting on whether the ruling of the chair is to stand as the decision of the committee. An appeal is debatable under the five-minute rule, although any member who has been recognized may make either of two non-debatable motions that, if adopted, end debate on the appeal. A member may move the previous question on the appeal. Instead, the member may move to table the appeal; if the committee votes to table an appeal, the ruling of the chair stands.

Reserving Points of Order.

During committee markups, the most common points of order are against amendments—on the grounds, for example, that an amendment is not germane. To make a point of order against an amendment, however, a committee member must be alert to make it at the proper moment. A point of order may be made against an amendment (or any other debatable motion) after it has been read or the committee has waived the reading of the amendment, but before debate on it has begun. Once the proponent of the amendment begins to explain it, a point of order no longer can be made against the amendment; the point of order would come too late.

This can present a problem during committee markups that are conducted rather informally, as they usually are. Often, when a member offers an amendment, the chairman responds by directing the clerk to distribute copies of it to all the members. While this is being done, the member offering the amendment sometimes begins to explain it. By the time the other committee members receive and review copies of the amendment, it is too late to make a point of order against it because debate on the amendment already has begun. To avoid this problem, members sometimes reserve points of order against amendments as soon as they are offered, and without having yet seen them. In this way, an amendment's sponsor may explain and defend it for five minutes, while other members examine it, determine whether it is subject to a point of order, and, if so, decide whether they want to make that point of order. After the sponsor has relinquished the floor, the member who reserved the point of order may make it, or withdraw the reservation and allow the debate to continue.

Parliamentary Inquiries.

When a committee member is uncertain about the procedures being followed during a markup, he or she may address the chair and, when recognized, make a parliamentary inquiry. This inquiry must be a question about procedure, not about the substance, meaning, or effect of the bill or amendment the committee is debating. A committee chairman is not required to entertain parliamentary inquiries, but chairmen usually do so unless convinced that an inquiry is repetitive or is being made for dilatory purposes. The chairman's reply to a parliamentary inquiry is not subject to appeal because it constitutes only an explanation, not a ruling.

---

[4](...continued)
answers to procedural questions as they arise.

From time to time, committee members may address the chairman to raise a "point of information" or a "point of clarification." Neither exists under the procedures of the House of Representatives or its committees. Nonetheless, chairmen sometimes reply as a courtesy to their fellow committee members.

Challenging Committee Procedures.

The procedural rulings of the chairman usually are final, unless reversed on appeal by majority vote of the committee. In most circumstances, a committee member who disagrees with a ruling made in committee may not challenge it on the floor of the House. It is generally left to each committee to enforce or disregard its markup procedures. In *Procedure in the House* (ch. 17, sec. 11.1), the House parliamentarian has stated that "a point of order does not ordinarily lie in the House against consideration of a bill by reason of defective committee procedures occurring prior to the time the bill was ordered reported to the House. Such point of order, if made in the House, may be overruled on the ground that the rules of a particular committee are for that committee to interpret unless they are in direct conflict with the rules of the House or unless the House rules specifically permit the raising of such objections." In general, if the committee votes to order a bill reported to the House, that vote (if properly conducted) cures procedural defects that may have occurred at earlier stages of the committee's consideration of the bill.

Motions to Conclude Markups

It bears repeating that no House committee has the authority to actually change the text of a measure that has been introduced and referred to it, nor do committees vote directly on the merits of bills and resolutions. The committee votes instead on the amendments that it will recommend to the House. The House then considers and votes on these committee amendments when it acts on the bill itself.

Markups may begin with an amendment in the nature of a substitute being offered by or on behalf of the chairman, sometimes for the tactical reasons discussed above. Members then offer their amendments to that complete substitute, rather than to the text of the underlying bill. In such a case, the final vote the committee takes on amendments is on agreeing to the amendment in the nature of a substitute, as it may have been amended. When the committee reports the bill back to the House, the bill will be accompanied by only that one amendment in the nature of a substitute, even though the committee may have adopted several or even many amendments to it during the course of the markup.

Ordering the Bill Reported.

The committee does not conclude its markup by voting on the bill itself. After voting on the last amendment to be offered, the chairman recognizes a majority party member to move that the committee order the bill reported to the House with whatever amendments the committee has adopted during the markup, and with the recommendation that the House agree to those amendments and then pass the bill as amended. The bill is actually reported (as opposed to the committee *ordering* it reported) when the committee chairman takes the bill and the accompanying committee report to the floor when the House is in session, files the report, and returns the bill to the House. The committee report then is printed, the bill is reprinted to show the committee's action and its recommended amendments, and the bill is listed on the Union Calendar if it authorizes or appropriates funds or affects revenues, or otherwise on the House Calendar.

The Committee's Reporting Options.

A House committee has several options in deciding how it will report to the House after it has completed a markup.

Committee Amendments. If the committee has marked up a bill that was introduced and referred to it—H.R. 1, for example—the committee may vote to order H.R. 1 reported with one or more amendments.

If, as its last vote on amendments, the committee agreed to an amendment in the nature of a substitute (perhaps as amended), the committee may vote to order H.R. 1 reported with that one amendment, even though the amendment constitutes an entirely new text of the bill that may not resemble the text of H.R. 1 as it was introduced and referred to the committee.

If the committee has marked up H.R. 1 and agreed to several different amendments to it, each amendment affecting a different provision of the bill, the committee may vote to order H.R. 1 reported with those separate amendments. Instead, though, the committee may authorize the chairman to incorporate those amendments into a single amendment in the nature of a substitute. The reason for doing so is that it is more convenient for the House, when considering a bill on the floor, to act on a single committee substitute than to act on a series of discrete committee amendments. The committee may agree to a unanimous consent request that the committee report an amendment in the nature of a substitute instead of the several amendments. Alternatively, a member may offer the amendment in the nature of a substitute as the last amendment to be considered during the markup. (In the latter case, however, any committee member has the right to insist that the substitute actually be drafted and available in writing at the time it is offered.)

Clean Bills. Alternatively, the committee may vote to report what is known as a *clean bill* instead of reporting H.R. 1 with one or more amendments. A clean bill is a new bill that has a new number instead of H.R. 1 and that typically lists as its sponsor the committee chairman, not the Member who had introduced H.R. 1. This new bill is known as a clean bill because it incorporates all the amendments that the committee adopted during its markup of H.R. 1. For this reason, the committee reports the new bill without amendment; in this sense, it is "clean."

The effect of reporting a clean bill is much the same as reporting the marked-up bill with an amendment in the nature of a substitute. In either case, all the committee's proposed changes in the marked up text are incorporated into a single new text. Then why would a committee report a clean bill?

There are at least two reasons. First, if the committee has marked-up a staff draft (discussion draft, chairman's mark) instead of H.R. 1, that marked-up text must be introduced and reported as a bill before the House can consider it. Second, there are instances in which the committee (or its chairman) decides to assume complete responsibility (and credit) for the bill it orders reported. Imagine, for example, that the committee has marked up H.R. 1 in ways that the original sponsor of the bill finds unacceptable. In that case, the sponsor may wish to disavow further responsibility for H.R. 1, and so welcomes the committee's decision to report a clean bill instead of reporting H.R. 1 with a committee substitute. In other cases, the chairman may prefer a clean bill in order to have his or her name most closely associated with it.

Technically, the committee must have the clean bill in its possession before it can vote to order it reported. This means that, at the conclusion of the markup, the marked up text must be prepared as a bill, it must be introduced while the House is in session, and the newly introduced clean bill must be numbered and referred back to the committee before the committee may act on it. In practice, committees sometimes short-circuit this process if no one objects. Immediately after the committee completes its markup, it may authorize the chairman to report the clean bill. So long as the clean bill is introduced on that same calendar day, the official records of the House's proceedings do not indicate whether the clean bill actually was introduced and referred to committee before or after the committee's markup ended.

Other Views.

Immediately after the committee votes to order the bill reported, the ranking minority member or another minority party member usually claims the right for all committee members to submit their own supplemental, minority, or dissenting views for printing as part of the committee's report on the bill. Clause 2(l) of Rule XI provides that:

> If at the time of approval of a measure or matter by a committee (other than the Committee on Rules) a member of the committee gives notice of intention to file supplemental, minority, or additional views for inclusion in the report to the House thereon, that member shall be entitled to not less than two additional calendar days after the day of such notice (excluding Saturdays, Sundays, and legal holidays except when the House is in session on such a day) to file such views, in writing and signed by that member, with the clerk of the committee.

Preparing for Conference.

There is one final action that House committees sometimes take concerning bills that they have just marked up and ordered reported. A committee can adopt a motion that authorizes its chairman to take the actions necessary to send the bill to conference when that time comes—in other words, after both houses have passed different versions of the bill or another bill on the same subject. For this purpose, the chairman may recognize a majority party member to move that, pursuant to clause 1 of Rule XXII, the committee authorizes its chairman to make such motions in the House as may be necessary to go to conference with the Senate on H.R. 1 or a similar Senate bill.

If and when the time comes to take H.R. 1 to conference, the House usually agrees to a unanimous consent request that the House create a conference committee with the Senate to negotiate a compromise between their differing positions on the bill. If unanimous consent cannot be secured, one option is to obtain a special rule from the Rules Committee for that purpose. A second alternative lies in Rule XXII, clause 1:

> A motion to disagree to Senate amendments to a House bill or resolution and to request or agree to a conference with the Senate, or a motion to insist on House amendments to a Senate bill or resolution and to request or agree to a conference with the Senate, shall be privileged in the discretion of the Speaker *if offered by direction of* the primary committee and of all reporting committees that had initial referral of the bill or resolution (italics added).

Under the terms of this rule, the committee chairman can make this motion on the House floor only if the committee has adopted a motion authorizing him to do so. And the vote in committee on this motion requires that a majority of the committee actually be present, just as does the vote to order the bill reported back to the House. By adopting the motion to go to conference at the same meeting at which the committee has marked up the bill and voted to order it reported, the committee avoids the need to schedule another meeting and assemble a majority of the committee's members when the time actually arrives, perhaps months later, to arrange for the conference with the Senate.

The committee must agree to such a motion with respect to each bill or resolution on which it may eventually want to go to conference. Committees cannot give their chairmen the authorization required by clause 1 of Rule XXII in a blanket form that applies to some or all of the bills that the committee may order reported during the course of the Congress.

Related CRS Products

Other CRS reports that discuss aspects of the legislative process in House committees include: *House Rules Affecting Committees* (Report 97-524), *Hearings in the House of Representatives* (Report 96-623), and *House Rules and Precedents Affecting Committee Markup Procedures* (Report 97-1045). In addition, a series of related fact sheets are available online as part of the "CRS Guide to the Legislative and Budget Process" (lcweb.loc.gov/crs/legproc/newformat/HomeNF.html). The fact sheets also are available in printed form. All these CRS products will be revised when necessary to reflect significant changes in relevant House rules, precedents, and practices.

THE AMENDING PROCESS IN THE HOUSE OF REPRESENTATIVES

Stanley Bach

Summary

Most amendments that Representatives propose to legislation on the House floor are offered in Committee of the Whole. Measures considered under suspension of the rules are not amendable on the floor, and few amendments are proposed to bills and resolutions considered in the House, in the House as in Committee of the Whole, or under the Corrections Calendar procedures.

The House's procedures recognize distinctions between first and second-degree amendments, between perfecting and substitute amendments, and among amendments in the forms of motions to strike, to insert, and to strike out and insert. An amendment in the nature of a substitute proposes to replace the entire text of a bill or resolution. All amendments must be germane to the text they would amend, and they are subject to other general prohibitions such as that against proposing only to re-amend language that already has been fully amended. Additional restrictions apply to appropriations and tax amendments, and the budget process creates various other points of order that Members may make against certain amendments. In general, a Member must make a point of order against an amendment before debate on it begins, unless that point of order is waived by a special rule.

In Committee of the Whole, measures usually are considered for amendment one section or title at a time. Members must offer their amendments to appropriate parts of a bill when it has been read or designated. Each amendment is debated under the five-minute rule. After the first 10 minutes of debate, Members obtain additional time for debate by offering pro forma amendments in the form of motions to strike the last word. Each amendment in Committee of the Whole may be amended by a perfecting amendment or a substitute amendment or both. A substitute for an amendment also is amendable. After the Committee of the Whole disposes of the last amendment to be offered to the bill, it rises and the House then votes again on all the amendments the Committee has approved. A recommittal motion usually offers a final opportunity to amend the bill before the House votes on passing it.

Introduction

The amending process on the floor of the House of Representatives gives Members an opportunity to change the provisions of the bills and resolutions on which they are going to vote. This report summarizes many of the procedures and practices affecting this process, which can be among the most complex as well as the most important stages of legislative consideration.[1] The discussion that follows is intended to be a useful introduction; however, it is not exhaustive and it cannot substitute for a careful examination of the House's rules and precedents themselves, for close observation of the House in daily session, and for consultation with the parliamentarian and his associates on specific procedural problems and opportunities.

The way in which the House considers each measure affects Members' opportunities for amending it and the procedures that govern the amending process. There are essentially five alternative sets of procedures, or modes of consideration, by which the House considers public bills and resolutions on the floor: (1) under suspension of the rules, (2) by call of the Corrections Calendar, (3) in the House, under the hour rule, (4) in Committee of the Whole and the House, and (5) in the House as in Committee of the Whole.[2]

The overwhelming majority of the amendments on which Representatives vote are offered while measures are being considered in Committee of the Whole, before being reported back to the House for votes on final passage. Under two of the other modes of consideration, suspension of the rules and the Corrections Calendar, most

---

[1] This report only addresses the amending process that may take place on the floor before the House first votes on passing a measure. It assumes a basic familiarity with some of the other stages of the legislative process, such as committee hearings, markups, and reports, the manner in which measures reach the House floor for consideration, and the general purposes and uses of special rules. CRS reports that discuss some of these and related subjects are listed at the end of this report.

[2] Clause 5 of Rule XV provides procedures for considering private bills and resolutions. All citations in this report, which necessarily are selective, are to the rules of the 105th Congress, the annotations to the rules appearing in the *House Rules and Manual* for each Congress, and the recent precedents compiled and published in *Procedure in the U.S. House of Representatives* and the 1985 and 1987 *Supplements* (cited as *House Procedure*, *House Procedure, 1985 Supplement*, and *House Procedure, 1987 Supplement*). (See "Sources of Additional Information" for more complete references to these volumes.) The amendment process also is the subject of volume 9 of *Deschler's Precedents of the U.S. House of Representatives*, published in 1991.

floor amendments are prohibited; under the remaining procedures, floor amendments are in order but they are much less likely to be offered, either because of the procedures involved or because of the nature of the measures being considered.

There are several distinctions among different kinds of amendments as well as some general principles and prohibitions governing the amendments that Members and committees can offer. These distinctions, principles, and prohibitions can be important, whatever set of procedures the House is following, although they are more likely to matter when measures are considered in Committee of the Whole than under other circumstances.

This report begins, therefore, with a discussion of distinctions among amendments, followed by some observations on drafting amendments and on several general principles and prohibitions affecting the amending process. Next we examine the specific possibilities and procedures for offering and debating amendments under each of the five sets of procedures, beginning with measures that are debated and amended in the House, under the hour rule, and then those that are considered first in Committee of the Whole and then in the House. We next consider the possible "amendment trees" that may develop. The report also discusses several other elements of the amending process: the special procedures and rules governing appropriations and tax amendments and amendments affecting federal spending programs; the procedures for making points of order against amendments; and the effects of special rules on the amending process. At the end of the report is a list of sources of additional information.

This report concentrates on amendment procedures under the House's standing rules and precedents. It does not address the various ways in which special rules can affect the amending process, nor does it discuss the points of order that Members may make against amendments under the Congressional Budget and Impoundment Control Act of 1974 and subsequent laws, especially the Gramm-Rudman-Hollings Act of 1985 as amended and the Budget Enforcement Act of 1990. On these subjects, see two other CRS reports: CRS Report 96-938, *Special Rules in the House of Representatives* and CRS Report 97-865, *Points of Order in the Congressional Budget Process.*

Distinctions Among Amendments

Amendments are not all the same. We can distinguish among amendments in terms of their degree, their form, and their effects. Moreover, these are not merely analytical distinctions; they can help us understand what amendments Members may offer, under what circumstances, and with what consequences.

Degrees of Amendments

Whenever a bill or resolution can be amended on the House floor, it is subject to amendments in two degrees. An amendment in the *first degree* proposes to change the text of the measure itself. After a Representative offers a first-degree amendment but before the House votes on it, another Member may propose an amendment to that amendment.[3] An amendment to a first-degree amendment is an amendment in the *second degree*. The House then debates and votes on the second-degree amendment before voting on the first-degree amendment, which now may have been amended. As a general rule, third degree amendments (amendments to second-degree amendments) are not in order.[4]

Forms of Amendments

We also may distinguish among amendments in terms of their form.

First, an amendment may propose only to *insert* something into a bill or resolution (or first-degree amendment) without changing the provisions already in it. For example, the amendment may propose to insert a new section or title without affecting the existing sections and titles.

Second, the amendment may propose only to *strike out* something from a measure (or first-degree amendment) without inserting anything in its place. For example, the amendment may propose to strike out as little as one word or as much as one or more titles of a bill.

Third, and finally, an amendment may propose to both *strike out and insert* by replacing something that is already in the measure (or first-degree amendment) with something else. For example, the amendment may propose only to change a dollar amount, or it may replace a section or title of a bill with an entirely different version of that section or title.

Members sometimes refer to their amendments in terms of these effects; for instance, Representatives may state that they wish to offer a motion to strike out a particular section or that their amendment is a motion to strike out and insert. As this indicates, amendments are a special kind of motion.

Effects of Amendments

A third way of distinguishing among amendments is in terms of their effects.

With respect to first-degree amendments, an amendment may propose only to make some change in the portion of the bill or resolution being considered for amendment without affecting the rest of it. Such an amendment is a *perfecting amendment*; it proposes to change—and, therefore, presumably perfect—that portion of the bill without replacing it altogether. For instance, a section of a bill may authorize an amount of money to be appropriated for certain purposes. An

---

[3] Unless otherwise noted, references throughout this report to the House also apply to the Committee of the Whole. Clause 12 of Rule XVIII states that "[t]he Rules of the House are the rules of the Committee of the Whole House on the state of the Union so far as applicable."

[4] *House Procedure*, ch. 27, sec. 6, p. 502-504. When the amendment to an amendment is a substitute, the substitute may be amended. See the section on "The Amendment Trees."

amendment to change only the dollar figure, but not the purposes for which that amount is authorized, would be a perfecting amendment.

On the other hand, an amendment may propose to strike out the entire pending portion of a bill—whether it be a paragraph, section, or title—and replace it completely. For instance, the amendment could propose to strike out a section of an authorization bill and replace it with a new section that changes both the amount that is authorized and the purposes for which it is authorized. Such an amendment may be designated an *amendment in the nature of a substitute*, although Members typically do not do so.[5]

Of greater practical importance are the differences in effects among amendments to amendments. An amendment proposing to make some change in the text of a first-degree amendment, without replacing it completely, is a *perfecting amendment*. By contrast, an amendment to replace the entire text of a first-degree amendment is a *substitute amendment*. The significance of this distinction will emerge from the discussion of the "amendment trees."

The difference between perfecting amendments and substitute amendments depends primarily on the way in which they are drafted and not on the magnitude of the policy changes they would make. A perfecting amendment may replace all but the first word, line, or sentence of a section of a bill (or a first-degree amendment) and so entirely change its substantive effect. Conversely, a substitute for a first-degree amendment would amend the text completely but might make only one minor substantive change and replace the remainder with precisely the same language.

A perfecting amendment may take any one of the three possible forms; it may propose to strike out, to insert, or to strike out and insert. On the other hand, a substitute amendment is a proposal to replace one thing with another, and so it always takes the form of a motion to strike out and insert.

Amendments in the Nature of Substitutes for Measures

Finally, a special kind of amendment, known as an *amendment in the nature of a substitute*, always proposes to replace the entire text of a bill or resolution, not some lesser portion of the measure. This amendment strikes out everything after the enacting clause of a bill, or the resolving clause of a resolution, and replaces the entire text of the measure with a different text.[6]

---

[5] "While an amendment in the nature of a substitute is in every instance a "motion to strike out and insert," the term "amendment in the nature of a substitute" applies only to those motions which propose to strike out an entire pending text and to insert new matter and is not used to describe those motions to strike out and insert which may be properly characterized as "perfecting amendments" and which go only to a portion of the pending text." *House Procedure*, ch. 27, sec. 23.1, p. 525.

[6] The enacting clause reads "Be it enacted by the Senate and House of Representatives of the United States of America in Congress assembled," and is followed by the text of the bill. There is a different resolving clause for each kind of resolution (simple, concurrent, and joint)

(continued...)

If a majority of Members vote for such an amendment, Representatives cannot offer any additional amendments to the measure because it has been amended in its entirety. When Members refer to an amendment in the nature of a substitute, they almost always have this kind of amendment in mind, although, as noted above, the same phrase can be applied to an amendment that proposes to replace whatever portion of the measure is then being considered for amendment.

There are several unique characteristics about the way in which the House considers amendments in the nature of substitutes for the entire text of measures.

First, most often this kind of amendment is recommended by a committee at the same time it reports the measure itself. And in practice, Members almost always want to devote far more of their time and attention on the floor to this committee alternative than to the text of the bill as introduced. For this reason, special rules reported by the Rules Committee usually give a committee substitute special standing during the amending process in Committee of the Whole by providing for Members to offer their amendments to that substitute rather than to the bill itself. The committee substitute is considered "as an original bill for the purpose of amendment," meaning that it is not treated as a first-degree amendment. Instead, it is amendable in two degrees as if it were the text of a measure.[7]

Second, if an amendment in the nature of a substitute for a bill or resolution is not given this special standing, a Member can propose it as a first-degree amendment at only two points during the amending process in Committee of the Whole. The amendment is in order either at the very beginning of the process or at the very end, after the Committee has voted on all other amendments to the text of the measure.[8] But even if a Member or committee offers an amendment in the nature of a substitute at the beginning of the amending process, the Committee of the Whole typically does not vote on it until the end of the process because Members will direct most—usually all—of their amendments to it.

Finally, when an amendment in the nature of a substitute for everything after the enacting or resolving clause is proposed at the beginning of the amending process, other Members can propose amendments to the pending portion of the measure as

---

[6](...continued)
that also precedes the text of the resolution.

[7] Special rules sometimes give the same special standing to such an amendment in the nature of a substitute that has been printed in a report of the Rules Committee or the *Congressional Record* or that is embodied as the text of another bill.

[8] "An amendment in the nature of a substitute for a bill is in order after the first section of the bill has been read for amendment...or following the reading of the final section of the bill....However, an amendment in the nature of a substitute for a bill is not in order at an intermediate stage of the reading.... Of course, if the bill is considered as having been read for amendment, then an amendment in the nature of a substitute may be offered at any time during consideration of the bill. An amendment in the nature of a substitute may ordinarily be offered after the reading of the first section of a bill being read by sections notwithstanding the pendency of committee amendments adding new sections to the bill." *House Procedure*, ch. 27, sec. 12.1, p. 510-511.

well as to the complete substitute; if so, they vote on any and all such amendments before voting on the amendment in the nature of a substitute. (This possibility, which rarely arises in practice, is discussed at the end of the section on "The Amendment Trees.")

Drafting Amendments

Clause 1 of Rule XVI requires that every amendment offered on the House floor must be in writing, and it must be drafted accurately to achieve its intended procedural and policy effects.[9] Each amendment must state precisely where and how it would amend the measure or other amendment, identifying the specific pages, lines, and words it would affect.[10] The text of every amendment reveals its form (whether it inserts, strikes out, or strikes out and inserts), and also may identify it as a perfecting or substitute amendment. The following examples illustrate some of the ways in which various kinds of amendments may be drafted.

Amendments to a measure:

To insert:

After line 8 on page 23, insert the following:

At the end of Title III, insert the following new section:

To strike out:

Beginning on page 3, strike out line 1 and all that follows through line 14 on page 4.

To strike out and insert:

On line 10 of page 7, strike out "$100" and insert in lieu thereof "$50".

To strike out all after the enacting (or resolving) clause and insert:

Strike out all after the enacting (or resolving) clause and insert in lieu thereof the following:

Amendments to an amendment:

Perfecting amendment—to insert:

At the end of the amendment offered by the gentleman from New York, insert the following:

---

[9] *House Procedure*, ch. 27, sec. 1.4, p. 489.

[10] *House Procedure*, ch. 27, sec. 1.7, p. 489-490.

Perfecting amendment—to strike out:

In the amendment offered by the gentlewoman from California, strike out Section 2.

Perfecting amendment—to strike out and insert:

In the amendment offered by the gentleman from Wisconsin, strike out "$100" and insert in lieu thereof "$50".

Strike out Section 1 of the pending amendment and insert in lieu thereof the following:

Substitute amendment:

In lieu of the matter proposed to be inserted by the gentleman from Texas, insert the following:

It is sometimes possible to draft an amendment in more than one way. It bears emphasizing that the distinction between perfecting and substitute amendments generally is a matter of drafting style, not substantive effect. For example, imagine an appropriations bill that includes the following on lines 6 and 7 of page 12:

> For the salaries and expenses of the Congressional Research Service of the Library of Congress, $500.

A Member who wishes to amend this appropriation to increase it to $1,000 could draft the amendment in at least two different ways:

> On line 7 of page 12, strike out "$500" and insert in lieu thereof "$1,000", or
>
> Strike out lines 6 and 7 on page 12 and insert in lieu thereof the following: "For the salaries and expenses of the Congressional Research Service of the Library of Congress, $1,000."

These two amendments would have precisely the same substantive effect, even though they are drafted differently. Representatives sometimes find it advisable to have amendments (and especially amendments to amendments) drafted in more than one way, especially when a bill or resolution is considered in Committee of the Whole, because the development of an "amendment tree" may permit or encourage a Member to propose an amendment in one form, but not in another.

The examples offered above are illustrative only. In drafting amendments, it is desirable to consult, whenever possible, with attorneys in the House's Office of Legislative Counsel for their expert advice and assistance. Under some circumstances, it also is advisable to consult with the House parliamentarian to ensure that an amendment meets the procedural requirements that will apply when the amendment is going to be proposed. When an amendment must be drafted on the floor, committee staff may be able to provide assistance.

Principles and Prohibitions

A number of general principles and prohibitions govern the amending process and restrict the amendments that committees and individual Representatives may propose on the floor. Many of these principles and prohibitions derive from House precedents, but the best known restriction on amendments—the germaneness requirement—is embodied in the House rules themselves. Like most other House procedures, Members generally must enforce these principles and prohibitions, and thereby protect their own rights and interests, by making appropriate points of order. The procedures for doing so are discussed in a later section of this report.

In General

The House's published precedents are the source for many of the principles and restrictions affecting the amending process. For example, the prohibition against third degree amendments is one of the most basic limitations on the amendments that Members may offer, but it is not stated explicitly in the standing rules.[11] Precedents govern the amending process in several other important respects.

Committee Amendments.

Standing committees do not actually amend measures during their markups; instead, a committee votes on what amendments it wishes to recommend to the House. These amendments then have the status of committee amendments. If the committee reports a measure with one or more amendments, they receive priority consideration on the floor and they are considered automatically.[12] The House considers each of them at the appropriate time; it is not necessary for a committee member to offer them from the floor. When and how the committee amendments are considered depends on the set of procedures under which the bill or resolution itself is being considered.

Under several possible procedures for considering amendments to a measure, it is "open to amendment at any point"—that is, amendments can be offered to any part of the bill in any order. In such a case, the Speaker directs the clerk to read the first committee amendment as soon as the bill is considered for amendment. After the House votes on this amendment, it considers any additional committee amendments in turn.[13] Members may be able to offer their own amendments to each committee amendment, but they generally may not propose amendments to the text of the bill itself until the House has completed action on the committee amendments. The

---

[11] In Section XXXIII of his *Manual of Parliamentary Practice*, Jefferson held third degree amendments to be out of order, and Rule XXVIII states in part that the "rules of parliamentary practice comprised by Jefferson's Manual shall govern the House in all cases to which they are applicable and in which they are not inconsistent with the Rules and orders of the House."

[12] *House Procedure*, ch. 27, sec. 10.1, p. 508.

[13] *House Procedure*, ch. 27, sec. 11.5, p. 509-510.

amending process under these procedures usually is routine; typically, no more than one committee amendment is to be considered.

On the other hand, the particularly important procedures governing the amending process in Committee of the Whole usually are governed by the principle that a measure is to be "read for amendment"—that is, only one paragraph, section, or title of the measure is open to amendment at a time. In this case, the Committee of the Whole automatically considers any committee amendment(s) to each part of the bill as soon as it is read.[14] Again, Representatives may propose amendments to each committee amendment, but the Members must dispose of the committee amendments to each part of the measure before they can offer other amendments to that part of it.[15]

An exception to this principle arises whenever the committee amendment takes the form of a motion to strike out some language or provision of the bill. While such a committee amendment is pending, a Member may offer an amendment to change the part of the bill that the committee proposes to strike out altogether. This possibility is considered in more detail during the discussion of the "amendment trees."

Also, the committee's recommendations for changes in a bill or resolution often are embodied in a single amendment in the nature of a substitute. As already noted, the special rules for considering measures often make special arrangements for Members to consider a committee substitute in Committee of the Whole by designating it as a proposal that Members may amend in two degrees.

General Principles.

Several other general principles govern the amending process.

First, clause 2 of Rule XVI requires that the clerk is to read each amendment when it is offered and before debate on it begins, whether it is a committee amendment or one proposed by an individual Member.[16] The sponsor or principal proponent of the amendment very often asks unanimous consent that the amendment be considered as read, and there usually is no objection unless an interested Member is not familiar with it and wants time to examine the amendment before it is debated. In addition, a Member may move to dispense with the reading, under circumstances discussed in a later section, but only if Members already have access to a printed copy of the amendment.

Second, an amendment should not affect the measure in more than one place. This principle protects the House against having to cast one vote on two or more

---

[14] *House Procedure*, ch. 27, sec. 9.1, p. 506-507.

[15] "While committee amendments to a pending section are normally considered prior to amendments offered from the floor, a floor amendment to the text of a pending section is considered before a committee amendment adding a new section at the end of the pending section." *House Procedure*, ch 27, sec. 24.1, p. 526.

[16] *House Procedure*, ch. 27, sec. 20.1, p. 521.

propositions that may be unrelated. Thus, an amendment to replace the text of Section 201 and add a new sentence at the end of Section 203 is subject to a point of order if the bill is being read by sections. Instead, the sponsor of the amendment could offer each part of it as a separate amendment, or the sponsor could ask unanimous consent that the two amendments be considered en bloc—that is, as if they were one amendment.[17] There often is no objection to such a request if both amendments are necessary to achieve a single purpose. Alternatively, if the title containing Sections 201 and 203 has been read for amendment, or if the bill is open to amendment at any point, the sponsor could avoid a point of order by drafting a single amendment to strike out Sections 201-203 and replace them with the preferred provisions.[18]

Third, any Member may demand, as a matter of right, the *division* of an amendment proposing to insert additional provisions into (or strike provisions from) a measure or first-degree amendment, but only if the amendment to be divided (or the matter to be stricken) consists of two or more parts that, in the judgment of the chair, could stand as independent propositions. When an amendment is divided, the House considers each division of the amendment in turn, as if each were a separate amendment. This right, which also protects the House against having to cast a single vote on two or more separable proposals, is conveyed by clause 5(a) of Rule XVI; however, clause 5(c) of the same rule states in part that a motion to strike out and insert is not divisible.

Fourth, the same amendment may not be offered more than once. If the House has considered and rejected an amendment, it may not be offered again unless it has been changed substantively.[19] Otherwise, the House could not be sure of its ability to dispose of questions conclusively. However, a part of a rejected amendment may be offered as a separate amendment, and the entire text of the rejected amendment may be included as part of a larger amendment.[20] In addition, it is sometimes possible to offer two amendments that are substantively identical. For example, a Member may propose to add a new title to the text of a bill, and also move to insert the same new title into the text of an amendment in the nature of a substitute for the bill. These amendments are different procedurally because each seeks to amend a different text.

Fifth, it is not in order for a Representative to offer an amendment that proposes only to amend language that already has been amended.[21] If not for this principle also, the House would have difficulty resolving issues once and for all. Thus, if a dollar number in an appropriations bill has been amended, another amendment that would only change the same number again is subject to a point of order. Or if the House agrees to a substitute for a section or title of a bill, no further amendments only to that

---

[17] *House Procedure*, ch. 27, sec. 9.4, p. 507.

[18] If so, the text of Section 202 proposed in the amendment would be identical to the text of Section 202 already in the bill.

[19] *House Procedure*, ch. 27, secs. 33.1-33.2, p. 537.

[20] *House Procedure, 1985 Supplement*, ch. 27, sec. 33.5, p. 72.

[21] Annotations to Section XXXV of *Jefferson's Manual* in *House Rules and Manual*.

section or title are in order because it has been fully amended.[22] Any further amendment to it would constitute a prohibited attempt to re-amend. An important implication of this principle is that adoption of an amendment in the nature of a substitute precludes all further amendments to the measure. This complete substitute replaces the entire text of the bill or resolution, so any new amendment would propose to re-amend something that already has been fully amended.

An exception to the prohibition against re-amendment is what is sometimes called the principle of "the bigger bite." Representatives may seek to amend something already amended if they do so as part of an amendment to change a larger part of the text.[23] For example, a Member may re-amend a dollar figure in an appropriations bill by offering a substitute for the paragraph containing that number, so long as the amendment also makes some other substantive change in the paragraph. Similarly, after the House has agreed to a substitute for a section of a bill, a Member may propose a substitute for the title containing that section, and thereby re-amend the section in the process of amending other sections of the same title. Each of these amendments takes a bigger bite out of the text than the amendment the House already has considered and adopted.

The Germaneness Rule

Clause 7 of Rule XVI states in part that "no motion or proposition on a subject different from that under consideration shall be admitted under color of amendment."

This brief and somewhat obscure clause constitutes the germaneness rule—a rule that is simple and straightforward in principle, but complex and sometimes difficult to apply in practice. Indeed, determining whether or not an amendment is germane can be the most challenging, and even perplexing, task in interpreting the House's legislative procedures. The four-line rule is accompanied by 25 pages of commentary and explanation in the *House Rules and Manual* for the 105th Congress, and discussions of precedents on this subject consume all the 1,957 pages of volumes 10 and 11 of *Deschler's Precedents of the House of Representatives.*[24]

The principle underlying the germaneness rule is that the House should consider one subject at a time. While debating authorizations for military weapons systems, for example, the House should not be distracted by amendments concerning food stamps, mass transit, or other unrelated subjects. The object of the rule is not simply orderliness. If not for the germaneness requirement, Members could offer amendments on subjects of their choice, thereby bypassing the standing committee system and depriving the House of the committees' expert appraisals, recommendations, and reports. Furthermore, Members could be compelled to vote on unanticipated questions without adequate time for preparation. In sum, the

---

22 *House Procedure*, ch. 27, sec. 27.1, p. 529.

23 Annotations to Section XXXV of *Jefferson's Manual* in *House Rules and Manual*; *House Procedure*, ch. 27, secs. 27.3-27.10, p. 529-531.

24 For a more digestable selection of recent precedents on germaneness, see *House Procedure*, ch. 28, p. 543-625, and *House Procedure, 1985 Supplement*, ch. 28, p. 73-82.

germaneness rule is designed to encourage systematic and thoughtful legislative decisions.

Germaneness is a requirement that applies to all amendments originating in the House, whether proposed by individual Representatives or recommended by House committees. It does not apply to provisions of measures; anything contained in a bill or resolution is immune to challenge on grounds of germaneness. Also, Members generally may not make points of order against nongermane Senate amendments until the House has reached the stage of disagreement with the Senate over a measure—and usually when the House begins to consider a conference report.[25]

In determining whether an amendment proposed on the House floor is germane, the chair normally is concerned with the relationship between the amendment and the text it proposes to amend. In general, a second-perfecting amendment or a substitute for an amendment must be germane to the amendment it would affect. So it may be ruled nongermane even though it could be germane to the underlying text of the measure. And a first-degree amendment to a section or title of a bill must be germane to that section or title; the chair may rule it nongermane even though it might be germane to some other portion of the bill.[26] On the other hand, an amendment proposing to add a new section or title at the end of a measure may be subjected to a broader test: whether it is germane to the text of the measure as a whole.

Also, an amendment must be germane to the text it would amend as that text reads at the time the amendment is proposed. Thus, it is not sufficient that an amendment be germane to the bill as originally introduced (or to the first-degree amendment as originally proposed). Instead, the amendment must be germane to the bill (or amendment) as it already may have been amended. By its votes on amendments offered earlier, the House may have broadened or narrowed a bill (or amendment) in ways that affect the germaneness of other amendments that Members then propose. This situation adds to the difficulty of anticipating, evaluating, and protecting against germaneness challenges. The parliamentarian and his associates can offer a Representative expert advice on the germaneness of a prospective amendment. But by the time the Representative actually offers the amendment on the floor, the House may have amended the bill (or amendment) in ways that change the relationship on which the germaneness ruling is based—the relationship between the proposed amendment and the text it proposes to amend.

The concept of germaneness is akin to that of relevance or pertinence, but more restrictive. The mere fact that the House is considering a tax bill, for instance, does

---

[25] The standing rules of the Senate do not require floor amendments to be germane except when proposed to general appropriations or budget measures or to matters on which the Senate has invoked cloture. On the other hand, the Senate sometimes imposes a germaneness requirement on itself, by unanimous consent, during consideration of individual measures. House procedures for dealing with nongermane Senate amendments appear in clauses 4 and 5 of Rule XXVIII. See also "Sources of Additional Information," and Stanley Bach, "Germaneness Rules and Bicameral Relations in the U.S. Congress," *Legislative Studies Quarterly*, v. VII, n. 3, August 1982, pp. 341-357.

[26] *House Procedure, 1985 Supplement*, ch. 28, sec. 16, p. 77.

not necessarily mean that any amendment affecting federal taxes is germane. Instead, case by case, the House has gradually developed an elaborate body of precedents to assist and guide the chair in ruling on points of order that particular amendments are not germane. No other question of order arises so often, and no other rulings can be as difficult for Members and staff to predict. The precedents on germaneness are voluminous and often based on rather fine distinctions, distinctions that the chair explains in making rulings but that are not always obvious from the concise way in which the rulings have been summarized in print.

Thus, although new rulings are always based on earlier ones, it is often possible to develop from the precedents plausible arguments both for and against the same point of order on germaneness. However, while germaneness decisions may appear to be contradictory if only the published headnotes are studied, there is more apparent consistency if the factual situations are carefully reviewed.

To help Members and staff understand how the germaneness rule has been interpreted and applied, the parliamentarian's commentary in the *House Rules and Manual* identifies three tests of germaneness: subject matter, fundamental purpose, and committee jurisdiction.

First, to be germane, "[a]n amendment must relate to the subject matter under consideration." For example, "to a bill seeking to eliminate wage discrimination based on the sex of the employee, an amendment to make the provisions of the bill applicable to discrimination based on race was ruled out as not germane ...." In this case, the chair evidently held that the subject matter of the bill was not wage discrimination in general, but sex discrimination in particular.[27] Thus, the amendment to extend the coverage of the bill to race discrimination proposed to raise a different subject and, therefore, was nongermane.

Second, "[t]he fundamental purpose of an amendment must be germane to the fundamental purpose of the bill." More specifically, "an amendment must not only have the same end as the matter sought to be amended, but must contemplate a method of achieving that end that is closely allied to the method encompassed in the bill or other matter sought to be amended...." Among amendments that have met this test, the commentary cites the following example: "to a proposition to accomplish a result through regulation by a governmental agency, an amendment to accomplish the same fundamental purpose through regulation by another governmental agency was held germane ...." On the other hand, "to a bill to aid in the control of crime through research and training an amendment to accomplish that result through regulation of the sale of firearms was held not germane...." In the first case, the method of action proposed by the amendment was "closely allied" to that of the bill; in the second case, it was not.

Third, "[a]n amendment when considered as a whole should be within the jurisdiction of the committee reporting the bill...." This test is most likely to be applied when the jurisdictional issues are clear—"when the pending text is entirely

---

[27] The remaining quotations in this section are taken from the annotations to Rule XVI, clause 7 in the *House Rules and Manual* for the 105th Congress.

within one committee's jurisdiction and where the amendment falls within another committee's purview...." For instance, "[t]o a bill reported by the Committee on Government Operations creating an executive agency to protect consumers, an amendment conferring on Congressional committees with oversight over consumer protection the authority to intervene in judicial and administrative proceedings (a rule-making provision within the jurisdiction of the Committee on Rules) was ruled not germane...." But committee jurisdiction is not the sole or exclusive test of germaneness, especially in cases in which "the proposition to which the amendment is offered is so comprehensive (overlapping several committees' jurisdictions) as to diminish the pertinency of that test and the amendment as offered does not demonstrably affect a law within another committee's jurisdiction..., or where the portion of the bill also contains language, related to the amendment, not within the jurisdiction of the committee reporting the bill...."

As this last statement suggests, no one of these three tests is always conclusive, nor is one of them necessarily more controlling than the others. An amendment may satisfy one test but not one or both of the others, so the chair must look to the particular case in deciding how much weight to give to each of them. Moreover, even when these three tests are taken together, they do not constitute a complete standard of germaneness. "[A]n amendment and the matter to which offered may be related to some degree under the tests of subject matter, purpose, and jurisdiction, and still not be considered germane under the precedents."

To help understand this conclusion, the parliamentarian's commentary on the rule elaborates other principles of germaneness, of which three are particularly clear and explicit. The essence of these three principles turns on the relationship between the scope of the amendment and the scope of the matter to be amended.

First, "[o]ne individual proposition may not be amended by another individual proposition even though the two belong to the same class...." For example, "[t]o a bill proposing the admission of one Territory into the Union, an amendment for admission of another Territory" was not germane. Similarly, "to a proposition to appropriate or to authorize appropriations for only one year (and containing no provisions extending beyond that year), an amendment to extend the authorization or appropriation to another year is not germane...." The first bill applied to only one territory; the second concerned only one fiscal year. Extending either bill to another item in the same class—a second territory or a second fiscal year—violated the prohibition against amending one individual proposition with another, even though the amendments may have met one or more of the three tests discussed above.

Second, "[a] specific subject may not be amended by a provision general in nature, even when of the class of the specific subject...." Under this principle, which applies to amendments that would expand the general applicability of measures that are limited in scope, the following illustrate the kinds of amendments that would not be germane: "to a bill relating to all corporations engaged in interstate commerce, an amendment relating to all corporations...; to a bill proscribing certain picketing in the District of Columbia, an amendment making the provisions thereof applicable throughout the United States...; and to a bill authorizing funds for radio broadcasting to Cuba, an amendment broadening the bill to include broadcasting to all dictatorships in the Caribbean Basin...."

These two principles limit the amendments that satisfy the germaneness rule; the third, related principle, on the other hand, provides a basis for holding amendments germane. "A general subject may be amended by specific propositions of the same class...." "Thus, the following have been held to be germane: To a bill admitting several Territories into the Union, an amendment adding another Territory...; to a bill providing for the construction of buildings in each of two cities, an amendment providing for similar buildings in several other cities...;" "and to an amendment prohibiting indirect assistance to several countries, an amendment to include additional countries within that prohibition...." Generally, if a bill already deals with several items in a class, amendments to add additional items in the same class may be germane under this principle.

Germaneness rulings may be based on a combination of two or more of these tests and principles, or perhaps others. And their application and the relationships among them cannot be reduced to a formula or obviously predictable standard. Furthermore, the illustrative examples quoted above are quite clear and simple ones; they do not fully reflect the difficulties and subtleties that can arise in applying these six tests and principles. A bill may amend so many provisions of an existing law, for example, that an amendment affecting any other provision of that law may be germane, but there is no simple test to determine when this point is reached. Thus, germaneness determinations often are difficult to make and even more difficult to anticipate.

Offering and Debating Amendments

In the House

We naturally think of all legislative action that occurs on the House floor as taking place "in the House." In the conventional language of the legislative process, however, this phrase refers to one of the five modes of consideration by which the House may act on a public bill or resolution. A bill considered "in the House" is not debated and amended in the same way as it would be if considered in Committee of the Whole or under suspension of the rules, for example. And for reasons that will become evident, only a few kinds of bills and resolutions—most notably, the special rules reported by the Rules Committee to affect the order of business—usually are considered "in the House." One of the most important reasons is the difficulty Members have in proposing amendments under this set of procedures.

The essential rule governing debate on the House floor is the "*hour rule*"—the provision of clause 2 of Rule XVII which states that "[a] Member, Delegate, or Resident Commissioner may not occupy more than one hour in debate on a question in the House...." A Representative who has been recognized to speak may not hold the floor for more than an hour, under normal House rules, without the unanimous consent of all colleagues who are present. Equally important, under this rule, each Member may speak for an hour on each debatable question; and a bill or resolution and each amendment to it are different debatable questions, as are a variety of motions that Members may make. A Representative can offer an amendment only when the

Speaker has recognized him to control the floor for an hour, or when another Member who controls the floor has yielded to him for that purpose.[28]

A measure considered in the House, under the hour rule, is "open to amendment at any point." If a Member controls the floor and chooses to offer an amendment, that amendment may propose to affect any part of the bill. And if another Member were to offer a second amendment at a later time, that amendment also could address any part of the bill that has not already been amended. For instance, if the first amendment changes Section 3 of the measure, a second amendment could propose to change Section 1. In other words, the order in which Members offer amendments "in the House" generally is not determined by where or how the amendments would affect the measure.

Most measures that the House considers under the hour rule are "*privileged.*" Clause 5(a) of Rule XIII grants certain committees "leave to report" measures on certain subjects or for certain purposes "at any time." For example, this authority extends to general appropriations bills reported by the Appropriations Committee, to budget resolutions and reconciliation measures reported by the Budget Committee, to committee funding resolutions reported by the Committee on House Oversight, and to amendments to House rules reported by the Rules Committee. Other measures are privileged under other rules—for instance, resolutions approved by the Republican Conference or Democratic Caucus to appoint members to House committees are privileged under clause 5(a)(1) of Rule X.

There are two differences between the treatment of privileged measures and the treatment of other bills and resolutions. First, a committee chair filing a report on a measure normally does so without comment, by merely submitting the report to the appropriate clerk on the floor while the House is in session. In the case of reports on privileged measures, however, the chair announces his action and files the report from the floor, and the Speaker refers it to the appropriate calendar. More important, when a committee reports a nonprivileged bill or resolution, it is referred to either the Union or the House Calendar, where it remains until it can be made in order for floor consideration.[29] On the other hand, once a privileged measure has been reported and placed on one of the same two calendars, and the one- or three-day layover requirement has been met,[30] the committee (or subcommittee) chair may call it up for consideration at any time that another matter is not already pending.[31]

---

[28] *House Procedure*, ch. 27, secs. 4.2-4.4, p. 499.

[29] On the various calendars, see *House Procedure*, ch. 22, sec. 1.1, p. 339.

[30] Clause 4(a)(1) of Rule XIII generally requires that the House may not consider a measure until the accompanying report has been available to Members for at least three calendar days, excluding Saturdays, Sundays, and legal holidays. Clause 6(a) of the same rule imposes only a one-day layover requirement for most special rules reported by the Rules Committee, and the House may waive this requirement by a two-thirds vote.

[31] A privileged matter may interrupt the daily order of business specified in clause 1 of Rule XIV.

When the Speaker recognizes a chair (or another Member) to call up a privileged measure, at the direction of her committee, the chair is recognized to control the first hour of debate. The chair is certain to yield to other Members to participate in debate during this hour, but only the chair may offer an amendment or make any other motion during the hour she controls, unless she chooses to yield to another Member to do so.[32] At the end of the first hour, another Representative (usually the ranking minority member of the reporting committee) would be recognized to control the second hour of debate, and, if so, this Member becomes the only one with the right to offer an amendment or make another motion during that hour. And so the process could continue. Each Member can debate the measure for an hour, and the Member controlling each hour of debate determines whether an amendment is offered. If an amendment is proposed—whether it be an amendment in the nature of a substitute for the measure or a perfecting amendment to any part of it—each Representative then may debate the amendment for an hour.[33]

Thus, there could be more than 400 hours of debate on the measure itself and an equally lengthy debate on each amendment to it. In practice, however, when the House considers a bill or resolution "in the House"—and, therefore, under the hour rule—the House usually votes on passing it without considering any amendments except committee amendments, and after no more than a total of one hour of debate. The device for limiting the debate and precluding all floor amendments is the motion to order the *previous question*. A Representative who has been recognized to control the floor for an hour can make this non-debatable motion which immediately stops debate on the measure the House is considering. If a majority of Members vote to order the previous question, the House then proceeds to vote on pending amendments and on final passage of the measure without further debate and without considering any further amendments.[34]

In practice, the committee or subcommittee chair rarely proposes an amendment during the first hour of debate, which she controls, and is even less likely to yield to another Member to do so. As the majority floor manager, the chair typically supports the measure as it was reported by committee. But she always moves the previous question before or when her hour expires, and the House normally votes for this motion.[35] Thus, a Representative wishing to offer an amendment must obtain part of

---

[32] The majority floor manager often yields control of half of the first hour to the minority floor manager, but "for purposes of debate only." If the committee has reported an amendment to the measure, it is automatically presented to the House for consideration when the measure is called up.

[33] The sponsor of the amendment may withdraw it at any time, as a matter of right, before the House amends it, orders the previous question on it, or votes on it.

[34] After the House orders the previous question but before it votes on final passage, one Member usually has an opportunity to move to refer or recommit the measure to committee, with or without instructions. *House Procedure*, ch. 23, sec. 7.7, p. 355.

[35] In practice, measures considered under the hour rule often tend to divide the House along party lines, so a majority usually supports ordering the previous question. Bills and resolutions that many Representatives are eager to amend are unlikely to be considered in this

(continued...)

the first hour of debate and convince the House to vote against ordering the previous question when that motion is made. Only if the previous question is not ordered is a second Member—almost always a minority party Member—recognized for an hour, during which he may propose an amendment.[36]

If the previous question is not ordered (or in the very unlikely event it is not even moved) and a second hour of debate begins, the Member controlling it then may propose an amendment and debate on that amendment proceeds under the hour rule.[37] But the Representative offering the amendment is almost certain to move the previous question, on both the measure and the amendment thereto, before or at the end of the hour she controls. And if the House votes for this motion, it then votes without further debate on the amendment and finally on the measure as it may have been amended.[38]

In daily practice, therefore, the hour rule does not operate to permit one hour of debate per Member on each measure considered "in the House," and another hour of debate per Member on each amendment to the measure. Instead, because the previous question is routinely moved and normally ordered, there is only one hour of debate in total on the bill and no floor amendments may be offered, unless the floor manager yields for this purpose. The House must vote against ordering the previous question before there can be a second hour of debate, when the Member controlling that second hour can propose an amendment.[39] And then the House is virtually certain to order the previous question on both the bill and the amendment during the second hour, precluding still more debate and still other amendments.

In short, the procedures governing consideration of measures in the House, under the hour rule, are not well suited—in theory or in practice—for permitting many Members to participate in debate and offer their amendments. It is largely because of this problem that the House considers most major bills instead in Committee of the Whole.

In Committee of the Whole and the House

The Committee of the Whole House on the State of the Union is a committee on which all Representatives serve and which meets on the House floor. The House resolves itself into Committee of the Whole to consider a particular measure and amendments to it. Then it transforms itself back into the House, and the House proceeds to vote on whatever amendments the Committee of the Whole has recommended and then votes on final passage of the bill or resolution itself. The

---

[35](...continued) way.

[36] *House Procedure*, ch. 29, sec. 5.7, p. 637; *House Procedure, 1985 Supplement*, ch. 23, sec. 10.6, p. 45.

[37] *House Procedure*, ch. 29, sec. 20.5, p. 650.

[38] *House Procedure*, ch. 27, sec. 4.6, p. 499.

[39] *House Procedure*, ch. 23, secs. 8-10, p. 356-358.

House uses the device of the Committee of the Whole largely because it provides a set of procedures for debating measures and for offering and debating amendments that are more flexible and accommodating than the procedures that govern the four other modes of consideration.

Because of these advantages, the House first considers most major bills and resolutions in Committee of the Whole before voting on them in the House. Clause 3 of Rule XVIII requires that certain kinds of measures be considered in this way; these are essentially the authorization, appropriations, and tax measures that are placed on the Union Calendar after being reported from committee. In addition, most other important and controversial measures are called up on the floor only after the House first agrees to a resolution, or special rule, reported by the Rules Committee, that makes the measure in order for consideration and provides for debating and amending it in Committee of the Whole.[40]

Considering a bill in Committee of the Whole involves a four-stage process. First, the House resolves itself into Committee of the Whole for the sole purpose of considering the bill. Second, there is a period of time for general debate. Third, the bill is considered for amendment; the Committee of the Whole votes on whatever amendments are proposed, and then it "rises" and reports the bill back to the House with the amendments the Committee has adopted. Fourth, the House votes on these amendments and, shortly thereafter, votes on passing the bill. The following discussion concentrates on the latter two stages during which Members consider and vote on amendments.

There are two ways in which the House resolves itself into Committee of the Whole to consider a measure. A special rule typically authorizes the Speaker, pursuant to clause 2(b) of Rule XVIII, to declare the House resolved into Committee of the Whole for that purpose at any time after the House adopts the resolution. On the other hand, the special rule governing consideration of a general appropriations bill need not include such a provision; its sole or primary purpose often is to waive points of order against the bill or amendments or both.[41] Instead, the chair of the Appropriations Committee makes a non-debatable motion that the House resolve into Committee of the Whole to consider a measure his committee has reported. In either case, the Speaker designates another majority party Member to serve as chair of the Committee of the Whole during its consideration of that measure.[42] The chair then directs the clerk to report the bill by title before general debate begins.[43]

General Debate.

The special rule governing consideration of the measure normally specifies the length of general debate. Typically it is one hour though there may be more time

---

[40] *House Procedure*, ch. 17, sec. 34.1, p. 240.

[41] *House Procedure*, ch. 25, sec. 23, p. 435-438.

[42] Clause 1 of Rule XVIII.

[43] The bill is to be read at this point, but this reading is routinely waived by the terms of the special rule or by unanimous consent.

provided for debating particularly important and controversial bills. In other instances, the amount of time is controlled by a unanimous consent agreement (in the case of a general appropriations bill), or it may be governed by a provision of a rule-making statute (for example, in the case of a budget resolution or reconciliation measure). Control of the time usually is divided equally between the chair and ranking minority member of the committee of jurisdiction, each of whom yields part of her time to other Members during the course of the debate. When a bill had been referred to two or more committees, there often is a longer period for general debate, with part of it controlled by each committee chair and ranking member. In unusual circumstances, a special rule also may allocate control of some general debate time to other, individually named Members who oppose the committee's position in an important respect.[44]

The Committee of the Whole does not consider and act on any amendments during general debate. This period is reserved for discussions of the state of existing law, the conditions stimulating new legislation, the provisions of the measure, and the advisability of enacting it. Members may debate the merits of committee amendments and the amendments individual Representatives intend to propose, but the amendments are not formally proposed or considered during this time. At the conclusion of general debate, the Committee of the Whole may vote to rise, which temporarily concludes its business and transforms the Committee back into the House. Then the House may resolve back into Committee of the Whole at some later hour or date to resume consideration of the measure. Alternatively, the Committee may move directly from general debate to the third stage of consideration, during which the amending process takes place.

During this third stage, the Committee of the Whole considers and votes on amendments to the measure and on amendments to those amendments. The Committee never votes directly on any section or title of the measure itself or on the measure as a whole. This amending process is somewhat akin to the markup of a bill that has been reported by one committee and then referred sequentially to another. After a standing committee reports the bill, it is referred sequentially to this unique committee on which all Members serve. The Committee of the Whole debates and votes on all the amendments recommended by the standing committee and then on whatever additional amendments individual Members offer. But neither a standing committee nor the Committee of the Whole actually has the authority to amend the bill; that is the exclusive power of the House. Both committees only recommend amendments for the House to consider.

The text that Members can attempt to amend usually is the text of the bill as it was introduced. However, the special rule for considering it may provide instead for amendments to be directed to an amendment in the nature of a substitute that is to be considered "an original bill for the purpose of amendment." Typically, this is a committee substitute, though it may be an amendment in the nature of a substitute printed in the Rules Committee's report on the rule or in the *Congressional Record*, or it may even be the text of another measure on the same subject. Whatever form it may take, an amendment in the nature of a substitute considered in this way almost

---

[44] *House Procedure*, ch. 29, sec. 7.5, p. 640.

always reflects the position of the committee or committees of jurisdiction, or at least their leading majority party members.

Reading Measures For Amendment.

The flow of the amending process is governed by the requirement that a measure considered in Committee of the Whole is to be read for amendment. Members may propose amendments only to the part of the bill that the clerk has read, and they may no longer offer amendments to it (except by unanimous consent) after the clerk has read the next part.[45] The typical procedure is for a bill or resolution to be read for amendment section by section (or paragraph by paragraph, in the case of a general appropriations bill). When a special rule states that a measure shall be "read for amendment under the five-minute rule," it is to be read by sections. Alternatively, the special rule may specify that the measure is to be read by titles. And especially when a special rule prohibits most or all floor amendments, it may state that each section shall be considered as having been read or that the entire measure "shall be considered as having been read for amendment." There would be no point in the clerk reading each section or title in turn if Members may not offer amendments to it after it is read.

These alternatives affect what kinds of amendments Members can propose, and when. If a measure is being read or considered for amendment by sections, Representatives may offer amendments only to each section when the clerk has read or designated it. It is no longer in order to propose an amendment to a section that had been read previously, and it is premature to offer an amendment to a section not yet reached, unless the Members agree by unanimous consent to consider such an amendment. Thus, after the clerk reads or designates Section 4, only amendments to Section 4 are in order. It is now too late to offer an amendment to Section 3, and it is not yet appropriate to amend Section 5.[46] Furthermore, an amendment affecting Sections 4 and 5 would not be in order because the bill is being considered for amendment one section at a time.[47]

Thus, Members must accommodate themselves to the pace of the amending process in Committee of the Whole, protecting their own rights to propose amendments by being on the floor and by seeking recognition at the appropriate times.

---

45 *House Procedure*, ch. 27, sec. 8.1, p. 505-506.

46 *House Procedure*, ch. 27, sec. 10.3, p. 508. "When it is proposed to offer a single amendment in the nature of a substitute for several paragraphs of a bill which is being considered by paragraphs, the substitute may be offered to the first paragraph provided that notice is given that if it be agreed to, motions will be made to strike out the remaining paragraphs." *House Procedure*, ch. 27, sec. 12.4, p. 512.

47 *House Procedure*, ch. 27, secs. 9-10, p. 506-509. "The Chair inquires whether any Member seeks to offer an amendment to the pending portion of a bill before recognizing a Member to offer an amendment inserting a new section or title thereafter....An amendment adding a new section at the end of a bill is in order when the last section of the bill has been read for amendment and no amendments to that section are offered....Where an amendment adding a new title to a bill has been adopted, an amendment to the title of the bill that was pending when the amendment was offered comes too late and may be offered only by unanimous consent...." *House Procedure, 1985 Supplement*, ch. 27, sec. 8.4, p. 68.

The same procedures govern a measure being considered for amendment by titles; amendments are in order only to the title that the clerk has read or designated most recently. Considering a measure by titles gives Members somewhat more latitude, because they can offer amendments that span more than one section of the title or that propose to strike or replace the entire title. Thus, when a bill is divided into titles, which in turn are subdivided into sections, a special rule frequently provides for it to be considered for amendment title by title.

The one exception to these procedures concerns amendments in the nature of substitutes. A Member can offer this kind of amendment after the clerk reads or designates the first section of the measure, even though the amendment also would affect all its other sections or titles. But once this opportunity passes, an amendment in the nature of a substitute is not in order again until the Committee has acted on all amendments to the last section or title of the bill. On the other hand, when a measure is open to amendment at any point, Members may propose amendments to any part of it in any order, so long as the amendments meet the other requirements of House rules and precedents and are not prohibited by a special rule.

The Committee of the Whole sometimes expedites consideration of amendments by adjusting the process of reading for amendment.[48] If a bill containing several titles is being read section by section, the majority floor manager may ask unanimous consent that a title be considered as read and open to amendment at any point.[49] Or the manager may extend this request to cover several titles or the entire measure. The manager is most likely to make such a request when few amendments are anticipated and no useful purpose is served by having the clerk read each section or title individually.

---

[48] *House Procedure*, ch. 27, sec. 7.1, p. 504.

[49] *House Procedure*, ch. 27, sec. 11, p. 509-510.

Offering Amendments.

After the clerk reads or designates the first section, the chair directs the clerk to read the first of any committee amendments to it. The majority floor manager typically asks unanimous consent that the reading be dispensed with. The Committee of the Whole debates and votes on this amendment, and any floor amendments to it, after which the clerk reads and the Committee acts in turn on any other committee amendments to that section. Individual Members then may propose their own amendments to the section.[50] After the Committee debates and votes on all of them, the clerk reads or designates the next section and the process is repeated. When a bill is being considered by titles, a comparable process occurs, as the Committee first considers and acts on each committee amendment (and amendments to it) to a title before individual Representatives' amendments to the title are in order. When a bill is open to amendment at any point, on the other hand, the Committee first considers and acts on all the committee amendments, in the order in which they would affect the measure, before Members propose their own amendments to the measure.

In most cases, there are not very many committee amendments. If the committee wishes to amend a measure extensively, it may report the bill or resolution with a long series of amendments. However, it is more likely to recommend an amendment in the nature of a substitute by which the committee incorporates all its proposed changes to the measure in a single amendment. Or the committee may propose a "clean" measure, carrying a different bill or resolution number, that addresses the same subject in the way the committee prefers.

When the Committee of the Whole has disposed of all committee amendments to the section or title being considered (or to the entire bill, if it is open to amendment at any point), the chair looks to the majority and minority tables on the floor for Members seeking recognition to offer amendments of their own. It is the responsibility of a Member wishing to offer an amendment to seek recognition for that purpose.[51] If two or more Members are seeking recognition, the chair has the discretionary authority to recognize one or the other.[52] However, the chair is guided in decisions regarding recognition by practices that are very well-established, if not actually binding as precedent.[53]

The chair almost always gives preference in recognition to members of the committee and subcommittee that reported the measure, in approximate order of seniority, alternating between Democrats and Republicans.[54] Thus, the majority floor manager is recognized in preference to anyone else, followed by the minority floor manager. If neither of the managers seeks recognition, the chair tends to recognize

---

[50] *House Procedure*, ch. 27, secs. 3.7-3.8, p. 498.

[51] "In order to obtain recognition to offer an amendment, a Member must not only be standing but must also actively seek recognition by addressing the Chair at the appropriate time." *House Procedure, 1985 Supplement*, ch. 29, sec. 4.1, p. 83.

[52] *House Procedure*, ch. 29, sec. 4, p. 634-635.

[53] *House Procedure*, ch. 27, sec. 3.5, p. 498; ch. 29, sec. 5, p. 635-638.

[54] *House Procedure*, ch. 27, sec. 3.1, p. 497.

a senior committee member before a more junior member, and any committee member before another Representative. The chair also attempts to give Members of both parties a roughly equal opportunity to propose amendments.[55] These practices promote fairness, and also focus the attention of the Committee of the Whole first on amendments sponsored by Members who are presumed to have an expert knowledge of the subject.

Every amendment offered must be in writing. In addition, clause 5(b) of Rule XVIII states:

> When a Member, Delegate, or Resident Commissioner offers an amendment in the Committee of the Whole House on the state of the Union, the Clerk shall promptly transmit five copies of the amendment to the majority committee table and five copies to the minority committee table. The Clerk also shall deliver at least one copy of the amendment to the majority cloak room and at least one copy to the minority cloak room.

Although this rule places the responsibility on the clerk, it is good practice for Members to bring multiple copies of amendments with them to the floor, or to arrange for copies to be made of amendments they or their staff prepare on the floor during debate. This permits the sponsor of an amendment to distribute copies of it to colleagues who want to examine it. In most cases, Representatives find it advisable to alert the majority and minority floor managers of the measure, and other interested Members, of the amendments they plan to offer. This is not done only as a matter of courtesy. Floor managers who support the bill often are inclined to oppose amendments that they have not had an opportunity to study. But if the floor managers have copies of an amendment in advance, they may decide to support it or at least discuss possible changes that would make it acceptable to them.

Clause 8 of Rule XVIII also provide for Members to submit their amendments in advance for printing in the *Congressional Record*. Under clause 8(c),

> Material submitted for printing in the Congressional Record under this rule shall indicate the full text of the proposed amendment, the name of the Member, Delegate or Resident Commissioner proposing it, the number of the bill or resolution to which it will be offered, and the point in the bill or resolution or amendment thereto where the amendment is intended to be offered. The amendment shall appear in a portion of the Record designated for that purpose. Amendments to a specified measure submitted for printing in that portion of the Record shall be numbered in the order printed.

And clause 7 permits a non-debatable motion to dispense with the normal requirement that an amendment be read before it is debated, but only if the amendment has been printed in the *Record* in this way or printed in a measure as reported from committee:

> It shall be in order in the Committee of the Whole House on the state of the Union to move that the Committee of the Whole dispense with the reading of an amendment that has been printed in the bill or resolution as reported from a

---

[55] *House Procedure*, ch. 29, secs. 5.1-5.5, p. 635-637.

> **committee, or an amendment that a Member, Delegate, or Resident Commissioner has caused to be printed in the Congressional Record. Such a motion shall be decided without debate.**

House rules do not accord any special priority for consideration on the floor to an amendment that has been printed in the *Record*; the rules do not require, for example, that a Member with a printed amendment be recognized to offer it before another Representative whose amendment is merely handwritten. As we shall see, however, Members who submit their amendments for printing in the *Record* do gain some assurance of time for debate when they actually propose the amendments in Committee of the Whole. Also, recent special rules sometimes have authorized the chair to give priority in recognition for offering amendments in Committee of the Whole to Members who did submit them in advance for printing.

Special rules for considering particularly complicated or technical measures, such as tax bills, sometimes permit consideration of only those amendments that have been printed in the *Record* by a date certain or at least one day before they are offered. This requirement gives committee members and others an opportunity to study the amendments in advance and evaluate their implications. More generally, the Rules Committee may ask Members to submit to it copies of the floor amendments they want to offer to a bill. Amendments not submitted in response to such a request are very unlikely to be made in order under the special rule for that bill.

Debating Amendments.

The essential rule governing debate on amendments in Committee of the Whole is the *five-minute rule*, contained in clause 5(a) of Rule XVIII:

> A Member, Delegate, or Resident Commissioner who offers an amendment shall be allowed five minutes to explain it, after which the Member, Delegate, or Resident Commissioenr who shall first obtain the floor shall be allowed five minutes to speak in opposition to it. There shall be no further debate thereon, but the same privilege of debate shall be allowed in favor of and against any amendment that may be offered to an amendment. An amendment or an amendment to an amendment may be withdrawn by its proponent only by the unanimous consent of the Committee of the Whole.

The five minutes for opposing a first-degree amendment often are claimed by one of the floor managers who supports the measure in its present form; in turn, the sponsor of a first-degree amendment often seeks recognition for the five minutes to speak against an amendment to her amendment.

This rule clearly states that there shall be only 10 minutes for debating each amendment. Yet debate on an amendment often continues for much longer, sometimes for hours at a time. The explanation for this apparent contradiction lies in the use of *pro forma amendments*.

A Representative offers a pro forma amendment when he or she *moves to strike the last word*. In theory, this motion is an amendment that proposes to strike out the last word of whatever the Committee of the Whole is then considering—a measure or a portion of it, a first-degree amendment, or an amendment to an amendment. In practice, however, the Committee recognizes pro forma amendments to be only a well-accepted device by which Members secure time for debate.

After two Representatives have consumed the 10 minutes provided by Rule XVIII for debating an amendment, any other Member whom the chair recognizes can obtain five minutes to speak simply by moving to strike the last word. A Member also can move to strike the last word when no amendment is pending, if the Member wishes to discuss the measure itself. Technically, the next Member wishing to speak for five minutes should move to strike the last two words because the same amendment cannot be proposed more than once. This leads some Members to move to strike "the requisite number of words," in order to make certain that they are not offering an amendment for the second time. However, the Committee recognizes that there is no point in prohibiting Members from offering the same pro forma amendment more than once because these amendments are not substantive. Thus, many Representatives may move to strike the last word.

Because a pro forma amendment is not substantive, no Member claims five minutes to speak against it, and the Committee does not vote on it. When a Member who has made such a motion has used her five minutes or has yielded back the balance of her time, the amendment is deemed to have been withdrawn by unanimous consent.

The time for debating any amendment, whether substantive or pro forma, may be extended by unanimous consent. When offering an amendment, for example, a Member may expect that five minutes will not be sufficient to explain it. So even before beginning the statement, the Member may ask unanimous consent that an additional five minutes or more be granted. Alternatively, when the chair informs the Member that the five minutes have expired, the Member then may ask unanimous consent to proceed for an additional minute or more. The one who has the floor may yield to others who want to speak; and in turn, a Representative to whom the Member has yielded may ask unanimous consent that the Member be granted additional time so they may continue their exchange.[56] Representatives usually do not object to such unanimous consent requests, but they can do so.

At any time after the sponsor of an amendment has consumed or yielded back the balance of his five minutes for debate, other Members may seek recognition either to propose a substantive amendment that is in order or to offer a pro forma amendment (even instead of seeking recognition for the five minutes provided by Rule XVIII to speak against the amendment).[57] However, a Representative who has been recognized for one of these purposes may not use it for another; thus, a Member who has been recognized to speak against the amendment under Rule XVIII, or who has

---

[56] During general debate in Committee of the Whole, and during debate in the House under the hour rule, a Member controlling time may yield a specific number of minutes to a colleague or he may yield such time as the other Member may consume. During debate under the five-minute rule, however, the Member controlling the floor may yield but not for a specified period of time. However, a Member who has been recognized for five minutes and then yields to another may reclaim his time whenever he chooses.

[57] *House Procedure*, ch. 27, sec. 16.10, p. 518; ch. 29, sec. 5.10, p. 637.

moved to strike the last word, may not offer a substantive amendment during that five-minute period.

In Committee of the Whole, the chair must recognize a Representative before he or she can propose an amendment or control five minutes for debate. The chair's exercise of the power of recognition is not subject to challenge or appeal, but normally the same priorities are followed in recognizing Members to move to strike the last word as in recognizing them to offer substantive amendments. Committee members are recognized before others, and the chair usually recognizes them in an order consistent with their committee or subcommittee seniority. The chair also makes an effort to assure that Members of both parties have roughly the same opportunities to offer amendments and to speak. But it is each Member's responsibility to seek recognition at the appropriate time; the chair cannot protect Members' rights unless he knows that they wish to exercise them.

Pro forma amendments permit each Representative to speak for five minutes on each portion of the measure as it is considered for amendment and on each amendment that Members propose. If every Member took advantage of this opportunity, there could be more than 36 hours of debate per amendment, which would make it impossible for the House to conduct its legislative business in a timely way.[58] However, the rules and practices of the House protect against this possibility through a device for bringing debate under the five-minute rule to an end. This device can effectively prevent a minority from filibustering in Committee of the Whole by debating amendments at great length.

By unanimous consent or by motion, the Committee may decide to conclude the debate on (1) an amendment, (2) an amendment and all amendments thereto, or (3) the measure, or a portion of it, and all amendments thereto. In the last case, however, the Committee can close debate only on whatever part of the measure has been read or designated for amendment. If a bill is being considered by sections or titles, the Committee can end debate only on each section or title as it is considered.[59] But if the measure is open to amendment at any point, the Committee may close debate on it as a whole, as well as on any amendments that are pending at the time and all other amendments that Members intend to offer.

After a Representative has proposed an amendment and concluded his five minutes for debate, and at any time that another Member does not control the floor, the majority floor manager may ask unanimous consent that all debate on that amendment (and any amendments to it) be brought to an end. He may request that the debate end immediately, or at a certain hour, or at the expiration of a specified additional period of time. While any Representative may make such a request, it is unusual for anyone other than the majority floor manager to do so. If another Member objects, or reserves the right to object, that Member and the floor manager may discuss whether the amendment and the issues it raises have been fully argued,

---

[58] Pro forma amendments are not in order when a measure or amendment is being considered under a closed or restrictive rule that does not explicitly provide for them. *House Procedure*, ch. 27, sec. 2.7, p. 491.

[59] *House Procedure*, ch. 29, sec. 27.1, p. 656-657.

and they attempt to find a mutually acceptable accommodation. If the floor manager cannot obtain unanimous consent to his request, he then may make a non-debatable motion to close the debate—immediately, at a time certain, or after a specified period of time.[60] The Committee agrees or disagrees to the motion by simple majority vote. Again, any Member whom the chair recognizes may make such a motion, but this is a prerogative normally exercised only by the majority floor manager.[61]

If the Committee agrees to a unanimous consent request or votes for a motion that leaves some time remaining for debate, the chair may continue recognizing Members for five minutes each but also has the authority to dispense with the five-minute rule.[62] Instead, the chair may divide the remaining time between the control of two Members (for example, the sponsor of a pending amendment and the majority floor manager) and allow them to yield part of their time to others as they choose. Or the chair may divide the remaining time equally among the Members who stand to indicate their desire to be recognized. Thus, if the Committee agrees to a motion that permits thirty minutes more for debate and fifteen Members still want to be recognized, the chair has at least three options: to recognize each of the 15 Members for two minutes each, to recognize only six of the Members for five minutes each, or to recognize only two Members to control 15 minutes each.[63]

When all the time for debate has expired, pursuant to a motion or unanimous consent agreement, Members may continue to offer amendments that are otherwise in order but they have no time to explain their amendments, which obviously puts them and their amendments at a significant disadvantage.[64] Anticipating this potential problem, clause 8(b) of Rule XVIII offers Members some protection by reserving five minutes for one of them to explain, and then five minutes for another to oppose, any amendment that has been printed in advance in the *Congressional Record*:[65]

> If the Committee of the Whole House on the state of the Union closes debate on any portion of a bill or resolution before there has been debate on an amendment that a Member, Delegate, or Resident Commissioner has caused to be printed in the Congressional Record at least one day before its consideration, the Member, Delegate, or Resident Commissioner who caused the amendment to be printed in the Record shall be allowed five minutes to explain it, after which the Member, Delegate, or Resident Commissioner who shall first obtain the floor shall be allowed five minutes to speak in opposition to it. There shall be no further debate thereon.

---

[60] Clause 8(a) of Rule XVIII.

[61] *House Procedure*, ch. 29, sec. 27.5, p. 657.

[62] *House Procedure*, ch. 29, sec. 31, p. 661-665.

[63] *House Procedure*, ch. 29, sec. 6.6, p. 638.

[64] *House Procedure*, ch. 29, sec. 33.1, p. 667.

[65] *House Procedure*, ch. 27, sec. 1.9, p. 490.

This rule permits only 10 minutes of debate on each amendment; Members cannot extend the debate through pro forma amendments.[66] Furthermore, clause 6 may be superseded by the special rule for considering a bill if, for example, that resolution prohibits consideration of all but certain specified amendments.

From time to time, a Member who is opposed to a bill or pending amendment secures time for debating it that otherwise would not be available by moving that the Committee rise and report the measure back to the House with the recommendation that the *enacting (or resolving) clause be stricken.* When a Representative makes this motion, the chair recognizes him and another Member to debate it for five minutes each, after which the Committee votes without further debate.[67] If the Committee agrees to the motion and the House then concurs, the bill is thereby rejected because striking the enacting clause removes from it the language required by law that would be necessary to give the bill statutory force.[68] However, Members rarely make this motion with any serious expectation that it will carry. Instead, it is another device to obtain five minutes for debate.

The motion proposing that the enacting clause of a bill be stricken is in order in Committee of the Whole only once each legislative day, unless the bill has been materially changed. And it is in order only so long as there remains time for debating the measure itself. If the Committee has agreed to limit further debate on an amendment, for example, and all that time has expired, a Member can still debate the amendment and the bill for five minutes by making this motion.[69] On the other hand, the motion is no longer in order once the Committee has concluded debate on the bill and all amendments thereto.

After The Committee Rises and Reports.

When the Committee of the Whole has acted on the last amendment to be proposed, the Committee rises and reports the bill or resolution back to the House with whatever amendments to the measure it has agreed to. Most special rules provide for the Committee to rise and report automatically; in the case of general appropriations measures, the majority floor manager makes a non-debatable motion that the Committee rise and report.[70] Once the Committee rises, the Speaker again presides over the House, and the chair reports to him that the Committee has had the bill under consideration and now reports it back to the House, usually with an amendment or several ("sundry") amendments. The Committee also recommends that the House agree to the amendment or amendments and then pass the bill as amended.

The Committee of the Whole only reports the amendments to the measure that it adopted. It does not report any amendments that it rejected nor does it report any

---

66 *House Procedure*, ch. 27, sec. 4.7, p. 499-500.

67 *House Procedure*, ch. 19, sec. 12, p. 279.

68 Clause 9 of Rule XVIII.

69 *House Procedure*, ch. 19, secs. 12.9-12.10, p. 280.

70 *House Procedure*, ch. 19, sec. 9, p. 276-278.

amendments to amendments. Thus, if the Committee perfects and then adopts a first-degree amendment, it reports only the perfected first-degree amendment. And if the Committee concludes the amending process by agreeing to an amendment in the nature of a substitute, as amended, it reports only that amended substitute.[71]

The House then must vote on the amendments recommended by the Committee of the Whole because only the House itself actually has the authority to amend the bill. More often than not, the House agrees to all these amendments "en gros," by one single voice vote. If Members wanted a record vote on one or more of them, they probably obtained it when the Committee of the Whole voted on each amendment. However, any Member has a right to demand a separate vote in the House on any amendment the Committee has recommended, and this is very likely to be a roll call vote.[72] The goal is to reverse the result of the earlier vote in favor of the amendment. If the Committee agreed to an amendment by a very narrow margin, an opponent may believe that a second, and later, roll call vote will produce the opposite result and defeat the amendment. When Members demand one or more separate votes, the House first agrees to the other amendments en gros by voice vote, and then acts on each of the amendments that require separate votes.

Members normally may demand separate votes in the House only on the amendments proposed by the Committee of the Whole to the bill or resolution itself, not on any amendments to those amendments that the Committee may have adopted.[73] But this right to vote a second time on the Committee's proposals could be effectively nullified when the Committee recommends an amendment in the nature of a substitute. In this situation, the Committee reports the bill back to the House with only that one amendment, even though most or all of the other amendments on which the Committee voted probably were amendments to the substitute. There are no separate amendments on which Members could demand separate votes in the House. For this reason, whenever a special rule anticipates or provides that the Committee of the Whole is to consider an amendment in the nature of a substitute, it also permits Members to demand separate votes in the House on amendments to the bill itself or to that substitute.

When the Committee of the Whole has reported a bill or resolution and the House acts on the Committee's recommended amendments, the measure and the amendments are considered under the set of procedures that govern consideration in the House, especially the hour rule. In theory, therefore, the amending process that took place in Committee of the Whole could be repeated under the hour rule. Each amendment the Committee of the Whole reported could be debated for one hour or more and perhaps even amended, depending on when and if the House orders the previous question on the bill and all amendments to it. Then, if the House failed to order the previous question after acting on all the Committee's amendments, Members could offer their own amendments, each of which would be debatable for at least an hour. But this would not only be repetitious; it would effectively nullify the

---

71 Annotations to Section XII of *Jefferson's Manual* in *House Rules and Manual.*

72 *Ibid.*

73 *House Procedure*, ch. 27, sec. 34.1, p. 537-538.

value of having already considered the bill and amendments to it in Committee of the Whole.

To avoid this situation, the special rules for considering measures typically provide that, after the Committee of the Whole rises, "the previous question shall be considered as ordered on the bill and amendments thereto to final passage without intervening motion except one motion to recommit." The effect of the previous question is to preclude further debate and amendments. Thus, ordering the previous question in advance requires the House to vote on each Committee amendment without debate or amendment and precludes Members from proposing additional amendments.[74] In addition, this provision prevents consideration of any other motion except one motion to recommit (to be discussed shortly).

Consequently, after the House votes on the Committee's amendments—usually en gros, but with the possibility of one or more separate votes on individual amendments—it votes on engrossment and third reading, and the clerk then reads the title of the measure. This vote, which is never contested, also directs the clerk to engross the bill: to have it printed as the House has amended it.[75] After acting on a motion to recommit, if one is made, the House then completes action on the bill by voting to pass or defeat it. A motion to reconsider that vote is routinely tabled, making the vote on final passage conclusive.[76]

---

[74] If a special rule governing consideration of a general appropriations bill only waives points of order, it does not include this provision. Instead, the House orders the previous question, on motion of the bill's majority floor manager, as soon as the Committee of the Whole reports the bill.

[75] *House Procedure*, ch. 24, sec. 5, p. 375.

[76] Clause 3 of Rule XIX provides one opportunity for a Member to move to reconsider the vote on final passage or on most other motions and questions decided in the House, but not in Committee of the Whole. The motion to reconsider must be made on the same day as the vote or on the following day, and by a Member who voted on the prevailing side. In the overwhelming majority of cases, the motion is made and routinely tabled, thereby disposing of it adversely. (Normally, the Speaker merely states that, "without objection, a motion to reconsider is laid on the table," and no Member objects.) Rollcall votes on reconsideration motions are rare because few votes are decided by such narrow margins that a sufficient number of Members actually might change their positions and reverse the outcome.

The Motion To Recommit.

Under clause 6(c)(2) of Rule XIII, not even a special rule may prevent a ***motion to recommit*** from being made after engrossment and third reading and before the vote on final passage. This motion almost always proposes to recommit the bill or resolution to the committee that reported it. In practice, however, the motion takes one of two forms; one is designed to reject the measure, the other to amend it.

A simple or "straight" motion to recommit only proposes to send the bill back to committee. This motion is not debatable.[77] If a majority of the House votes for it, the bill is considered as having been rejected. In other words, this motion offers Members an indirect opportunity to defeat the bill, and the opportunity arises immediately before they would vote directly on final passage. For these reasons, simple motions to recommit are not made frequently and they rarely succeed.

The alternative is a motion to recommit the bill to committee "with instructions." These instructions may take various forms. For example, they may direct the committee to hold additional hearings on some issue relating to the bill before reporting it back to the House.[78] Almost always, however, the instructions direct the committee to report the bill back to the House immediately ("forthwith") with one or more amendments stated in the motion. Clause 2 of Rule XIX provides for ten minutes of debate on a motion to recommit with instructions, but also permits the majority floor manager to demand that the debate be extended to an hour. In either case, the time for debate is divided between the Representative making the motion and the majority floor manager or another Member opposing it.[79]

A motion to recommit with instructions usually constitutes one last attempt to amend the bill before the House votes on passing it. The instructions typically direct the committee to report the bill back to the House "forthwith" with a certain amendment. When the House votes for such a motion, it is telling one of its committees exactly what it must do, and it also is requiring the committee to act immediately. Under these circumstances, there is no point in the committee actually meeting to comply with the instructions because it has been given no time or discretion. Instead, the committee chair immediately rises on the floor and states that, pursuant to the motion and on behalf of the committee, the bill is reported back to the House with the amendment. The House then votes on the amendment itself, normally agreeing to it by voice vote because the amendment presents the same policy choice as the motion to recommit on which the House just voted. Finally, the House votes on passage of the bill as it now has been amended by the motion to recommit with instructions.

---

[77] *House Procedure*, ch. 23, sec. 16.5, p. 366.

[78] *House Procedure*, ch. 23, secs. 14.8-14.11, p. 363.

[79] The instructions are amendable if the House votes against ordering the previous question on the motion.

Only one motion to recommit is in order; but if one is ruled out of order, another can be proposed.[80] In addition, two other important kinds of constraints on the recommittal motion affect who may make it and what instructions it may contain.

First, a Representative who makes a recommittal motion must be opposed to the measure, at least in "its present form." Equally important, this motion is the prerogative of the minority party; the Speaker recognizes any Member of the minority to make it before recognizing any Member of his own party. The Speaker also gives preference in recognition to a minority party Representative who serves on the committee that reported the bill. If the ranking minority member of the committee wishes to make a recommittal motion, therefore, the Speaker is most likely to recognize him.

Second, when the instructions contain an amendment, that amendment must comply with the principles and prohibitions that apply to amendments under other circumstances. Members may not propose as instructions anything that they could not have proposed directly as amendments. For instance, a Member may make a point of order against a motion to recommit with instructions if the instructions require the committee to report the bill back with an amendment that is not germane. Similarly, a recommittal motion may not propose instructions to amend a part of the bill that the House already amended when it agreed to the amendments recommended by the Committee of the Whole.

Once again, a special problem could arise when the Committee reports a bill or resolution back to the House with a single amendment in the nature of a substitute. When the House agrees to this amendment, it thereby amends every part and provision of the measure. This common occurrence could preclude any recommittal motion with instructions containing an amendment, because such a motion would be subject to the point of order that it violates the prohibition against amending something that already has been amended.[81] With this potential problem in mind, when a special rule anticipates or provides that the Committee of the Whole is to consider an amendment in the nature of a substitute, it normally provides explicitly for a motion to recommit "with or without instructions." This additional phrase permits the instructions to contain an amendment, even if the effect of agreeing to the recommittal motion would be to re-amend the text of the measure.[82]

In the House as in Committee of the Whole

As its name implies, "the House as in Committee of the Whole" is a hybrid set of procedures, involving some of the characteristics of consideration under the hour rule in the House and some of those applicable to consideration under the five-minute rule in Committee of the Whole. These procedures are not used very often, except for acting on measures concerning the District of Columbia, reported by the Committee on Government Reform. When the chair of this committee calls up a

---

[80] *House Procedure*, ch. 23, sec. 14.4, p. 362.

[81] *House Procedure*, ch. 27, sec. 30.3, p. 534-535.

[82] *House Procedure*, ch. 23, sec. 15.3, p. 364.

measure, which is privileged on the second and fourth Mondays of each month under clause 4 of Rule XV, he may ask unanimous consent that it be considered in the House as in Committee of the Whole. The House occasionally acts on other public bills and resolutions under these procedures, either by unanimous consent or pursuant to a special rule.[83]

When the House acts on a measure in this way, the Speaker continues to preside over the House. There is no general debate and the bill or resolution is considered as having been read for amendment. It is immediately open to amendment at any point and all debate is governed by the five-minute rule.[84] Thus, the majority and minority floor managers secure time for making their opening statements by moving to strike the last word. Other Members then may offer substantive or pro forma amendments, the Speaker normally following the same priorities for recognition as does the Chair of the Committee of the Whole. In general, the same rules, principles, and practices governing the amending process in Committee of the Whole also apply in the House as in Committee of the Whole, except that measures are not read for amendment.

There is one other important exception. In the House as in Committee of the Whole, a Member may move the previous question on an amendment (and all amendments thereto) or on the measure as a whole (and all amendments thereto), just as in the House.[85] This motion, which is invariably made by the majority floor manager, permits the House to decide by majority vote whether it wishes to consider amendments and how long it wishes to debate the bill and any amendments that Members do offer. After the House orders the previous question, or if no one seeks recognition, the House votes on engrossment and third reading of the measure, then on a recommittal motion if offered, and finally on passing the bill.[86]

By Call of the Corrections Calendar

There is only one opportunity for a Member to offer a floor amendment to a bill called from the Corrections Calendar.

After a committee has reported a bill and it has been placed on the House or Union Calendar, the Speaker may have it placed on the Corrections Calendar as well. On the second and fourth Tuesdays of each month, the Speaker may direct that the

---

[83] "Where the House grants unanimous consent for the immediate consideration of a bill on the Union Calendar, or which would belong on the Union Calendar if reported, the bill is considered in the House as in Committee of the Whole...." Annotations to Section XXX of *Jefferson's Manual* in *House Rules and Manual.*

[84] *Ibid.*; *House Procedure*, ch. 27, sec. 11.6, p. 510.

[85] *House Procedure*, ch. 23, sec. 6.3, p. 354.

[86] Also, "a motion is in order in the House as in Committee of the Whole to close debate on the bill or on an amendment...." Annotations to Section XXX of *Jefferson's Manual* in *House Rules and Manual.* However, the previous question is used more often than the motion to close debate because the latter does not preclude Members from proposing additional amendments.

bills that have been on this special calendar for at least three legislative days shall be called up for consideration on the floor.

A bill called up in this way is considered in the House, under the hour rule, and is debated for no more than one hour. Clause 6(b) of Rule XV provides for the previous question to be considered as ordered after the first hour of debate. The same rule also prohibits all amendments to the bill except amendments proposed by the primary committee of jurisdiction or its chair, but the rule does permit a motion to recommit, with or without instructions. In other words, bills called up from the Corrections Calendar are protected against all floor amendments that other Members might want to offer, except whatever amendment might be included in a motion to recommit with instructions. It requires a three-fifths vote to pass a bill under this procedure.

Under Suspension of the Rules

Individual Representatives may not offer floor amendments to a measure considered under suspension of the rules.[87]

However, amendments to the measure may be included as part of the motion itself. A Member often moves to suspend the rules and pass a certain bill "as amended." After the 40 minutes of debate permitted on a suspension motion, the House then casts one vote on suspending the rules and passing the bill as proposed to be amended under the terms of the motion. No separate vote on the amendments, individually or collectively, is in order.[88] Support by two-thirds of the Members present and voting is required to pass a measure under suspension of the rules.

A suspension motion typically is made by a committee or subcommittee chair. Consequently, the amendments proposed as part of the motion usually are committee amendments, or at least amendments supported by the chair of the committee or subcommittee of jurisdiction. The amendments also enjoy the support or acquiescence of the Speaker, because the Speaker has discretion in deciding whether or not to recognize a Member to offer a suspension motion.

---

[87] Clause 1 of Rule XV addresses suspension of the rules.

[88] *House Procedure*, ch. 21, sec. 17.3, p. 320.

The Amendment Trees

The amending process on the House floor normally does not become very complicated. Amendments usually are not proposed to measures considered in the House, under the hour rule, because the House precludes them by voting to order the previous question. Members are somewhat more likely to propose amendments to bills and resolutions considered in the House as in Committee of the Whole, but they do not do so with great frequency and the amendments offered usually do not generate very much controversy. When a bill is called from the Corrections Calendar, the only amendments in order are those proposed by the primary committee of jurisdiction or its chair. Finally, the House acts on more measures under suspension of the rules than under most other procedures, and no floor amendments are in order at all under the suspension procedure.

It is when the House has resolved into Committee of the Whole to consider a measure that Representatives are most likely to offer amendments, some of which Members may debate at length. More often than not, however, there are few, if any, procedural complications. A Member proposes an amendment and other Members join her in debating it; the Committee of the Whole eventually votes on the amendment and proceeds to consider the next one to be proposed. Alternatively, another Member may offer a second-degree amendment to the amendment, and the Committee then votes on the second-degree amendment before voting on the first-degree amendment, as it may have been amended.

Yet from time to time, the amending process does become complicated, as Members take advantage of the opportunities afforded by clause 6 of House Rule XVI:

> When an amendable proposition is under consideration, a motion to amend and a motion to amend that amendment shall be in order, and it also shall be in order to offer a further amendment by way of substitute for the original motion to amend, to which one amendment may be offered but which shall not be voted on until the original amendment is perfected. An amendment may be withdrawn in the House at any time before a decision or amendment thereon. An amendment to the title of a bill or resolution shall not be in order until after its passage or adoption and shall be decided without debate.

This rule creates the possibility for as many as four (and sometimes even five or more) amendments to be proposed before Members must vote on any of them. It would be extraordinary for such a situation to develop when bills are considered in the House or in the House as in Committee of the Whole, and it arises infrequently in Committee of the Whole. Nonetheless, Rule XVI, clause 6, creates a number of strategic possibilities that Members can employ when they believe it to be in their interests to do so. The situation that may result can be depicted graphically and is often described as the "*amendment tree*."

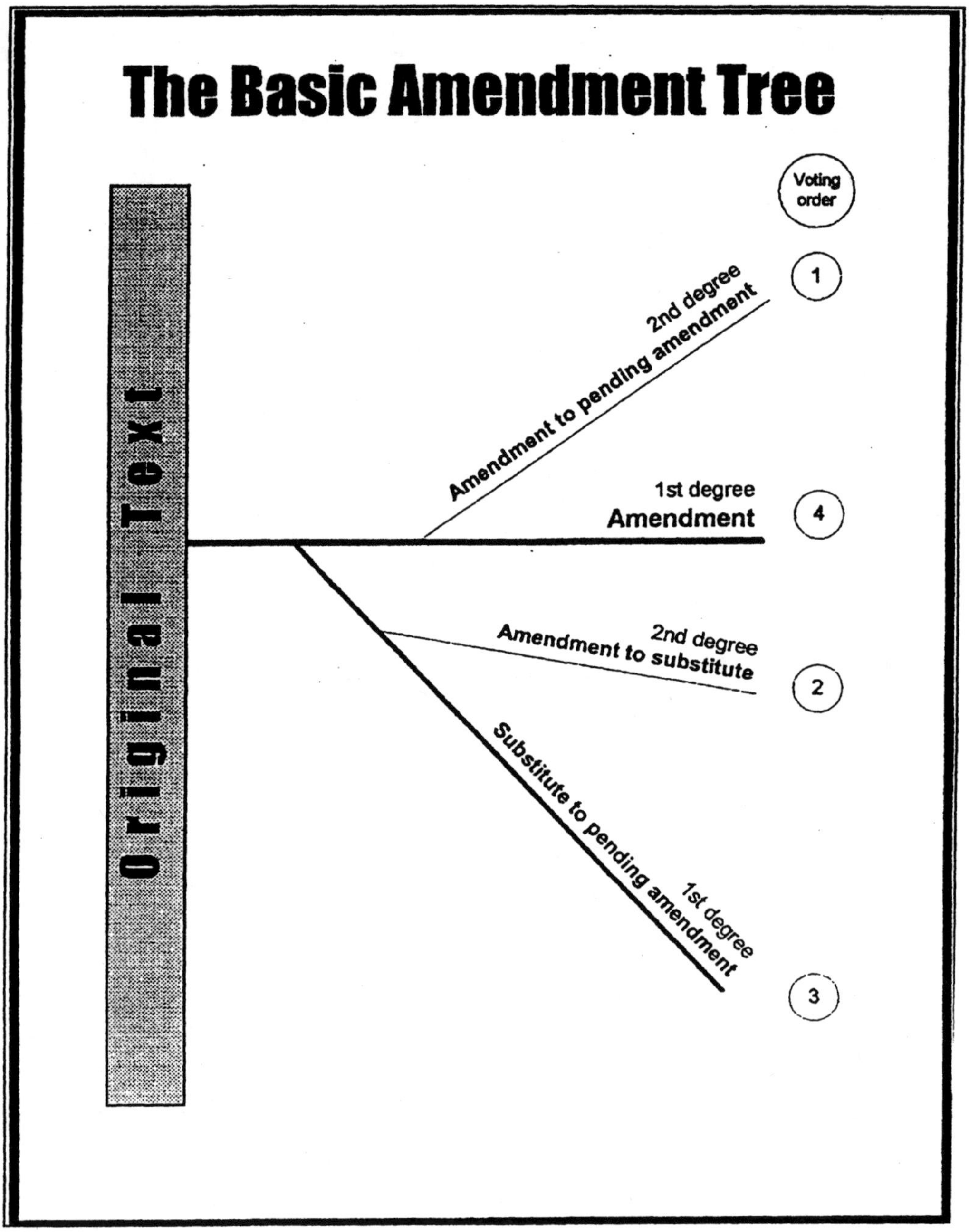
The Basic Amendment Tree
Voting order
Original Text
2nd degree
Amendment to pending amendment
1
1st degree
Amendment
4
2nd degree
Amendment to substitute
2
Substitute to pending amendment
1st degree
3

The amending situations that may develop depend primarily on the form of the first-degree amendments that Representatives offer. If a Member proposes a first-degree amendment in the form of a *motion to insert* or, in most cases, in the form of a *motion to strike out and insert*, this amendment tree depicts the kinds of amendments, and the maximum number of amendments, that Representatives may propose before the Committee of the Whole (or the House) must vote on any one of them. Somewhat different situations, to be discussed later, may arise if the first-degree amendment is a *motion to strike out* or if it is an *amendment in the nature of a substitute* proposing to replace the entire text of the measure.

Motions to Insert and to Strike Out and Insert

Let us assume, then, that a Representative proposes an amendment that would insert something into a measure, or that would replace part but not all of it. No other first-degree amendment may be offered until after the Committee votes on this amendment. And this being a first-degree amendment, it is amendable. The amendment to the amendment may either be a *second-perfecting amendment* that would strike from, add to, or replace something in the first-degree amendment, or it may be a *substitute amendment* that proposes a complete alternative to what the first-degree amendment would insert or strike and insert.

Under Rule XVI, both of these amendments are in order. After one Member proposes a second-perfecting amendment, and before the Committee votes on it, another Representative may offer a substitute for the first-degree amendment. And it is equally possible for Members to propose these two amendments in the opposite order. Thus, Members can offer two different amendments, each directed toward the first-degree amendment, before the Committee votes on either of them. In addition, Rule XVI provides that the substitute for the same first-degree amendment also is amendable. Another Member may propose an amendment to the substitute, either before or after the second-perfecting amendment is offered. And the amendment to the substitute is in order even though it could be construed to be a third degree amendment (an amendment to a substitute amendment for an amendment), which normally is prohibited.[89]

In this way, Members may propose four different amendments before any votes must occur. The Representative offering the first-degree amendment may not propose the perfecting amendment to, or the substitute for, her amendment, because a Member may not amend her own amendment. However, this Member may amend the substitute for her amendment.

After Representatives have offered these four amendments, they and other Members may continue to debate them. When there is no more debate or when the Committee has voted to end the debate, Rule XVI specifies the order in which the Committee votes on the amendments. First Members vote on the second-perfecting amendment, thereby perfecting the first-degree amendment. Next comes the vote on

---

[89] For this reason, it is not wholly accurate to characterize each amendment to an amendment as a second-degree amendment. Under Rule XVI, a substitute for a first-degree amendment is also treated as a first-degree amendment in that it is amendable.

the amendment to the substitute, which perfects the alternative to the first-degree amendment. Third, the Committee votes on the substitute amendment, as it may have been amended. And finally, a vote occurs on the original first-degree amendment, again as it may have been amended.[90]

In this way, the Committee can perfect two alternatives before choosing between them. The substitute for the first-degree amendment presents the Committee with a choice between two alternatives. One alternative, the first-degree amendment, is perfectible by a second-degree amendment. Therefore, Rule XVI also permits the Committee to perfect the other alternative, the substitute amendment.[91] Both alternatives are perfected before the Committee votes on the substitute and thereby chooses between the two of them. If the substitute wins, the last vote—on the first-degree amendment, as amended by the substitute—is nothing more than a second vote on the same substantive proposal made by the substitute. On the other hand, if the substitute loses, the Committee usually ratifies its decision by agreeing to the first-degree amendment (perhaps as perfected). The Committee may reject the first-degree amendment, whatever the outcome of the preceding votes, but the decisive vote more often occurs on the substitute amendment.

By their amendments, Representatives may create only part of this amendment tree. For instance, different Members may offer a perfecting amendment to, and a substitute for, a first-degree amendment, but no amendment to the substitute. Or they may propose a substitute for the first-degree amendment and an amendment to that substitute, but no second-perfecting amendment. In any event, the order in which the Committee votes on the amendments that Members do offer remains the same: the first votes are to perfect either or both alternatives before the Committee votes on a substitute, if any.

Furthermore, the situation depicted by the amendment tree is not necessarily a static one. There may only be one amendment on each "branch" of the amendment tree at a time.[92] But after the Committee votes on each amendment, a Member can offer a different amendment on the same branch, subject to the prohibition against attempting only to re-amend matter that already has been amended.[93] A Member who seeks recognition may offer an amendment on any unoccupied branch of the tree, if it is otherwise in order, and no Member can claim a right to be recognized before another because of the nature of the amendment he wishes to offer.

After the Committee votes on a second-perfecting amendment, for example, it does not necessarily proceed to act immediately on the next amendment in the voting

---

[90] *House Procedure*, ch. 27, sec. 21.1, p. 523.

[91] "While a perfecting amendment to a pending substitute should retain some portion of the substitute so as not to be in effect a substitute in the third degree, the Chair does not look behind the form of the amendment absent a timely point of order from the floor to determine whether it is a proper perfecting amendment.... *House Procedure, 1985 Supplement*, ch. 27, sec. 6.7.

[92] *House Procedure*, ch. 27, secs. 5.1-5.4, p. 500-501.

[93] *House Procedure*, ch. 27, sec. 21.2, p. 523.

order. Instead, a Member may propose another second-perfecting amendment, so long as it would not only re-amend something already amended.[94] The Committee then debates and votes on this new amendment, and any other subsequent perfecting amendments, even if a substitute amendment and an amendment to it had been offered previously. In other words, Members may offer a series of second-perfecting amendments, each addressed to matter in the first-degree amendment that has not yet been fully amended, and the Committee acts on each of these amendments in turn before voting on the amendment to the substitute and the substitute itself.

If no Member seeks recognition to offer another second-perfecting amendment, the Committee votes on the amendment to the substitute, after which a Representative may propose a different amendment either to the substitute or to the first-degree amendment. The vote on an amendment to the substitute does not preclude additional perfecting amendments to the first-degree amendment. And should the Committee eventually reject the substitute, the first-degree amendment remains open to another substitute and to other perfecting amendments. The amending process may continue until the first-degree amendment has been fully amended or until Members have no further amendments they wish to offer.[95]

The opportunities that Rule XVI offers suggest several strategic considerations. If Member A plans to offer an amendment to a bill and knows that Member B is likely to have a different amendment on the same subject, it is not necessarily advantageous for Member A to offer his proposal as a first-degree amendment. Member B then can offer her amendment either as a perfecting amendment or as a substitute, and should it win, there will be no "clean," direct vote on the unamended version of Member A's original first-degree amendment.

If Member A does offer his amendment as a first-degree amendment to the bill, Member B may decide to propose her amendment as a second-perfecting amendment (if that can be done in a way that makes substantive sense), so that the Committee of the Whole will first vote on Member B's position. But if Member B adopts this strategy, Member A can attempt to re-coup the situation by having Member C offer a slightly changed version of Member A's amendment as a substitute for that amendment. Thus, even if the Committee votes for Member B's second-perfecting amendment, it could vote for Member A's basic position as well by adopting Member C's substitute. And if the Committee votes for both amendments, it is Member C's amendment that ultimately prevails, because the effect of adopting a substitute for an amendment is to fully replace the text of that amendment as it already may have been amended by one or more perfecting amendments.

Of course, Member C's substitute also is amendable. So Member B or a colleague could offer the substance of her proposal a second time, as an amendment

---

94 *House Procedure*, ch. 27, sec. 27.9, p. 530.

95 "Under the five-minute rule, no debate may intervene after a substitute for an amendment has been adopted and before the vote on the amendment, as amended, except by unanimous consent (since the amendment has been amended in its entirety and no further amendments including pro forma amendments are in order)." *House Procedure, 1985 Supplement*, ch. 27, sec. 27.18, p. 71.

to the substitute. Although a Member may not offer the same amendment twice, Member B may propose equivalent amendments to both the first-degree amendment and the substitute for it, because each of her amendments would amend a different text. Anticipating this development, Member A or another ally could seek recognition first to offer an amendment to the substitute that is consistent with Member A's original proposal. Finally, after the Committee votes on both perfecting amendments—one to the first-degree amendment, the other to the substitute—Members might still be able to offer additional perfecting amendments to either.

Alternatively, Member B could propose a substitute for Member A's first-degree amendment. To ensure that the eventual vote on the substitute would not preclude a vote on Member A's position, an ally of his could offer a second-perfecting amendment on which the Committee will vote first. If the Committee votes for this perfecting amendment, it may be unwilling to vote also for a substitute that is inconsistent with the amendment already adopted. But if the substitute prevails, the victory achieved by the second-perfecting amendment is lost, because the substitute will replace the text of the first-degree amendment as perfected. Member A's ally also has the option of amending Member B's substitute; if the Committee supports that amendment, there will be no "clean" vote on the substitute. In response, however, Member B or an ally might obtain a vote on the essence of their position in the form of a second-perfecting amendment to Member A's original amendment.

As these possibilities suggest, there is no ideal strategy for Representatives to adopt when they anticipate the development of an amendment tree. A Member's preferred strategy can depend on such considerations as the amount and intensity of the support for the Member's position and the importance of having the Committee vote first on that position. The nature of the issue also may matter. In some cases, Members may be inclined to vote for more than one approach to responding to a widely shared concern; in others, Members are less likely to vote for one approach and then to vote as well for a second, inconsistent approach. In addition, the positions of the Representatives offering the amendments can make a difference. The sequence in which the amendments actually are offered depends on the order in which the chair recognizes Members to propose them. And the chair traditionally gives preference in recognition to the senior members of the committee that reported the bill being considered.

Another implication of these possibilities is that the way in which an amendment is drafted—whether as a perfecting or a substitute amendment—depends not only on the nature of the proposal but also on the parliamentary circumstances under which it is likely to be offered. This is particularly true of amendments to amendments, which Members and staff may have to prepare after the floor debate has begun. It sometimes is advisable to draft the same amendment in several different forms, to preserve procedural flexibility and to maximize the likelihood that the Member actually will have an opportunity to offer it. Even then, the amendment's sponsor may have to complete the drafting process on the floor by "keying" it to the appropriate page and line numbers of the text she intends to amend.

Thus far, this discussion of the amendment tree has assumed that the first-degree amendment from which the tree "grows" is either (1) a motion to insert or (2) a motion to strike out and insert which affects only part of the measure's text. Somewhat different opportunities arise if, instead, the first-degree amendment is a motion to strike out or an amendment in the nature of a substitute (proposing to strike out the entire text of the measure and insert a different version in its place).

Motion to Strike Out

A motion to strike out usually is not amendable; in the conventional practice of the House, Members do not offer perfecting amendments to, or substitutes for, such motions. However, House precedents do permit Members to propose amendments to the part of the measure that the motion would strike. In other words, the House can perfect a part of a bill or resolution before deciding whether to strike it.[96] In this case, therefore, two Members can propose first-degree amendments to the text of a measure before the Committee of the Whole votes on either of them—the amendment to strike and the amendment to change the text proposed to be stricken. The latter amendment can be a perfecting amendment—replacing, striking, or adding to part of the language to which the motion to strike is directed.[97] Or the amendment may be a substitute for whatever the first amendment offered would strike.

In either case, the amendment to the text proposed to be stricken is a first-degree amendment that is amendable, and the other three branches of the amendment tree may "grow" on this amendment. Thus, five amendments may be offered before any votes occur: first, the motion to strike; second, an amendment to the text proposed to be stricken; and then, a perfecting amendment to the second amendment, a substitute for it, and an amendment to the substitute.[98]

All of the preceding discussion of the amendment tree applies to this situation, with one exception. After the Committee votes on all the other amendments, there also may be a final vote on the original motion to strike. If the amendment that comes behind the motion to strike is a perfecting amendment, the Committee votes on the perfecting amendment and then on the motion to strike.[99] But if the amendment proposes to replace the whole text at which the motion to strike is directed, and if it attracts a majority vote on the floor, no vote occurs on the motion to strike. The matter proposed to be stricken has been completely amended, so the motion to strike becomes an attempt to re-amend something that the Committee already has amended. The chair announces that the motion to strike "falls" without the need for a vote because the motion is no longer in order.[100]

---

[96] *House Procedure*, ch. 27, secs. 13.1-13.3, p. 513-514.

[97] *House Procedure*, ch. 27, sec. 22.3, p. 524.

[98] *House Procedure*, ch. 27, sec. 5.14, p. 502; ch. 27, sec. 13.12, p. 515.

[99] *House Procedure*, ch. 27, sec. 5.17, p. 502.

[100] Annotations to Section XXXV of *Jefferson's Manual* in *House Rules and Manual*.

Amendment in the Nature of a Substitute for a Measure

Finally, a considerably more elaborate amendment tree can develop when a Member offers an amendment in the nature of a substitute for the entire text of a bill or resolution, though there are procedural reasons why this rarely occurs.

Such an amendment in the nature of a substitute presents the Committee of the Whole with a choice between two versions of the bill: the version embodied in the bill as it was introduced and brought to the floor, and the version embodied in the complete substitute. The amendment in the nature of a substitute is a first-degree amendment, and so it is amendable to the same extent as any other first-degree amendment. The amendment is perfectible; in addition, it is subject to a substitute (in effect, a third version of the bill) which also is amendable. After the Committee votes on all amendments to the amendment in the nature of a substitute, it then votes on that complete substitute as it may have been amended. If the Committee adopts the amendment in the nature of a substitute, it replaces the entire text of the measure, amending it fully. This precludes any further amendments to the bill because of the prohibition against re-amendment.[101]

If this were the extent of the amendments in order, the Committee of the Whole would be able to perfect one version of the bill but not the other. It could vote on amendments to the amendment in the nature of a substitute before voting on it, and thereby choosing between it and the other version, the text of the bill. But it could not perfect the text of the bill itself before making this choice. For this reason, House precedents allow Members to offer amendments to the bill itself as well as to the complete substitute for it.[102] The result is the potential for Members to offer eight amendments before the Committee begins to vote: the amendment in the nature of a substitute and three amendments relating to it, and four amendments relating to the original text of the bill.

After a Representative proposes the complete substitute, another Member may offer an amendment to the substitute or a first-degree amendment to perfect the pending part of the original version of the bill. If the latter is offered, it is subject to the same amendment tree as any other first-degree amendment (unless, of course, it is a motion to strike).[103] If any or all of this two-trunk tree develops, the Committee votes first on amendments to the perfecting amendment and then on the perfecting amendment (perhaps as amended), before it acts on amendments relating to the amendment in the nature of a substitute. And after the vote on the perfecting amendment to the bill, Members may propose additional perfecting amendments, one at a time, and amend and vote on them, while the complete substitute and any amendments to it remain pending.

Fortunately, there are at least two reasons why such extremely complicated situations rarely develop.

---

[101] *House Procedure*, ch. 27, sec. 30.1, p. 534.

[102] *House Procedure*, ch. 27, sec. 13.8, p. 514.

[103] *House Procedure, 1985 Supplement*, ch. 27, sec. 13.8, p. 68.

Most amendments in the nature of substitutes for measures are committee amendments (or substitutes supported by committee chairmen) which special rules regularly make in order as the original text to be amended. Under such a rule, it is the substitute, not the bill, that is read for amendment and may be amended in two degrees.[104] Members may not offer amendments to the text of the bill as introduced until after voting on all amendments to the amendment in the nature of a substitute and on the substitute itself, and then only if the Committee rejects it. Because the Committee of the Whole rarely, if ever, rejects an amended committee substitute, it rarely reaches the original text of the bill. And even if this were to happen, both versions would not be open to amendment at the same time. First the Committee would act on the substitute and all amendments to it, and then on amendments to the original version of the bill.

The two-trunk amendment tree is unlikely to develop even if a special rule does not provide for the Committee of the Whole to consider the amendment in the nature of a substitute as original text, and, instead, a Member offers it as a first-degree amendment. The reason lies in two elements of the amending process. First, as already noted, a Representative may propose an amendment in the nature of a substitute at only two points during the amending process in Committee of the Whole: either at the very beginning, after the first section has been read, or at the very end, after the Committee has disposed of all other amendments. Second, Members may only propose amendments to that portion of the measure itself that has been read or designated for amendment, and bills and resolutions typically are considered for amendment section by section or title by title.

If the substitute is offered at the beginning, after the clerk reads or designates the first section of the bill, Members can propose amendments to any part of the substitute but only to the first section of the bill (which often does nothing more than state its short title).[105] The clerk resumes reading the remaining sections or titles of the bill for amendment only after the Committee acts on all amendments to the substitute and then rejects it. Unless the Committee agrees, by unanimous consent, to consider the entire bill as read and open to amendment at any point, this situation effectively precludes substantive amendments to the text of the bill while the amendment in the nature of a substitute is pending. If, on the other hand, a Member proposes the substitute at the end of the process, the Committee already will have considered and voted on whatever amendments to the bill itself Members wished to offer. There is little likelihood that they would want to propose many additional amendments to it after the complete substitute is finally offered.

Except under the most extraordinary circumstances, therefore, only the first of the two amendment trees develops on the House floor. Also, while in theory this tree could grow during consideration of measures in the House or in the House as in Committee of the Whole, this is even more unlikely. In practice, Members do not create amendment trees very often, and then only in Committee of the Whole.

---

104 *Ibid.*

105 *House Procedure, 1985 Supplement*, ch. 27, sec. 7.12, p. 505.

Special Procedures for Tax and Appropriations Measures

In addition to the principles and prohibitions that apply to all amendments, House Rule XXI imposes certain special restrictions and procedures governing floor amendments to tax and appropriations measures.

Clauses 4 and 5 are intended to ensure that Members offer tax and appropriations amendments only to measures on those subjects that have been reported by the appropriate House committees. Clause 4 prohibits consideration of "an amendment proposing an appropriation...during the consideration of a bill or joint resolution reported by a committee not having that jurisdiction"—namely, any committee other than the Appropriations Committee. And similarly, clause 5(a) provides for a point of order against "an amendment in the House or proposed by the Senate carrying a tax or tariff measure...during the consideration of a bill or joint resolution reported by a committee not having that jurisdiction"—namely, any committee other than the Ways and Means Committee.

The same clause contains two other provisions affecting tax measures. First, no amendment, measure, or conference report is in order if it proposes a retroactive increase in federal income tax rates. Second, a three-fifths vote is required to approve any amendment, bill or joint resolution, or conference report that carries a federal income tax rate increase.

Clause 2 also includes provisions, which are invoked more often than those of clause 4 or 5, that restrict amendments to general appropriations measures. Their essential purposes are (1) to enforce the requirement that appropriations are to be authorized by law and (2) to preserve a separation between policy and funding decisions. These restrictions do not apply to continuing appropriations resolutions or to special appropriations bills for one purpose or a very limited number of related purposes.[106]

Clause 2(a)(1) states that almost all appropriations must have been authorized by law before they may be considered on the House floor, whether as provisions of bills and resolutions or as amendments to them:

> An appropriation may not be reported in a general appropriation bill, and may not be in order as an amendment thereto, for an expenditure not previously authorized by law, except to continue appropriations for public works and objects that already are in progress.

Furthermore, clause 2(c) provides in part that:

> An amendment to a general appropriation bill shall not in order if changing existing law....

---

[106]*House Procedure*, ch. 25, secs. 1-2, p. 393-394.

Enforcing the second of these prohibitions depends on what constitutes a change in existing law, or "legislation." The House has traditionally distinguished between "legislation" and a "*limitation*," which is an appropriations provision or amendment that restricts the purposes for which or the means by which appropriations may be used. An amendment limiting the availability of appropriations may be in order if it meets the requirements of a complex body of precedents:[107] for example, if it applies only to the funds appropriated by the bill or resolution to which it is offered (and not to the funds appropriated by "this or any other act"), and if it does not impose any new duty or responsibility on an official of the federal government.[108]

However, clause 2(d) imposes special procedures relating to limitation amendments. A Member wanting to offer a limitation to a certain paragraph of a general appropriations bill may not do so after the clerk has read that paragraph, even though that normally would be the appropriate time for offering an amendment in Committee of the Whole. Instead, as the bill is read for amendment, the Committee of the Whole considers and acts on all amendments except limitations. Then, after the bill has been completely read for amendment and the Committee has voted on the last amendment, a Representative may propose a limitation amendment relating to any paragraph of the bill or to the bill as a whole. But clause 2(d) provides a means by which the House can vote not to consider this or any other limitation.

Either before a Member proposes a limitation amendment, or after she offers it but before debate begins, the majority floor manager can offer a preferential and non-debatable motion that the Committee rise and report the bill back to the House with whatever amendments the Committee already has adopted.[109] The Committee of the Whole normally does not rise and report until after it has considered all the amendments that Members wish to offer. In this case, however, the Committee can vote against considering a limitation amendment by agreeing to a motion to rise and report before the limitation is proposed or before debate on it begins. If the motion is rejected, the limitation amendment is in order. But after the Committee votes on that amendment, the floor manager again may move that the Committee rise and report, and thereby preclude consideration of the next or any subsequent limitation.[110]

Thus, this special procedure under clause 2(d) permits the Committee of the Whole to cast a vote which, in effect, can preclude Members from proposing one or all limitation amendments that otherwise would be in order.

Clause 2(f) of Rule XXI also contains an exception to the general principle that, when a bill is being read amendment in Committee of the Whole, Members may offer amendments only to the part of the bill that has been read (or designated) and is open to amendment. Clause 2(f) permits a Member to offer amendments *en bloc* if the combined effect of the amendments is to "transfer appropriations among objects in the

---

107 See, for example, *House Procedure*, ch. 25, secs. 9-17, p. 409-427.

108 Annotations to Rule XXI, clause 2.

109 *House Procedure, 1985 Supplement*, ch. 25, sec. 22, p. 57.

110 These same procedures apply to "germane amendments which retrench expenditures by reduction of amounts of money covered by the bill." Annotations to Rule XXI, clause 2.

bill without increasing the levels of budget authority or outlays in the bill." Such amendments are in order even if they amend portions of the bill that have not yet been read for amendment, and the amendments are not subject to a demand that they be divided and considered separately.

Making and Reserving Points of Order

Several sections of this report have identified points of order to which amendments may be subject. If a Representative makes a point of order against an amendment and the point of order is sustained, the amendment may not be considered. The Speaker or the chair of the Committee of the Whole usually does not rule an amendment out of order until after a Member makes a point of order against it. It is the responsibility of each Member to enforce the procedures of the House, and thereby protect her own rights, by making appropriate points of order. If no Member makes a point of order, an amendment normally may be considered even though it violates some requirement of the House's legislative procedures.

When a Representative wants to make a point of order against an amendment, she usually does so as soon as the amendment is offered, or she may reserve the point of order before the debate begins and then make it at a later time during debate on the amendment. However, the special rule under which a measure is being considered may waive applicable points of order against specific amendments that Members are expected to propose. Furthermore, no point of order lies against an amendment presented to the House as part of a motion to suspend the rules and pass a measure as amended; the suspension procedure has the effect of waiving all points of order that otherwise might lie against the bill or any amendment incorporated in the motion.

In almost all cases, there is only one appropriate moment for making a point of order against an amendment: after the clerk has finished reading the amendment, or after the reading has been dispensed with by unanimous consent, but before the sponsor of the amendment begins to debate it.[111] In some cases, therefore, a Member may insist on having an amendment read in full to give him time to examine it. Once debate begins on the amendment, in most cases it is too late to make a point of order against it.

The exceptions to this general rule are points of order made under clauses 4 and 5 of Rule XXI, prohibiting an appropriations or tax amendment to a measure that was not reported by the appropriate committee. Such a point of order "may be raised at any time;" a Member may make it at any time that the Committee of the Whole is considering the amendment under the five-minute rule.

Instead of making a point of order against an amendment at the appropriate time—before there has been any debate on it—a Member may seek to "reserve" the point of order, and then make it after there have been five or more minutes of debate

---

[111] *House Procedure*, ch. 31, sec. 5, p. 700-702.

on the amendment.[112] There are two primary reasons for doing so. First, the Member may want more time to study the amendment, to decide if it is subject to a point of order and, if so, whether she chooses to make it. Second, the Member may intend to make a point of order but prefers to allow the amendment's sponsor (and perhaps other Members) some time to discuss it. If a Member reserves a point of order and a colleague then demands "the regular order," the "chair hears and rules on the point of order as expeditiously as possible."[113]

Members do not have any right to debate points of order; instead, the chair has discretion to entertain as much or as little debate for his information as he wishes. Traditionally, the Speaker or the chair recognizes the Member making the point of order to explain the basis for it—identifying the principle, rule, or precedent that the amendment violates—and to argue in favor it. The sponsor of the amendment next has an opportunity to defend it against the point of order, after which the chair may recognize other Members to speak on the procedural question. The Speaker or chair then makes a ruling, with the advice of the parliamentarian, which reflects past interpretations of the applicable rules and precedents.

Any Member may appeal the ruling of the chair on a point of order against an amendment, in which case the House then decides by majority vote whether to sustain or overturn the ruling.[114] But this is rarely done, and virtually never done successfully. The presiding officer of the House has not been overruled against his will in more than fifty years. Thus, rulings of the chair, either in the House or in Committee of the Whole, are conclusive for all practical purposes.

---

[112] *House Procedure*, ch. 31, sec. 2, p. 698-699.

[113] *House Procedure*, ch. 31, sec. 2.5, p. 698.

[114] *House Procedure*, ch. 31, sec. 8, p. 703-704.

Summary of the Effects of Special Rules

There have been references throughout this report to the usual or possible impact of special rules on the amending process. These effects are summarized here.[115]

First, special rules usually specify the set of procedures under which the House considers a measure. The overwhelming majority of rules provide for consideration in Committee of the Whole, but they may state instead that a bill or resolution is to be considered in the House or in the House as in Committee of the Whole. Special rules concerning general appropriations measures, which are privileged for floor consideration, may only waive points of order against the measure, its provisions, and amendments to it.

Second, special rules specify the length of general debate in Committee of the Whole and allocate it between or among committee chairmen, ranking minority members, and sometimes other Members as well.[116]

Third, special rules may provide for an amendment in the nature of a substitute, usually recommended by the committee that reported the measure, to be considered as an original bill for purpose of amendment. The effect of this provision is to make the substitute amendable in two degrees and to direct all amendments to it, rather than to the text of the measure as introduced, except in the unlikely event that the Committee ultimately rejects the substitute.[117]

Fourth, special rules may restrict the amendments that Representatives can offer in Committee of the Whole. A "closed rule" precludes all amendments, or all but those offered at the direction of the committee of jurisdiction. A "modified closed" rule or a "modified open" rule is a restrictive special rule that either permits only the amendments identified by the special rule or prohibits amendments on certain subjects or to certain parts of the measure. Special rules also may prohibit amendments to amendments.[118]

Fifth, special rules may waive points of order against one or more committee amendments or amendments that Members intend to offer.[119]

Sixth, and finally, special rules typically provide for the previous question to be considered as ordered when the Committee of the Whole rises and reports the measure back to the House. This provision prohibits debate on the amendments that

---

[115] See CRS Report 96-938, *Special Rules in the House of Representatives*, and Stanley Bach and Steven S. Smith, *Managing Uncertainty in the House of Representatives: Adaptation and Innovation in Special Rules*. Washington: The Brookings Institution, 1988.

[116] *House Procedure*, ch. 21, sec. 19.1, p. 324.

[117] *House Procedure*, ch. 21, sec. 19.12, p. 326.

[118] *House Procedure*, ch. 21, secs. 19.23-19.46, p. 328-331; ch. 27, sec. 2.33, p. 496.

[119] *House Procedure*, ch. 21, sec. 19.6, p. 325.

the Committee has recommended and prevents Members from offering additional amendments at this late stage of the process.

Sources of Additional Information

House of Representatives

The following official publications of the House contain further information on the amending process and related procedures:

Constitution, Jefferson's Manual, and Rules of the House of Representatives of the United States, published each Congress as a House document. (Cited in the notes as *House Rules and Manual.*)

House Practice: A Guide to the Rules, Precedents and Procedures of the House, by Wm. Holmes Brown. 104th Congress, 2nd Session. Washington, D.C., U.S. Govt. Print. Off., 1996.

Procedure in the U.S. House of Representatives, 97th Congress. Washington, D.C., U.S. Govt. Print. Off., 1982. (Cited in the notes as *House Procedure.*)

Procedure in the U.S. House of Representatives, 1985 and 1987 Supplements. Washington, D.C., U.S. Govt. Print. Off., 1985 and 1987. (Cited in the notes as *House Procedure, 1985 Supplement, House Procedure, 1987 Supplement.*)

Cannon's Procedure in the House of Representatives, 87th Congress, 2nd Session (House Document No. 610). Washington, D.C., U.S. Govt. Print. Off., 1963.

Hinds' and Cannon's Precedents of the House of Representatives of the United States (in 11 volumes). Washington, D.C., U.S. Govt. Print. Off., 1907 and 1936.

Deschler's Precedents of the U.S. House of Representatives and *Deschler-Brown Precedents of the U.S. House of Representatives* (in 14 volumes to date), 94th Congress, 2nd Session (House Document No. 94-661). Washington, D.C., U.S. Govt. Print. Off., 1977.

House Parliamentarian

The parliamentarian and his assistants welcome inquiries about House procedures, and offer expert assistance compatible with their other responsibilities.

Congressional Research Service

The Congressional Research Service has prepared various other complementary reports on legislative procedures, including:

CRS Report 98-853, *The Amending Process in the Senate*. (Updated periodically)

CRS Report 96-708, *Conference Committee and Related Procedures: An Introduction*. (Updated periodically)

CRS Report 97-856, *The Discharge Rule in the House of Representatives*. (Updated periodically)

CRS Report 97-301, *The House's "Corrections Calendar."* (Updated periodically)

CRS Report 97-825, *Legislative Procedures and the Legislative Agenda in the House of Representatives*. (Updated periodically)

CRS Report 95-563, *The Legislative Process on the House Floor: An Introduction*. (Updated periodically)

CRS Report 98-696, *Resolving Legislative Differences in Congress: Conference Committees and Amendments Between the Houses*. (Updated periodically)

CRS Report 96-938, *Special Rules in the House of Representatives*. (Updated periodically)

CRS Report 98-796, *Suspension of the Rules in the House of Representatives*. (Updated periodically)

CRS Report 96-421, *Voting and Quorum Procedures in the House of Representatives*. (Updated periodically)

The staff of CRS is available to consult with Representatives and staff; CRS also presents periodic staff seminars and institutes on legislative procedures.

Congress of the United States:
Powers,Structure, and Procedures

LEGISLATIVE PROCEDURES AND THE LEGISLATIVE AGENDA IN THE HOUSE OF REPRESENTATIVES

Stanley Bach

Summary

This report depicts a process of legislative agenda-setting in the House in which the standing committees first screen the possible agenda of all bills that are introduced, evaluating them and selecting from among them a potential agenda of bills that, in the judgment of the committees, deserve floor consideration. Priorities for considering these bills on the floor are controlled both by the operation of standing rules and by the adoption of special rules proposed by the Rules Committee. These priorities are transformed into short-term schedules and the daily order of business through the political influence of the majority party leaders and especially through the procedural discretion of the Speaker. The House's legislative agenda is embodied primarily in the bills it considers. Individual Representatives may propose floor amendments that present alternatives or additional options, but opportunities to offer amendments are constrained by the germaneness rule, among others, and can be limited by majority vote. Underlying these procedural arrangements is the axiom that the agenda of the House is generally for the House to decide, and the corollary that these decisions generally reflect whatever collective preferences can be assembled from the individual preferences of its Members.

Introduction

Analyzing the legislative process in the House of Representatives, or any dimension of it such as the development of its agenda, involves abstracting one aspect of this process from its context.[1] This report focuses primarily on the internal arrangements of the House—the procedures and practices by which the House decides what issues it will consider, and how and when it will consider them. Before turning to these matters, several elements of the constitutional and political context within which the House conducts its business deserve brief consideration.

The Constitutional Context.

The Constitution imposes some restrictions on the subjects of national legislation and, therefore, on Congress's legislative agenda. Article I enumerates certain powers of Congress, including the powers to raise revenue, to provide for an army and navy, and to regulate commerce among the states and with foreign nations. Congress also is empowered to make all laws which are "necessary and proper" for carrying out its enumerated powers and all other powers that the Constitution assigns to the federal government.[2] On the other hand, the Constitution distinguishes in general terms between the powers of Congress and the powers of the executive and judicial branches, and reserves remaining powers to the individual states and the people. Article I, including the "necessary and proper" clause, has been interpreted by the

---

[1] This report considers the legislative agenda only from a procedural perspective. From a broader perspective, the process of agenda-setting can include the development, definition, and evolution of issues as they attract the attention of, and provoke action by, Congress and the federal government generally (or as they fail to do so). For different approaches to the analysis of agendas and agenda-setting, see, for example: John W. Kingdon, *Agendas, Alternatives, and Public Policies*. Boston, Little, Brown and Company, 1984; Paul Charles Light, *The President's Agenda*. Baltimore, The John Hopkins University Press, 1982; Nelson W. Polsby, *Political Innovation in America*. New Haven, Yale University Press, 1984; Barbara Sinclair, "Agenda, Policy, and Alignment Change from Coolidge to Reagan," in Lawrence C. Dodd and Bruce I. Oppenheimer (editors), *Congress Reconsidered* (3rd Edition). Washington, Congressional Quarterly, Inc., 1985; and Jack L. Walker, "Setting the Agenda in the U.S. Senate: A Theory of Problem Selection," *British Journal of Political Science*, v. 7, 1977, p. 423-445.

[2] The text of the Constitution, with useful commentary by the House parliamentarian, is included in U.S. Congress. House of Representatives. *Constitution, Jefferson's Manual, and Rules of the House of Representatives of the United States, 105th Congress*. House Document No. 104-272. 104th Congress, 2d Session.

Supreme Court to permit legislation on a wide range of subjects that are not specifically enumerated in the Constitution. But the "elastic" clause cannot be stretched in all directions and without limit. Moreover, there are subjects on which Congress is expressly forbidden to legislate; for example, the familiar constitutional protections in the Bill of Rights limit Congress's legislative discretion.

The Constitution also defines the formal relationship between Congress and the President. The President may not be a Member of Congress, nor does Congress have any part in electing the President, except under the most extraordinary circumstances.[3] The Vice President is also the president of the Senate but rarely presides and may vote only in the infrequent event of a tie. The President may nominate federal judges and senior officials of the executive branch, but all judicial and many executive branch nominees must be confirmed by majority vote of the Senate, just as treaties negotiated by the President require approval by a two-thirds vote of the Senate before they may be ratified. The President is directed to report to Congress from time to time (in practice, annually) on the "State of the Union" and to recommend such legislative action as he considers "necessary and expedient." He also shares in the legislative power more directly in that he may veto acts of Congress; but a presidential veto may be overridden by a two-thirds vote of both the House and the Senate.

Thus, the President may propose and may veto legislation, but neither of these powers is conclusive. Furthermore, neither the Constitution nor the rules of Congress make any other provision for the President or other executive branch officials to participate in the legislative process (except for the Vice President's position as president of the Senate). Presidential proposals for legislation have no special standing under the Constitution or congressional rules; they enjoy no procedural advantage or priority. Congress is under no constitutional obligation to consider, much less approve, presidential recommendations for legislation; and, if Congress fails to act, the President has no constitutional recourse other than to exercise whatever discretion he already has been granted by law.

Presidential proposals for legislation may take the form of general statements in speeches or written messages. During the 20th century, however, and especially during recent decades, Presidents and executive branch officials acting with the President's concurrence also have proposed specific drafts of legislation they wish to see enacted. Nonetheless, the limits on the President's formal legislative powers are epitomized by the fact that each of his legislative proposals must be introduced by a Representative or Senator if it is to receive formal congressional consideration. This obstacle is easily overcome; a presidential proposal is introduced by his supporters in Congress or, as a courtesy, by the chairmen of the House and Senate committees with jurisdiction over the subject of the proposal. But this obstacle is as important in principle as it is trivial in practice.

---

[3] The Twelfth Amendment to the Constitution provides that, if no presidential candidate receives a majority of the electoral votes, the House of Representatives shall vote by state delegation to elect the President from among no more than three persons receiving the greatest number of electoral votes. Under the comparable provision of the Constitution as originally ratified, the House elected Thomas Jefferson as President in 1801, neither Jefferson nor any other candidate having received a majority of the electoral votes.

The President is an influential participant in the legislative process, of course; he can have as much or more influence on the legislative agenda as any Member or entity of Congress. Nonetheless, presidential influence over the congressional agenda, and over legislative decisions as well, is grounded more in his political strength than in his constitutional or other formal powers. A President bases his election campaign on a agenda for government action, however general it may be. Once elected, he can use the resources of his office and the public attention he commands with great effect in attempting to persuade Congress to act—directly by negotiating with Representatives and Senators, or indirectly by mobilizing public support for his program. Congress is likely to give serious consideration to the proposals on which the President lays greatest stress, but Congress responds to presidential initiatives by choice—or by political, not constitutional, necessity.

In a celebrated analysis of the presidency, Professor Richard Neustadt characterized presidential power as the power to persuade:[4]

> The separateness of institutions and the sharing of authority prescribe the terms on which a President persuades. When one man shares authority with another, but does not gain or lose his job upon the other's whim, his willingness to act upon the urging of the other turns on whether he conceives the action right for him. The essence of a President's persuasive task is to convince such men that what the White House wants of them is what they ought to do for their sake and on their authority.

Although Congress always has been concerned with preserving its constitutional powers and position, it has come to accept and even welcome presidential efforts to persuade. For reasons to be developed later in this report, Congress as an institution has difficulty in setting priorities among the many and often conflicting demands made upon it. Effective presidential persuasion, direct or indirect, helps to focus congressional attention in ways that presumably respond to public preferences. By the same token, however, the President also must be selective in his attempts to persuade Congress to act (or not to act). His resources for persuasion are limited, so his efforts must be targeted. A President who attempts to overload the congressional agenda may achieve little because he diffuses his persuasive efforts and fails to convey a clear and consistent sense of direction and priority.

Congressional agenda-setting, however much influenced by presidential persuasion, is complicated by its constitutional context in another important respect. By constitutional arrangement, the House and Senate differ in size, length of terms, and constituencies. These differences are accompanied by deeply entrenched differences in legislative procedures and occasional differences in partisan control. As a result, relations between the two halves of Congress involve competition and conflict as well as cooperation.

In constitutional powers, the two houses of Congress are roughly equal; each has unique prerogatives that it usually guards jealously. Both houses must agree before a bill can become law, and neither house consistently dominates the other; nor is

---

[4] Richard E. Neustadt, *Presidential Power*. 1980 ed. New York: John Wiley & Sons, Inc., 1960. p. 27.

there any authority, other than an electorate fragmented by state and district boundaries, to which both are accountable. Each chamber has the constitutional power to select its own officers, devise its own rules, and, by implication, set its own agenda. There are no congressional leaders; there are only House leaders and Senate leaders, with no formal mechanisms for coordination between them. For many purposes, each house is autonomous. The House and Senate typically refer to each other as "the other body," reflecting a sense of separateness between the two houses that is far greater than the physical distance between the two wings of the Capitol building. When Representatives and Senators meet in a conference committee to resolve specific legislative differences between them, their discussions can take on the aura of bilateral treaty negotiations.

There is no congressional agenda as such. Each house generally is free to decide for itself what matters it will consider and when it will consider them. To be sure, there are constraints on this freedom of action. Certain laws must be enacted each year—the activities of the federal government must be funded before the new fiscal year begins—and presidential influence, popular sentiment, and national and international emergencies can provoke the House and Senate to give priority to the same matters. In such cases, however, the two houses are responding independently to the same requirements, pressures, or developments. Neither house has the constitutional power to compel the other to act. From time to time, the House or Senate will even act on a matter in the knowledge that the other house is unlikely to follow suit. The enactment of a law reflects independent decisions by majorities in the House and Senate that such action is necessary or desirable. It bears repeating that, in this most important sense, there is no congressional agenda; there is a House agenda and a Senate agenda, and they do not always coincide.

The Political Context.

If constitutional arrangements militate against a process of legislative agenda-setting that draws both houses of Congress together with each other and with the President, elements of the political context complicate the process of agenda-setting within the House of Representatives itself, and even among the members of the majority party in the House.

Political parties can unify what constitutions separate. However, the nature and condition of the national political parties in the United States, together with the single-member districts from which Representatives are elected, limit the impact of party priorities on arranging the agenda and policy choices of the House. The importance of party should not be underestimated. Representatives' party affiliations have been the best general predictor of how they will vote, and majority party leaders and their allies have a profound influence on the business the House conducts. But straight party-line votes are far more the exception than the rule—certainly in comparison with most European parliamentary regimes—and there are influences on the House's legislative agenda over which party leaders have no formal control and only limited influence.

While the form and condition of a party system cannot be attributed solely to any one set of factors, the structure of national elections and representation does not promote strong party government in the United States. A powerful presidency elected by a majority of the Electoral College (that almost always reflects a national plurality) has encouraged a coalescence of factions into a two-party system. Historically, third parties have had great difficulty attracting, and especially maintaining, widespread support in federal elections because they have been unable to contest seriously for the single most visible and valuable prize, the presidency. The result has been two parties with different centers of gravity but overlapping national constituencies in Presidential elections.

At the congressional level, however, candidates of the two parties run for the House in 435 separate single-member districts that are geographically, economically, and socially diverse. An unequivocal party position that has strong appeal in some districts would be overwhelmingly rejected in many others. But party positions usually are not unequivocal, and they are not staked out by national party organizations, except for the platforms adopted at the quadrennial presidential nominating conventions. The national party organizations have tended to be skeletal, and their chairmen usually have been managers more than policy spokesmen or political leaders in their own right. The President is the acknowledged leader of his party, but there is no officially designated leader of the "opposition," nor are there any well-developed mechanisms for reaching and enunciating national party positions on issues as they arise. Between presidential elections, the contest between Democratic and Republican positions more often than not is really a contest between the position of the President and the predominant position of the opposing party's members in Congress, as articulated by the leaders they have elected.

In the absence of strong national party organizations and mechanisms for setting and promoting party positions, party discipline in Congress can be difficult to define and still more difficult to enforce. The majority party in the House enjoys organizational control and, if it is sufficiently unified, procedural control as well; and it is on organizational and procedural votes that Representatives are most expected and likely to support their House party leaders. Because there are no authoritative positions of the national parties *per se*, the same degree of party unity often is neither expected nor achieved on policy matters. Furthermore, national party organizations, Presidents, and party leaders in Congress have relatively little direct influence over Representatives' re-election prospects (and even less impact on Representatives' nominations), and House party leaders have only limited control over Representatives' prospects for achieving their personal and policy objectives in the House.

At the same time, Representatives have become less and less beholden to state and local party organizations. Like the national parties, state and local parties generally are organized to win elections more than to promote specific policies. Historically, they have been better organized than the national parties, but subnational party organizations are not as strong today as in decades past. They also tend to be more concerned with the election of state and local officials than with the election of Representatives, whose districts may not coincide with state or local political boundaries; so, many of these organizations can do, or choose to do, relatively little to aid House candidates.[5] For example, they usually can provide only a small fraction

---

[5] "The task of the congressman's personal organization is to keep him in Congress. The task (continued...)

of the increasing amounts of money needed to wage an effective campaign in a closely contested district. Party support can be valuable but rarely is it decisive.

Primary elections for the House also tend to weaken control of nominations by the party organizations. In most states, anyone who can meet low threshold requirements can compete for a party's nomination, and the winner of the primary becomes the party nominee, whether he or she has the support of the local party leaders. In most districts, the costs of campaigns and the impact of mass media have reduced the value of endorsements by party organizations, encouraging some local party leaders to remain neutral in congressional primary contests. In short, most Representatives and congressional candidates have become political entrepreneurs—deciding for themselves to run for office, developing their own positions and campaign organizations, devising their own campaign strategies, attracting their own supporters and contributors, and linking themselves to other party candidates only when it serves their own interests.

These political conditions have profound meaning for the incentives and calculations of Representatives, the position of their party leaders in Congress, and the influence of individual Representatives on the legislative agenda. Members of the House have the political freedom as well as the political reasons for advocating policies that their party colleagues and leaders may oppose. In deciding where they stand, Representatives tend to look to their constituents before their party leaders, especially national party leaders. District interests do not always prevail but they can never be ignored, and they are to be protected and promoted whenever possible. Representatives are bound to their fellow party members in Congress by shared loyalties and usually by shared convictions, as well as by a common desire to achieve or maintain majority control in Congress and win the presidency. They cooperate with each other and support their congressional leaders whenever, in their individual judgments, they can do so.

The task of leadership in Congress is much like that of presidential leadership—to lead by persuasion, not merely by exercise of formal powers. The powers of a cohesive majority and its leaders are formidable, but the procedures of the House recognize that the political system promotes congressional individualism. The agenda-setting procedures and practices that are discussed in the remainder of this report reflect the fact that, to a greater or lesser degree, every Representative has his or her own legislative agenda and considerable independence to promote it, though not necessarily to achieve its enactment.

The Committee System and Agenda Control

During the 105th Congress (1997-1998), 5,014 bills and joint resolutions were introduced in the House of Representatives; another 301 such measures were passed by the Senate and sent to the House for consideration. Of this total of 5,315 bills and

---

[5](...continued)
of the local party organizations is to keep the party in control of local offices." Richard F. Fenno, Jr. *Home Style: House Members in Their Districts*. Boston, Little, Brown and Company, 1978. p. 113.

joint resolutions—which represented the possible legislative agenda for that two-year Congress—only 394, or about 7.4%, became law.[6] Any Representative may introduce virtually any bill at any time during the two-year life of a Congress. The introduction of a bill is a matter of right; no special permission is required. It is also a routine act. The Representative sponsoring a bill need not make any statement about it; he or she has only to present it on the House floor when the House is in session. And at introduction, all bills enjoy the same standing regardless of the party or position of their sponsors.

Thus, the legislative process in the House of Representatives (and the Senate) is in part a process of agenda control—a process of selecting from among the thousands of measures introduced the relatively few that will reach enactment. The rules of the House assign primary responsibility for the initial screening and filtering to its system of standing legislative committees (and their subcommittees), each of which has jurisdiction, pursuant to House rules, over bills that address certain subjects. In most cases, a bill that is introduced (or received from the Senate) is immediately referred to the appropriate committee.[7] In some cases, a bill may be referred to two or more committees if each has jurisdiction over part or all of it.

The committees constitute a system of division of labor by which the House designates certain of its Members to become experts in certain arenas of policy and to make recommendations to the full membership. But the committees are equally important for what they do not do. During the 105th Congress, the standing committees of the House reported (or recommended for passage) a total of only 511 bills and joint resolutions. What makes this figure so significant is that a measure that is not reported stands little chance of becoming law. Committee approval is not necessarily conclusive; committee disapproval usually is.

Constraints on Committee Agenda Decisions.

This first agenda decisions are made by each committee as it decides which of the many bills referred to it will be considered. The committees are creatures of the House and subject to its control, but it would be extraordinary for the House to formally direct one of its committees to give priority to a particular bill or to bills on a particular subject.[8] However, agenda decisions within each committee are

---

[6] A law may originate as either a bill or a joint resolution; joint resolutions usually are used for more limited purposes than bills. For simplicity, references in this report to bills should be understood to refer to joint resolutions as well. These totals include some bills and joint resolutions that are identical to others, but do not include House resolutions and House and Senate concurrent resolutions on which the House may act but which are not submitted to the President and so cannot have the force of law.

[7] The exceptions include the relatively few bills which are so noncontroversial that they are considered briefly by the full House and passed at the time they are introduced or received from the Senate.

[8] Exceptions are "reconciliation" bills, which result from instructions given by Congress in a budget resolution, directing House (and Senate) committees to propose changes in laws within their jurisdictions that will result in specified changes in federal spending, revenues, or both.

influenced by party leaders and the President; they also are constrained by emergency circumstances and recurring deadlines for legislative action.

The authority of the federal government to spend money to finance most programs and activities must be renewed at least once a year. For this purpose, appropriations bills usually are reported by the House Appropriations Committee during the spring of each year so that they can be enacted by October 1, the beginning of the new fiscal year. House and Senate rules also anticipate that Congress will complete action on a concurrent budget resolution each spring as a framework for subsequent consideration of spending and revenue bills. Thus, most actions of the Appropriations and Budget Committees, as well as the timing of their actions, are controlled by the fiscal calendar or the requirements of House rules.

With one significant exception, there are few such constraints on the agendas of the other legislative committees. That exception derives from the requirement of House rules—specifically, clause 2(a) of Rule XXI—that a law must first be enacted to authorize the appropriation of funds for a federal agency, program, or activity before the appropriation to carry out that purpose may be considered on the House floor. Because many of these authorizations are supposed to be renewed either annually or periodically, the sequence of authorizations before appropriations has a significant effect on the agendas of almost all the other legislative committees, which have jurisdiction over authorization bills, as well as on the floor agenda of the House itself. Ideally, committees should report their authorization bills during the first months of each year so they may be enacted in time to permit the orderly consideration of appropriations bills. However, the authorization requirement is not imposed by the Constitution; it is a requirement of House rules and can be waived or ignored if the House chooses to do so. And, because of the number and complexity of the authorization bills, and the controversy surrounding some of them, the House sometimes has found it necessary to act on appropriations for which the authorizations have not yet become law.

Thus, the authorization requirement need not constrain House committees if the House is prepared (as it often is) to waive that requirement in order to permit timely consideration of the related appropriations. Moreover, the time constraints on committees in reporting authorization bills do not affect the committees' latitude in deciding on the provisions of those bills. The committees may propose whatever authorization levels they consider necessary (which, if enacted, then become ceilings on the amounts that may be appropriated without violating House rules). Also, authorization bills almost always include changes in agency powers and responsibilities, program requirements and procedures, and similar matters. The committees are under few formal constraints in making these recommendations to the House.

Agenda-Setting in Committee.

Within these constraints, each committee is free to determine its own agenda. Early each year, the committees prepare reports that discuss the spending and revenue implications of the legislation they anticipate recommending during the remainder of the year. These reports assist the Budget Committee in proposing the budget resolution that Congress is to adopt by April 15. However, these reports are not always specific and detailed, and the committees are not bound by them. More generally, House rules neither require not anticipate that committees will develop a formal legislative agenda for one or both sessions of a Congress. Although committee members may share an understanding of what their priorities will be, their understanding usually is not given formal expression, and their priorities may change to accommodate unexpected developments, presidential requests, scheduling difficulties, and political exigencies.

Agenda decisions in committee need not be collective decisions. Clause 2(c) of House Rule XI authorizes committee chairmen to schedule meetings "for the consideration of a bill or resolution pending before the committee or the transaction of other committee business, subject to such rules as the committee may adopt." The same rule also includes provisions by which a majority of a committee's members may require that a meeting be called for a specific purpose, even over the chairman's opposition, but there are several reasons why this procedure is very unlikely to be invoked. First, committee members prefer not to confront their chairman in such a direct and public way, knowing that his or her support can be crucial if they are to achieve their own legislative objectives. Second, the majority party members of a committee are inclined to support their chairmen on organizational and procedural questions. And third, chairmen are selected every two years by the members of the majority party in the House. Chairmen who seriously thwart the will of their committees, including members of their own party, risk provoking opposition to retaining their leadership positions at the beginning of the next Congress.

In general, then, committee chairmen exercise considerable agenda control. But in doing so, they must take account of their committee colleagues. The power of committee chairmen was limited in recent years by a series of developments that enhanced the role and autonomy of subcommittees. No longer did committee chairmen appoint subcommittee chairmen and majority party subcommittee members; beginning in the mid-1970s and continuing for the next two decades of Democratic majorities in the House, Democratic committee members elected subcommittee chairmen and chose their own subcommittee assignments. Subcommittees also gained increased control over their budgets and staff, thereby giving them greater control over their own agendas. Finally, most subcommittees came to have fixed jurisdictions and to receive measures within their jurisdictions when they were referred to the committee.

Collectively, these developments meant that subcommittee agenda decisions became more difficult for the full committee and its chairman to control. Within each subcommittee, the chairman generally came to enjoy as much or more agenda control as did the chairman of the committee in deciding its priorities and schedule. A subcommittee decision to act—to hold hearings and then to report its recommendations for legislation—usually was not directly and formally controlled by the committee, although subcommittee agendas might be coordinated informally by subcommittee and full committee leaders. Committee rules might include a procedure by which the committee, by majority vote or decision of its chairman, could consider a bill on which the subcommittee to which it was referred failed to act. However, informal negotiations and accommodations always are considered preferable to any such formal action; committee members tended to protect subcommittee prerogatives because they held or could expect to hold positions of subcommittee leadership themselves.

The Republican majority that took control of the House in 1995 strengthened the influence of party leaders and the majority party conference over committees and their chairmen, and also returned to committee chairmen some of the authority over subcommittees that they had lost during the preceding two decades. Especially during the 104th Congress, committees and their chairmen often were guided by the majority party's legislative program, and subcommittees sometimes were bypassed in order to expedite the legislative process. To some extent, committees reasserted themselves during the 105th Congress as the House returned to a more typical legislative pace, but the imposition of term limits on committee chairmen may have an important long-term impact on the influence that chairmen are able to exercise *vis- à-vis* both their committees and the House as a whole.

Notwithstanding these recent developments, committee agendas still may reflect subcommittee agendas. When a subcommittee fails to act on a bill, its parent committee may not be inclined to take it up in the absence of compelling political necessity or an externally imposed deadline (such as the approaching end of the fiscal year). Indeed, subcommittee inaction may be welcomed as a way to protect the members of the full committee from issues they prefer not to confront. On the other hand, subcommittee action may create pressure for full committee action, and the timing of subcommittee action can limit committee control over its own schedule. The relationships between committees and their subcommittees continue to be characterized by cooperation more often than by conflict. Subcommittee chairmen who set agendas that fail to meet the needs and preferences of their party colleagues, on the committee and in the House, risk losing their chairmanships at the beginning of the next Congress.

The formal process of subcommittee or committee consideration normally begins with one or more public hearings at which other Representatives, executive branch officials, and leaders of private groups and organizations comment on the legislation and the issues it addresses. Even before these hearings, the subcommittee often requests a written statement of position from the executive branch department or agency that would be responsible for implementing the bill if it were to be enacted. Based on this record, the subcommittee may conclude that no legislative action is warranted, at least at that time, and the bill is removed from the active agenda. If the subcommittee decides to proceed, its chairman schedules a "markup" meeting at which the members vote on amendments to the bill they wish to propose to the House.

When the subcommittee reports its actions to the full committee, the same process may be repeated. Additional hearings at this stage are more the exception than the rule, but major bills are likely to be marked up again by the full committee, at which time the subcommittee's proposed amendments may be approved or rejected. The committee then votes to report the bill back to the House with the recommendation that the House pass it after first adopting the amendments the committee proposes. Alternatively, the committee may report a "clean" bill that already incorporates these amendments. The reported bill is accompanied by a written report that explains the committee's actions and recommendations.

The vast majority of bills do not survive the process of selection and consideration in committee. In fact, the process of hearings and markup can be so time-consuming and the time pressures on Representatives so great that hearings usually are not even scheduled on a bill unless the subcommittee chairman and at least some of his colleagues already believe that some legislative action may be necessary.[9] Similarly, not all bills approved by subcommittees are considered by their full committees. The time available for committee meetings also is limited, and committees generally consider it wise to be selective in the number of bills they recommend to the House for passage. Furthermore, subcommittee and committee agenda decisions are influenced by what their members believe will be acceptable to their other House colleagues. The reputation and influence of a committee, and especially its leaders, within the House depend in part on the willingness of the House to accept its recommendations. With this in mind, a committee may decide not to report a bill even though a majority on the committee may favor it, or the committee may report the bill but then not press for it to be considered on the House floor.

If the committee does not report a bill, the Representatives who support it have little in the way of effective recourse. House Rule XV, clause 2, does provide a procedure by which a majority of all Representatives may sign a petition to discharge the committee from further consideration of the bill. If sufficient signatures are obtained, the House votes on whether to discharge the committee and then on whether it wishes to consider the bill. This procedure rarely has been invoked successfully, though the prospect of being discharged sometimes may have provoked committees to act when they might not otherwise have done so. Some Representatives have been reluctant to sign discharge petitions even though they supported the bill at issue, arguing that the discharge procedure undermines the established prerogatives of committees generally and, implicitly, that a pattern of successful discharge efforts could ultimately jeopardize the prerogatives of their own committees. The House amended its rules in 1993 to make public for the first time the names of Members who sign discharge petitions. This was done in the expectation that it would become somewhat easier to attract the 218 signatures that a successful discharge petition requires.[10]

---

[9] On the other hand, a subcommittee or committee may hold hearings with no expectation of recommending legislation—for example, as a way of ventilating the issue, giving the bill's proponents an opportunity to be heard, or laying the groundwork for action at some later time.

[10] Another alternative that Representatives may pursue is to encourage the Senate to take the legislative initiative, in the hope of prompting House committee action or with the possibility of bypassing the recalcitrant House committee altogether. Also, the Rules Committee may report a resolution providing for floor consideration of a bill that has not yet been reported by

(continued...)

In light of the powerful veto that committees can and do exercise, proponents of legislation attempt to influence committee and subcommittee agendas. The President as well as private individuals and groups may lobby for committee action, both by arguing the merits of their case and by demonstrating the breadth and intensity of support for the bill they endorse. The bill's supporters in Congress may attempt to persuade their colleagues on the committee and demonstrate support for the bill within the House by such methods as seeking co-sponsors for the bill from a broad cross-section of the House and especially from influential Representatives—including, if possible, members of the committee itself. In some cases, the goal of such efforts is not to transform opponents into proponents, but instead to increase the visibility of a bill that otherwise might simply be lost in the press of other business. On the other hand, opponents can be equally successful in stressing the political and policy disadvantages of the bill, and in encouraging their allies on the committee to prolong the process of committee consideration, in the hope that the bill will be removed eventually from the committee's agenda in favor of more pressing and less controversial matters. By and large, the advantage normally rests with the opponents of legislative action.

Rules, Special Rules, and the Floor Agenda

When a House committee reports a bill—*i.e.*, when it returns the bill to the control of the full House with a recommendation that the bill be passed, with or without amendments—the bill normally is referred to one of two calendars. According to clause 1 of Rule XIII, authorization, appropriations, and tax bills are placed on the Union Calendar; other public bills appear on the House Calendar. The two calendars taken together may be thought of as a catalogue of bills that have survived committee scrutiny and are now available for consideration on the floor by the full House. If the bills that are introduced can be said to constitute a *possible* agenda for the House, the bills on these two calendars constitute a *potential* floor agenda.[11] Each reported bill has been studied and found worthy by the House's designated committee experts. At this stage, the agenda problem for the House becomes one of transforming this potential agenda into a *prospective* agenda of bills on which floor action is expected in the near term, and finally, into the *actual* agenda or schedule for the daily conduct of business.

The various legislative committees of the House can consider bills simultaneously, but the bills they report must be taken up on the House floor one at a time. Some bills on the calendar die at the end of each Congress for lack of time for floor consideration, so a selection process is unavoidable. A mechanical answer would be to call bills to the floor in the order in which they appear on the calendars,

---

[10](...continued)
the committee with jurisdiction over it. However, the Rules Committee rarely invokes this power of "extraction" over the intense opposition of another committee.

[11] Minor and emergency bills are the only ones that often reach the House floor without prior committee action. If a bill has been referred to committee, the House may not consider it until the committee reports it or is discharged from further consideration of the bill. The committee may be discharged by unanimous consent when possible or through the more elaborate procedures of Rule XV when necessary.

which is the order in which they are reported from committee. However, this procedure would not permit necessary differentiations between the critical and the insignificant, nor would it ensure timely action on bills that confront deadlines such as the beginning of the new fiscal year for appropriations bills. Some more discriminating procedure is required.

At one extreme, agenda decisions could be delegated to a single leader, and between roughly 1890 and 1910, it could be argued without much exaggeration that the Speaker enjoyed such power as the elected leader of the majority party. But this is no longer the case. At the other extreme, decisions affecting the floor agenda could require the unanimous concurrence of all Members; in daily practice, the Senate's rules encourage reliance on procedures that approach this limit. Generally speaking, the rules of the House seek the middle ground of majority control. Although the specific procedures to be discussed are varied and rather complicated, they are permeated by a single principle: when the votes of a simple numerical majority are sufficient to pass a bill, the decision to consider it also can be controlled by the same majority.

Privileged Business Under House Rules.

The rules of the House provide for arranging the floor agenda by applying the concept of "privileged" business. In brief, a bill that is privileged may be called up for consideration on the floor out of its order on the House or Union Calendar. To put it somewhat differently, privileged business may interrupt the daily order of business that is listed in the House's rules. In fact, this order of business under clause 1 of Rule XIV is never followed, save for the routine proceedings at the beginning of each day's session. Virtually all legislative business that is transacted on the House floor is an interruption of the regular order of business and is privileged by virtue of House rules, by vote of the House, or by unanimous consent. In practice, a bill that does not gain privilege by one of these means cannot be considered on the floor; a motion to consider it may not interrupt the regular order of business and, therefore, is not in order. Thus, House rules affect the floor agenda by designating certain classes of bills as privileged and by establishing procedures by which other bills become privileged.

General Privilege.

The rules grant privilege to bills and resolutions on certain subjects and for certain purposes, but only if those measures have been reported by the appropriate committees. Under clause 5(a) of Rule XIII, for example, privilege extends to general appropriations bills, to budget resolutions and budget reconciliation bills, and to House resolutions concerning changes in House rules, the conduct of Representatives and House employees, election challenges affecting Representatives, and certain expenditures for House operations. These matters generally concern either the integrity and proceedings of the House itself or the performance of what is usually considered to be the core constitutional power of Congress—the "power of the purse."

It is in order for the committee that has reported one of these privileged bills or resolutions to call it up for action on the floor at any time that another matter is not already under consideration. However, a variety of other matters also are privileged, including conference reports on legislative disagreements between the House and Senate, certain Senate amendments to House bills, and bills that the President has vetoed. Furthermore, House rules do not establish a fixed and certain order of precedence among all privileged matters; if each of two Representatives wishes to call up a privileged bill or other matter, the rules do not always determine which of them is to be recognized first. The effect of this situation is to leave some important discretion to the Speaker in arranging a specific order of business from among the various matters that enjoy privileged access to the House floor.

Putting the exercise of this discretion aside for the moment, the grant of general privilege by House rules has the effect of moving privileged bills from the potential agenda of bills on the Union and House Calendars to the prospective agenda of bills that can be expected to come to the floor in the near future.[12] But the rules do not require that privileged bills be considered, though they usually are. By one means or another, a numerical majority on the floor usually has an opportunity to vote to block consideration of a bill, thereby avoiding the need to vote for or against it on its merits. Such a vote is rarely necessary, however, because even privileged bills are not called up for floor action unless there is good reason to expect that the House is prepared to pass them. For these bills, unlike bills that are not privileged, the question affecting their fate usually becomes when, not whether, they will be considered on the floor.

Among the legislative measures that can become law, general appropriations measures and budget reconciliation bills are the only ones that frequently reach the floor by virtue of their general privilege under House rules. The rules do not grant such favored status to most bills. Instead, the rules include a number of devices by which the vast majority of non-privileged bills that the House considers are made in order. In the case of general appropriations bills and the other matters that are generally privileged, the House has determined over the years that privilege should extend to them as a class—because of their subjects and without regard to their specific provisions. Two additional devices to be discussed also are designed to facilitate floor action on certain limited classes of legislation—private bills and bills affecting the District of Columbia. There are five other devices by which bills are moved from the potential to the prospective agenda on a case-by-case basis, because of their individual merits and circumstances, not because of the general nature of the subjects they address.

These seven devices may be summarized as follows:

1. motions to discharge House committees from further consideration of bills they have not reported, making discharged bills eligible for floor consideration;

---

[12] House rules generally require that the written committee report on a bill, even a privileged bill, be available for three days before the bill may be considered on the floor. This delay permits time for Representatives and their staffs to become familiar with the committee's recommendations before they are debated.

2. procedures known as Calendar Wednesday, by which committees may call up nonprivileged bills they have reported but which have not reached the House floor by more conventional routes;

3. special procedures for considering bills concerning the District of Columbia;

4. procedures for the call of a special calendar of private bills affecting specific individuals or entities;

5. procedures for the call of the "Corrections Calendar" for bills that enjoy widespread support in the House;

6. procedures known as suspension of the rules for expeditious consideration of relatively noncontroversial bills; and

7. special rules adopted by the House, at the recommendation of its Rules Committee, that provide for consideration of individual, nonprivileged, bills.

These devices are not equally important, nor are they employed with equal frequency. Some are well-suited to relatively minor bills; others are used to consider more controversial bills. In a sense, the first six of these procedures are alternatives to the seventh, which usually is the most complicated and time-consuming, because it is through the Rules Committee that the most important nonprivileged bills usually reach the floor. The six alternative devices are generally used (if used at all) to deal with bills that are either routine or extraordinary, and they will be discussed first.

Special Days for Privileged Action.

House rules designate specific days of each week and month for transacting certain kinds of legislative business. The effect of these rules is to make the appropriate kinds of bills privileged for consideration on the designated days. Of the six rules with this effect, two are designed to protect the House against its own committees.

First, the second and fourth Mondays of each month are set aside for voting on motions by which a majority of Representatives can discharge a committee from further consideration of a measure that it has not reported (clause 2 of Rule XV). If the House votes to discharge, a motion to consider the measure at issue then is privileged.

Second, each Wednesday is available to committees that want the House to consider bills they have reported that have not otherwise become privileged for floor consideration. This procedure, known as Calendar Wednesday, usually is dispensed with each week by unanimous consent; the House also may dispense with Calendar Wednesday by a two-thirds vote (clause 7 of Rule XV.)

These two devices are designed to respond to unusual circumstances, and they are rarely used; but they are preserved in the rules as means by which a voting majority on the floor can retain control of its own agenda. Through a discharge motion, that majority can overcome the powerful negative influence of the standing committees over the potential floor agenda. The majority can propose to bring a bill directly and immediately to the floor over the opposition or disinterest of the committee of jurisdiction. Through Calendar Wednesday, the committee that has reported a bill can overcome the purported inaction or indifference of the Rules Committee or the majority party leadership (the implications of which are discussed below) if the full House is prepared to consider the bill. Any committee may use this procedure to propose one of its nonprivileged bills for floor consideration, but the House retains the authority to vote against considering it.

The other four devices are used to transact business that is far more routine; consequently, they are invoked more frequently. First, the first and third Tuesdays are set aside for the consideration of private bills—usually minor bills that affect only one individual or entity (clause 5 of Rule XV)—if any such bills have been reported and are awaiting floor action. On the designated days, each bill on the Private Calendar is called up and passed almost immediately—usually without any debate or amendments—but only if there is virtually no opposition to its passage. Second, the second and fourth Mondays are designated not only for considering discharge motions but also for considering bills concerning the District of Columbia—a subject of lower priority to most Representatives (clause 4 of Rule XV). Although only a majority vote is necessary to pass District bills, they usually require and consume less time on the floor than would be required in most cases if they were to be considered through more conventional procedures.

In short, by designating days for District of Columbia business and for the call of the Private Calendar, House rules set aside predictable and convenient opportunities for the House to act expeditiously on bills that are generally routine and non-controversial.

Third, on every Monday and every Tuesday, the Speaker may recognize Representatives to move to suspend the rules and pass a particular bill that usually is, but need not be, on the Union or House Calendar. When this motion is made, a special set of procedures is triggered by which the bill is debated for no more than 40 minutes, with no floor amendments to it in order, before a single vote occurs on suspending the rules and passing the bill. But to pass a bill under suspension of the rules requires a two-thirds vote (clause 1 of Rule XV).[13] Bills considered in this way are not expected to pass without opposition, but they are expected to enjoy such overwhelming support that there is no need to devote more than 40 minutes to each of them.

---

[13] A quorum (a simple majority of the Representatives actually serving) is supposed to participate in every vote. Thus, the minimal number of votes needed to pass a bill under suspension of the rules without violating this quorum requirement is 146 (two-thirds of a quorum of 218, assuming there are no vacancies in the House membership). However, a vote in which a quorum does not participate is considered conclusive unless a Representative makes a point of order that the quorum requirement was not met.

Finally, in 1995 the House created a new Corrections Calendar and fixed the procedure for considering bills placed on it (clause 6 of Rule XV). After a committee has reported a bill and it has been entered on the Union or House Calendar, the Speaker has the authority to have it placed also on the Corrections Calendar. On the second and fourth Tuesdays of each month, the Speaker may decide that the House will consider each bill that has been on this special calendar for at least three days. As each bill is called up, it is debatable for only one hour and it cannot be amended except for amendments proposed by the committee that reported it or by the committee's chairman (and one amendment included in a motion to recommit with instructions). Like suspension of the rules, the Corrections Calendar procedure limits Members' opportunities to debate and propose amendments. Also like the suspension procedure, therefore, the Corrections Calendar rules require more than a simple majority vote to pass a bill in this way. Instead of a two-thirds vote, however, a three-fifths vote is needed to pass a bill called up from the Corrections Calendar.

The six procedures just summarized merit several additional comments. First, three of these procedures—District of Columbia day, discharge motions, and Calendar Wednesday—each provide for a bill to be passed by simple majority vote, and in each case, the same majority can vote not to consider the bill. The House can defeat the discharge motion or it can vote against considering a bill called up on District day or on Calendar Wednesday. The question of consideration rarely is raised, but it remains available as a protection for the majority against being compelled to vote on a bill it does not wish to consider. The three procedures provide opportunities for committees or for a majority of Representatives (through a discharge petition) to propose bills for the House to consider, but it remains for the House to decide whether it will do so. These are majority vote procedures, and the majority retains ultimate control in deciding what bills to consider under them.

In the case of the Private Calendar, objections by only a few Members are sufficient to prevent bills from being considered. Under these procedures, therefore, the question of majority control of the floor agenda does not arise because consensus is required before a bill on this special calendar can be debated, much less passed. On the other hand, when a Representative moves to suspend the rules and pass a bill, that bill is immediately before the House for debate and disposition. There usually is no way that a majority can vote not to consider the motion and the bill.[14] Similarly, the Speaker is empowered to present a committee-reported bill from the Corrections Calendar for the House to consider. For a bill to pass under either procedure, however, more than a bare majority of the Representatives voting must support it. The majority loses a certain degree of agenda control, but only under conditions that require an extraordinary majority for passage. And a bill that fails to pass under any one of these three procedures may be considered on the floor again—this time under more elaborate procedures, permitting amendments and lengthier debate in Committee of the Whole, that require only a simply majority vote for passage.

---

[14] When the House amended its rules during the 1970s to minimize time-consuming procedural votes, it virtually eliminated a device by which Representatives had been able to demand a vote that had the effect of determining whether the House would consider a motion to suspend the rules and pass a particular bill.

Second, only four of the six procedures are used with any frequency—the discharge and Calendar Wednesday procedures are rarely attempted and less often successful—and these four are expediting procedures. Through them, House rules reserve regular and predictable occasions for disposing of business that is not especially contentious. District and private bills usually are noncontroversial because of the subjects with which they deal. Bills considered under the suspension and Corrections Calendar procedures are not expected to be very divisive because their proponents know that unusually high levels of support are necessary to pass them by either means. And it is usually pointless, and even self-defeating, for proponents of a bill to force it to a vote without reasonable prospects for success. Because of the nature and use of these procedures, therefore, they are not likely to provoke serious and recurring concerns about agenda control.[15]

Third, the availability of these expediting procedures affects the House floor agenda in another important respect. They relieve some of the pressure on the agenda by making it possible for the House to act on more bills than would be possible if the same, more elaborate, and time-consuming procedures were followed in every instance. While the fate of a bill obviously depends on *whether* it reaches the floor, its prospects also can be affected by *when* it reaches the floor. For example, a bill that the House passes during the first session of a Congress may have better prospects for ultimate enactment than one passed shortly before final adjournment, because there is ample time remaining for the Senate to act as well and for the two chambers to reach agreement. Thus, decisions to give priority to considering certain bills can damage the prospects of others that are not so favored.

In this respect, the suspension of the rules procedure has become particularly and increasingly important. In fact, as many as half of all the bills the House passed during some recent Congresses were considered in this way. Amendments to the House rules in 1973 and 1977 resulted in a four-fold increase in opportunities to offer suspension motions. Whereas such motions had been in order on every other Monday, they now can be made on any Monday or Tuesday that the House is in session. These rules changes recognized the utility of the suspension procedure as a way for the House to act quickly on the large number of measures that most Representatives are prepared to pass in the form recommended by their committees. Consequently, more time is available for prompt consideration of more bills that require more extended consideration. So in a sense, the use of the suspension procedure requires the majority to sacrifice a certain degree of agenda control over bills that matter less in return for greater agenda control over bills that matter more.

In summary, House rules designate certain days for certain purposes—either to allow opportunities for the majority to protect itself against inaction by its committees or leaders (discharge motions and Calendar Wednesday), or to facilitate the conduct of relatively routine business in a convenient and expeditious manner (the Corrections and Private Calendars and the District and suspension procedures). The first two procedures permit affirmative agenda control by a determined majority which can use

---

[15] From time to time, some Representatives have opposed passage of a bill under suspension of the rules on the grounds that the bill requires amendments and more extended debate, or that it combines elements that deserve separate consideration instead.

them to compel floor action, but these procedures cannot be used to compel such a majority to vote on a bill it does not wish to consider. Two of the other four procedures involve bills that usually evoke little if any controversy over their merits and, therefore, over the advisability of considering them (and in case of controversy over a District bill, the majority may vote not to consider it). The Corrections Calendar and suspension of the rules procedures, on the other hand, are used for bills that can evoke some opposition, and they are inconsistent with majority control of the agenda because a majority usually cannot prevent a bill from being considered in either way. However, both procedures are controlled by the majority party's leader and both require more than a simple majority vote for passage.

Special Rules Affecting the Order of Business.

The procedures discussed to this point are not applicable to most of the major bills that House committees report each Congress. These bills are not generally privileged under House rules, nor are they supported by large enough majorities to be passed under an expediting procedure such as suspension of the rules. Thus, these procedures are not sufficient to fully resolve the problem of transforming the large potential agenda of reported bills into the smaller prospective agenda of bills that are likely to reach the floor.

For this purpose, the House also has looked for the past century to one of its committees, the Committee on Rules. Like the other standing committees, the Rules Committee has jurisdiction over a class of measures, primarily bills and resolutions affecting House rules. But this committee also is authorized by clause 1(m) of Rule XI to report House resolutions that, if adopted by the House, affect the order of business on the floor. These resolutions, which also are known as rules or special rules, are privileged and so may be considered by the House at any time that another matter is not already pending. Because of both their provisions and their privilege, special rules constitute the critical link between most major legislation on the House and Union Calendars and the House's actual floor agenda.

A special rule usually begins by providing that, upon adoption of the resolution, the Speaker may declare the House resolved into the Committee of the Whole House on the State of the Union for the consideration of a particular bill designated by the resolution. (The nature of the Committee of the Whole and some of the other provisions of special rules are discussed later in this report.) In the absence of this provision, the Speaker would have no such authority because the bill at issue presumably is not privileged and, therefore, the regular order of business could not be interrupted to consider it in Committee of the Whole (except by unanimous consent). Adoption of the special rule concerning a bill has the effect of making the bill itself in order for consideration.[16]

Once the Rules Committee reports a special rule, it remains for the House to decide by majority vote whether to accept it or reject it. The special rule itself is debated for as much as an hour and it may even be amended, although with difficulty.

---

[16] Different forms of special rules are reported for other purposes, such as waiving points of order against conference reports.

The Rules Committee proposes moving individual bills from the potential floor agenda to the prospective agenda, but the House is not bound to accept these recommendations. The voting majority on the floor retains negative agenda control. The House usually cannot avoid considering a Rules Committee proposal but the majority may reject it (although this does not happen very often for reasons that will be discussed).

The Rules Committee also can exercise a certain degree of negative agenda control. The authority of the committee is not restricted to recommending the order in which the House should consider the bills reported by the other House committees. The Rules Committee also has the option of not acting—of declining to report the special rule that a bill may require if it is to reach the floor. The committee has often been characterized as a "traffic cop," regulating and directing the flow of legislative traffic to the floor. This metaphor is apt in some respects, but it also has one serious deficiency. The traffic cop decides *when* a car may pass, but not *whether* it may pass if its driver is obeying the "rules of the road." By contrast, the Rules Committee is not obliged to allow all bills to come to the floor; it may decide instead that individual bills do not merit floor consideration at all. If the committee fails to report a special rule for a bill, or fails to act promptly, the prospects for that bill becoming law fall precipitously.

The committee that reported the bill may resort to the Calendar Wednesday procedure, but Calendar Wednesday rarely is invoked in part because it is not difficult to prevent passage of a bill that is brought to the floor in this way. Alternatively, the bill's proponents may attempt to discharge the committee from further consideration of a special rule that would make the bill in order, but discharge petitions rarely have been successful. Thus, since much of the legislative activity in the House focuses on bills that are not privileged and that are too controversial to pass under suspension of the rules (with limited debate, no floor amendments, and a two-thirds vote required for passage) or by call of the Corrections Calendar, the position of the Rules Committee in arranging the floor agenda is absolutely pivotal.

In view of the importance of its decisions, how the Rules Committee makes these decisions requires attention. When one of the other committees reports a bill that does not enjoy enough support to pass under suspension of the rules of by use of the Corrections Calendar, the committee's chairman requests a hearing before the Rules Committee. If the committee obliges (and it need not do so), Representatives appear before it to speak for or against the bill. During the hearing, Rules Committee members may inquire into the merits of the legislation as well as into when and how it should be considered on the floor. The committee then decides, by majority vote, whether to grant a rule and, if so, what its provisions should be. Like any other committee, the Rules Committee bases its decisions on the views of its own members and on their perceptions of what a majority of the House is prepared to support. But in the contemporary House, the actions of this committee also have been shaped by its unique relationship with the House's majority party leadership.

Today this relationship is cooperative, but it has not always been so. In fact, the changes in this relationship during the 20th century have been at the heart of some of the most important developments that have taken place within the House.[17] At the beginning of this century, the Speaker also served as chairman of the Rules Committee and appointed its other members (as well as the chairmen and members of all other committees). Consequently, he and his allies controlled the committee and its decisions, and the flow of legislation to the floor. If the Speaker did not look with favor on a bill, it was all but certain to perish from Rules Committee inaction. The Calendar Wednesday procedure was adopted in 1909 to assuage critics of the Speaker's power; nevertheless, he soon was stripped of his chairmanship and appointment powers. This was truly a historic moment for the House, because the result was a fundamental redistribution of power from the Speaker and the majority party leadership to the standing committees and their chairmen.

The seniority system became the basis for much of the power of House committees and especially their chairmen. In search of a stable alternative to appointments by the Speaker, the House came to rely more and more on the length of continuous committee service by majority party Representatives as the criterion for selecting chairmen. Once appointed to committees, Representatives usually could remain on them as long as they wished and as long as they were members of the House. If they were members of the majority party, they could eventually expect to become chairman if they remained on their committees longer than any of their party colleagues. As a result, the seniority system tended to insulate committees from the short-term influence of elections as well as from the efforts of party leaders to draw their members together in support of a party program for legislation. And nowhere were the consequences of seniority more pronounced than on the Rules Committee.

Although the Democrats were the majority party in the House for all but four years between the mid-1930s and 1960, the Rules Committee could be dominated during most of that period by a coalition of Republicans and conservative Democrats. Although the Democrats enjoyed a nominal majority on the committee, their control over committee decisions was far from certain. The chairman of the Rules Committee during much of the 1950s has been credited with being one of the driving forces behind a bipartisan "conservative coalition" that could stymie the Democratic majority by refusing to report special rules. If this report had been written 40 years ago, it could very well have concluded that effective agenda control rested in the hands of this coalition, when it chose to exercise it, over which the leaders of the majority party had no real control and only uncertain influence.

This situation began to change in 1961 when the House voted narrowly to increase the size of the Rules Committee, giving the Democrats a tenuous one-vote majority on which it could rely more often than not. In 1975, the Democratic majority in the House changed its party rules to tie the Rules Committee more firmly to the party majority acting through its leader, the Speaker. Whereas a party committee nominated new members to other committees, subject to approval by all the Democrats meeting in a caucus, it was the Speaker who nominated the Democratic members of the Rules Committee. Because there now were more than

---

[17] On the history of the Rules Committee, see U.S. Congress. House of Representatives. Committee on Rules. *A History of the Committee on Rules*. Committee Print. 97th Congress, 2d Session (1983).

twice as many Democrats as Republicans on the committee, the effect of these changes was to transform the relationship between the committee and the majority party. With rare exceptions, the Rules Committee became allied with the Speaker and the other majority party leaders. Although the Speaker could not dictate committee decisions, he and the committee's Democratic members tended to share the same policy goals and a common desire to use the committee's powers to promote them.

Now that the utility of these arrangements has become well-established, they are likely to be preserved, no matter which party holds a majority of seats in the House. Rule 12B of the House Republican Conference for the 105th Congress authorizes the Speaker to nominate the chairman and other Republican members of the Rules Committee, subject to approval by the Republican Conference. Should the conference reject one of these nominations, the Speaker is to make another one. In other words, the Republican Speaker, like his Democratic predecessors, can ensure that a working majority of the committee will be responsive to the party leadership's priorities and to its short-term agenda preferences and strategic interests.

From the perspective of this report, these developments were critical because of their implications for majority control of the floor agenda. The majority party leadership selects more than a majority of the members of the Rules Committee, who in turn make decisions that meet the needs and interests of their party colleagues who can constitute a working majority on the floor.

The Rules Committee provides an excellent vantage point from which to look again at the implications for agenda-setting in the House of the organization of national parties generally and in Congress specifically. The House has relied heavily on the seniority system for allocating committee chairmanships in part because doing so has avoided the possibility of factional conflicts within the majority party. The Speaker lost his authority to appoint and reappoint majority party members to committees when a significant faction within his own party rebelled and joined forces with the minority party. The presumption that a Representative who serves on a committee may remain on that committee protects the interests of Members individually against the preferences of their party collectively.

This arrangement would not be as acceptable if there were consistently a coherent party position that Representatives were expected to support. But it has been acceptable in the House where party positions often have tended to emerge, if at all, from a weighing of what most party members in the House are willing to support, as they calculate their own electoral interests and as they evaluate national interests and balance them against constituency interests. When majority party unity is particularly strong, Members may delegate to its leaders more *de facto* authority over the selection of committee chairmen, even in violation of the seniority norm, and over appointments to fill committee vacancies. When unity is weaker, majority party leaders are likely to exercise less unilateral control over these decisions.

Changing the relationship between the Rules Committee and the majority party's leaders in the House narrowed the gap between agenda control by majority vote and agenda control by the majority party. Because members of the committee now are effectively chosen by the party leadership, their interests and decisions are likely to coincide, more often than not, with the preferences of most of their party colleagues.

When there is significant opposition on the floor to a special rule, the House tends to divide along party lines, and the outcome usually turns on the number of Members from each party who vote with most of the Members from the other.

In sum, the Rules Committee is the key instrument through which the House makes its agenda decisions affecting most major bills. Without a special rule from the committee, a bill that is not privileged cannot reach the floor for passage by majority vote (except through the rarely successful discharge and Calendar Wednesday procedures). The House accepts or rejects the committee's recommendations by majority vote, and thereby retains the power to refuse a bill a place on the floor agenda. Changes in the committee's membership and the procedures for selecting its members have made the committee more regularly and predictably responsive to the agenda preferences of the majority party, whether Republican or Democrat. The committee always has been reluctant to propose a bill for the floor agenda that a majority might oppose. In the House today, the committee also is reluctant to refuse a special rule for a bill when support for it centers in the majority party. Such a bill still may not reach the floor until the committee and party leaders can assemble the majority vote needed to pass it. But, the Rules Committee has become an ally of, not a potential obstacle to, control of the floor agenda by the majority party.

The Floor Agenda and the Daily Order of Business

The floor agenda of the House is governed by the application of standing rules and the adoption of special rules. Through these two types of rules, a prospective agenda of bills that probably will reach the floor is created from the potential floor agenda of bills that have been reported from committee and placed on one of the two primary calendars. Important as these rules are, however, they are not sufficient to define and control the daily order of business.[18]

House rules provide that a motion to suspend the rules and pass a bill is usually in order only on a Monday or Tuesday; but the rules do not control whether or when a particular bill is to be considered under this procedure. A privileged bill may be called up on the floor at the direction of the committee that reported it whenever there is no other matter pending. But various types of bills are privileged, as are a number of other matters, and House rules do not establish a firm order of priority among all of them. Other bills may not be debated and passed by majority vote until after the House adopts special rules for their consideration. But a special rule usually does not require that the bill it makes in order must be considered immediately after the House adopts the rule. So standing and special rules may create an agenda of bills with special claims on the attention of the House, but these rules generally do not determine the order in which the bills are considered. Additional procedures and authorities are required to transform the prospective agenda into the daily order of business—in other words, to develop an actual schedule for considering legislation on the floor.

---

[18] As noted earlier, House rules do designate certain days for considering bills on the Corrections and Private Calendars and bills concerning the District of Columbia.

During a 1983 debate, Speaker Thomas P. O'Neill Jr. declared that "[t]he power of the Speaker of the House is the power of scheduling."[19] In political terms, he exercises this power as the elected leader of the majority party; his scheduling decisions take account of the strategic interests and prevailing sentiments of his majority party colleagues. In procedural terms, his control over scheduling flows from certain provisions of House rules and generally from his responsibilities as the presiding officer of the House. In this capacity, he enjoys considerable discretion, but a discretion that is far from being unlimited, in recognizing Representatives to speak or to bring legislative business before the House for consideration.

The suspension of the rules procedure restricts the rights and powers of most Representatives by limiting debate and precluding amendments to bills that are considered in this way. On the other hand, it enhances the power of the Speaker. Suspension motions are in order on Mondays and Tuesdays, but Representatives do not have a right under House rules to make such motions. The Speaker has the discretion to decide whether to permit a bill to be considered in this way. If a committee or subcommittee chairman wants to bring a bill to the floor "under suspension," he or she must seek the consent of the Speaker; if a chairman sought to use the procedure without the Speaker's prior approval, the Speaker simply would refuse to recognize him or her for that purpose.

The Speaker's control over the suspension procedure usually does not provoke controversy. The procedure is attractive to committee chairmen because it protects their bills from amendments. It is equally attractive to the Speaker because it conserves time and, therefore, creates greater flexibility for scheduling more controversial bills. Also, bills considered in this way usually enjoy substantial bipartisan support because a two-thirds vote is required for passage. When controversy does arise, however, there usually is no way for a majority of the House to avoid debating and voting on a suspension motion (and, therefore, a bill) that it would prefer not to consider, at least under such procedural restraints. Both the Speaker and the committee chairmen are constrained in using the suspension procedure by a shared desire to avoid floor defeats, but the opportunity to limit debate on a bill, and especially to protect it against damaging amendments, can sometimes make the risk worthwhile.

The procedures governing bills on the Corrections Calendar also limit Members' opportunities to debate and offer amendments while requiring a three-fifths vote for final passage, and the Speaker exercises comparable control over the use of this calendar. Only the Speaker may place a bill on the Corrections Calendar after a committee has reported it favorably. And the Speaker has the discretion to decide whether bills that he has had placed on this special calendar actually should be called up for the House's consideration on the days the rules set aside for that purpose.

With respect to bills considered under special rules (or as generally privileged matters), the Speaker's powers are less direct and conclusive, but he and his party leadership colleagues still are primarily responsible for scheduling floor action on special rules and the bills they make in order. On matters of significant party interest,

---

[19] *Congressional Record* (daily edition), v. 129, no. 158, November 15, 1983. p. H9856.

the majority party members of the Rules Committee normally act in concert with their party leaders in deciding whether to hold hearings and grant rules and when to do so. On the infrequent occasions when another committee reports a bill that is unacceptable to the majority party leadership, the Rules Committee may decline to consider it, at least until some accommodation can be reached. Similarly, when two or more committees make conflicting proposals on the same subject, the committee can withhold action and urge the committee and subcommittee chairmen to seek common ground. In short, the Rules Committee as "traffic cop" can be expected to direct legislative traffic in the direction of, and at a speed consistent with, goals sought by the majority party leaders on behalf of their party colleagues.

Once the Rules Committee reports a special rule, it is privileged for floor consideration, as is any bill made in order by the standing rules or by a special rule the House already has adopted. However, the Speaker retains an important degree of discretion in arranging these matters into a daily and weekly schedule that meets the responsibilities of the House and the interests of his party. As noted earlier, a variety of bills and other matters are privileged for floor consideration. In some cases, they are of equal privilege. Thus, the Speaker may exercise discretion in deciding the order in which they are to be considered. If one Representative seeks to call up a privileged matter, the Speaker may decline to recognize him or her if there is another Representative on the floor who can be recognized instead to bring up some other matter that is at least equally privileged (and who, therefore, has an equal right to be recognized).

It is rarely necessary, however, for the Speaker to actually use his control over recognition on the floor to control the flow of legislative business. Scheduling decisions generally are made within the majority party through consultations by the Speaker and other party leaders with the appropriate committee and subcommittee leaders. A probable schedule for the week then is announced on the floor by a majority party spokesman. Representatives of the minority party also may be consulted. They may inquire about the status of certain bills, and they may complain that some bills are being held back while others are being propelled to the floor prematurely. But the minority has little effective recourse, other than to attempt to defeat the special rules providing for consideration of the bills they oppose.

By the time the House convenes each day, Representatives have been advised of the expected order of business, although it is always subject to change. When the House completes action on one bill, the Speaker knows which Representative should be the next to seek recognition. If another Member seeks recognition instead and the Speaker is unsure of his purpose, the Speaker may ask: "For what purpose does the gentleman rise?" If the response is not satisfactory, he may decline to recognize that Representative if there is an equally privileged matter available for consideration. Of course, the Speaker does not exercise this authority arbitrarily and for his own purposes; instead, he uses his powers as the presiding officer of the House to advance whatever legislative program he and his fellow party leaders construct from among the measures reported by the House's committees and the sometimes disparate interests and preferences of his party colleagues.

Thus, the arrangement of an agenda of privileged bills and other matters into a daily and weekly schedule for the order of business is a responsibility (and opportunity) for the majority party leadership—one that is usually exercised formally by the Speaker, but only after consultation with other party leaders, the party's members of the Rules Committee, and appropriate committee and subcommittee chairmen. The leverage over legislative decisions that flows from this influence over scheduling derives, to a considerable extent, from the tactical importance of timing for legislative success.

When party unity is strong and predictable, and defections are few, timing may be less significant unless the majority party's margin of votes is very narrow. In the House of Representatives, on the other hand, where majority coalitions are not always equivalent to party majorities and where substantial components of majority coalitions may have to be assembled vote by vote, timing can become critical. Sometimes, for example, floor action must be expedited before a bill's opponents and their allies outside of Congress can organize and bring the full weight of their influence to bear. At other times, critical floor votes must be delayed—sometimes for only a day, but sometimes for weeks or longer—while a few more Representatives are being convinced or cajoled. When a vote is expected to be particularly close, the decision to hold back or push ahead may even turn on the number of Representatives absent that day and how their absence will affect the outcome. Their control over the daily schedule allows majority party leaders to reap the marginal but sometimes decisive advantage that comes with determining not only what issues will be considered, but when critical votes will take place.

There are limits, to be sure, on the discretion that the Speaker, other majority party leaders, and the Rules Committee can exercise in constructing the House's legislative schedule and its daily order of business. The President, the media, and interest groups can press for prompt action, which the party in control of the House ignores at its political peril. Events over which the House has no direct control can force a re-shuffling of priorities and provoke legislative responses that the majority party might otherwise approach more slowly and cautiously. In addition, requirements for annual legislative action and deadlines such as the end of the fiscal year combine to load the floor agenda with bills (such as appropriations bills) that should or must be considered, and to dictate when at least some of those bills (such as continuing resolutions) must occupy the attention of the House.

Equally important, the Speaker and his colleagues in the majority party leadership must be ever alert to what can pass and what cannot. Like House committees, the reputations of House leaders rest in large part on their records of past successes and failures. On occasion, the Speaker and the Rules Committee have allowed controversial bills to reach the floor even while doubting that the votes could be found to pass them. But there usually is little to be gained from failure.

Amendments and the Floor Agenda

To this point, the discussion has focused on the agenda of measures that reach the House floor. However, the agenda problem may be posed not only in terms of bills and resolutions but also in terms of policy issues or choices. Looking at the problem from this perspective, the important question becomes whether a policy option can reach the floor for debate and decision. That option may be embodied in a bill, but it also may be presented as an amendment to a bill. Thus, the rules and practices of the House governing the amendments that Representatives may offer on the floor also affect the floor agenda by creating opportunities for, and imposing limitations on, expanding the agenda of policy decisions that the House may make.

As a general rule, any Representative may offer amendments to a bill while it is being considered on the House floor. However, there is a critically important limitation on the contents and subjects of these amendments. In addition, House rules prohibit amendments under some circumstances and make them difficult to propose under others. Finally, Representatives can and sometimes do vote to impose restrictions on their rights to offer amendments during consideration of specific bills.

The most important limitation that House rules impose on amendments is the germaneness requirement; clause 7 of Rule XVI requires that any amendment to a bill must be germane to that bill. The concept of germaneness is related to the concepts of relevance and pertinence, but it is generally narrower in application. For example, an amendment to change individual income tax rates would not be germane to every bill affecting federal tax laws, and it may not even be germane to a bill dealing with other aspects of the income tax. When an amendment is challenged on the grounds that it is not germane, the Representative presiding over the House often bases his ruling on rather fine distinctions that derive from a large and complex body of earlier rulings.[20] It is neither possible nor necessary to summarize these precedents here, but the principle underlying the germaneness requirement is simple. While the House is considering a bill on one subject, it should not be distracted by amendments on other subjects. Although the application of this principle to specific amendments is far more complicated, what is most important for present purposes is that the requirement exists and usually is enforced. Consequently, it can severely restrict (if not foreclose altogether) Representatives' opportunities to present policy questions and options on the floor that are not reflected in the bills the House considers.

Another general restriction on amendments is related to the special nature and standing of most appropriations bills. The basic theory underlying House rules governing these bills is that they are intended to fund departments and agencies that already have been established, as well as programs and activities that already have been approved, in authorizing legislation. Therefore, clause 2 of House Rule XXI prohibits amendments to (and provisions in) general appropriations bills that would appropriate funds for purposes that have not been authorized by law or that would change the existing laws governing how the appropriated funds may be used. Under some circumstances, a general appropriations bill can be amended to prevent funds from being used for a specific purpose or in a specific way that otherwise would be permitted under existing law. In general, though, amendments to appropriations bills are supposed to address the question of how much money Congress should provide for various purposes, and not to other issues even though they may be related to those purposes.

---

[20] In the most recent published compilations of House precedents, two full volumes comprising a total of 1,850 pages are devoted to the issue of germaneness. U.S. Congress. House of Representatives. *Deschler-Brown Precedents of the United States House of Representatives*. Volumes 10 and 11. House Document 94-661. 94th Congress, 2d Session.

In addition to these restrictions on amendments, certain House procedures prohibit amendments altogether. As noted earlier, when a motion is made to suspend the rules and pass a bill, no amendments to the bill may be offered from the House floor. Similarly, when the House considers a bill that the Speaker has placed on the Corrections Calendar, no amendments to the bill are in order unless offered by the committee or its chairman. Under certain other circumstances, the House may have to decide by majority vote that it wishes to consider a specific amendment before that amendment can be formally proposed. During consideration of a bill or resolution, for example, the House may have to vote against a motion to order the previous question before a Member can be recognized to offer an amendment to the measure.

The House's rules are designed to permit major bills to be considered under floor procedures that do allow for orderly consideration of whatever germane amendments individual Representatives choose to offer. These bills and amendments to them, are debated in the Committee of the Whole House on the State of the Union—a committee on which all Representatives serve and which meets on the House floor. The Committee of the Whole is really a parliamentary device to facilitate full and orderly deliberation by allowing Representatives to offer amendments to each part of a bill in sequence and by permitting each Member to speak for five minutes on each amendment. Under Rule clause 6 of Rule XVI, each amendment to a bill also may be amended, so Members can alter a proposal before deciding whether to include it in the bill. Within the constraints imposed by the germaneness requirement, the amending process in Committee of the Whole permits Representatives to propose alternatives to or improvements in the legislation recommended by their standing committees.

The House itself usually decides by majority vote whether to permit such an open amending process, and it does so by approving, amending, or disapproving the special rules recommended by the Rules Committee. The importance of these special rules for making bills in order for floor consideration already has been discussed. But special rules also contain other provisions that can be just as important, especially provisions governing the amending process in Committee of the Whole. The Rules Committee may propose, for example, that no amendments to a bill be permitted at all, except perhaps for amendments proposed by the committee that had studied and reported the bill. Alternatively, a special rule may restrict the amendments that Representatives can offer without foreclosing them completely.

In recent years, the Rules Committee often has recommended that the House restrict the amendments that Members may offer to a certain bill to only the series of specific amendments that are printed in a written report from the Rules Committee that accompanies its resolution. In other cases, the committee has proposed to restrict amendments only by prohibiting amendments on certain subjects or to certain provisions of a bill. At the other extreme, the committee may even propose that Members be allowed to offer certain amendments on the floor even though those amendments would violate the standing rules of the House. For example, a special rule may make an amendment in order, notwithstanding the fact that the amendment is not germane to the bill to which it will be proposed.

In short, the Rules Committee can propose to narrow or expand the range of amendments that Representatives may offer to individual bills. This enables the committee to define a special set of procedures and ground rules that it considers best suited to the parliamentary and political circumstances surrounding each bill. In the contemporary House, these decisions by the committee can be more important and controversial than its decisions to grant or not grant rules at all. While most Representatives may agree that a bill needs to be considered, there may be far more disagreement over the procedures that should govern its consideration, and especially over the amendments that should be considered on the House floor. The importance of special rules as they affect the amending process is difficult to overestimate. By permitting some amendments and prohibiting others, a special rule limits the range of alternatives and defines the choices that Representatives can make on the floor. Although the Rules Committee's proposals are cast in procedural terms, their substantive consequences can be profound. If an amendment cannot be proposed, it cannot be adopted.

It bears emphasizing that the committee proposes special rules to the House but it cannot impose its recommendations on the membership. It is for the House to decide, again by majority vote, whether it is prepared to accept the ground rules, including any restrictions on amendments, that the committee proposes. Historically, most special rules have been essentially "open rules"—rules that do not prohibit any amendments that would be in order under the normal operation of House rules and precedents. But more and more often during the 1980s and 1990s, the committee recommended more complex rules proposing to proscribe some amendments, or permit others to be offered, or both.

Restrictive special rules have been more controversial than simple open rules; nonetheless, the House has approved most of those the Rules Committee has proposed. In some cases, there has been bipartisan agreement that the bill to be considered is very complex and technical, and that it is in everyone's interests to take up only a limited number of amendments that focus attention and debate on the major policy choices at issue. In other cases, however, minority party Representatives have argued that the Rules Committee's proposed special rule would permit consideration of key amendments supported by the majority but not equally important amendments that minority party Members wished to offer. Thus, the most important vote on a particularly controversial bill may not be the vote by which the House finally passes the bill. Instead, that vote may come on ordering the previous question on the special rule—which determines whether the House wishes to consider an amendment to the rule, and thereby permit Representatives to offer amendments to the bill in addition to, or instead of, those contemplated in the special rule as reported by the committee.

Such are the powers of the Rules Committee, both procedural and political. Procedurally, the committee's special rules shape the House floor agenda in two respects. Not only does the committee recommend which bills should reach the floor, it also proposes which amendments to those bills should be considered. The first decisions affect the general issues on which the House acts; the second decisions affect the choices available for addressing those issues. Politically, the powers of the committee and the majority party leadership have been enhanced by their close and mutually supportive relationship. The committee's recommendations usually are approved with the support of most Representatives of the majority party, both because their interests tend to be well served and because majority party support for special rules can be portrayed as being part and parcel of the party's continuing control over the essential operations of the House. Nonetheless, party voting is far from being automatic, and the Rules Committee must be ever conscious of the need to fashion special rules that accommodate the political interests and policy preferences of a diverse House membership that normally does not vote strictly along party lines.

Senate Influence on the House Agenda

The constitutional and political context in which the House reaches its agenda decisions makes the House agenda highly permeable in political terms but highly autonomous in procedural terms. In the latter respect, presidential proposals enjoy no formal status or advantage under House rules, and both the standing rules and the special rules that have been discussed in previous sections do not take cognizance of institutions, persons, or events outside the precincts of the House. However, this picture of a House that is procedurally autonomous is not complete, in the same way that the legislative process is not yet complete when the House passes a bill. There remains the "other body" and the impact of the Senate on the agenda of the House.

The passage of a bill by the Senate creates no procedural imperatives for House action (and conversely), although action by one house may stimulate public attention and create political momentum that makes action by the other chamber more likely than it otherwise would be. But there are two respects in which Senate actions impinge in a more direct procedural way on the House agenda, and both derive from differences between House and Senate rules.

The first of these differences concerns appropriations. Senate rules and precedents are not as restrictive as those of the House in prohibiting unauthorized appropriations and keeping general appropriations bills free from changes in the laws that govern the ways in which, and the purposes for which, appropriations may be used. Unlike the House, for example, the Senate's Rule XVI permits it to consider an appropriation that is not yet authorized by law if that appropriation is recommended either by its Appropriations Committee or by the Senate committee with jurisdiction over the authorization bill. Thus, when the Senate considers a general appropriations bill that the House already has passed, the Senate may attach to it Senate amendments that were not and could not have been considered by the House because they would have violated basic House rules.

The second difference, which is probably even more important for bicameral relations, concerns the floor amendments that Senators can offer. Whereas House procedures require that all amendments must be germane (unless Members vote to approve a special rule that permits a specific non-germane amendment to be offered), there is no such general requirement in the Senate. Senate rules require that amendments be germane under certain limited circumstances, and the Senate sometimes imposes such a germaneness requirement on itself by unanimous consent during consideration of individual bills. As a general rule, however, Senators are free to offer whatever amendments they like, on whatever subjects, to most bills that reach the Senate floor.

This situation has obvious and profound implications for attempts to define and control the legislative agenda in the Senate. Although Representatives usually are free to offer amendments, the subjects of their amendments are limited by the germaneness requirement. It is fair to say that, in the House, the basic agenda decisions are those that determine which bills will be considered. Amendments to a bill may present alternatives and raise closely related issues, but only on subjects already raised by the bill itself. This is not the case in the Senate. If the Senate does not consider a bill on a subject that is of special interest to even one Senator, that Senator may bring the subject to the floor in the form of a nongermane amendment to a bill on a wholly unrelated subject. Consequently, the bills that the Senate passes can address a wider and more diverse range of subjects than the bills approved by the House. Furthermore, amendments play a far more significant and independent part for the Senate than the House—and Senate committees play a far less conclusive part than House committees—in defining the issues that reach the floor agenda.

The requirements of the legislative process compel the House to respond to the consequences of these two differences between House and Senate rules, especially when the Senate attaches amendments to a bill that the House already has passed. Before a bill can become a law, the House and Senate must reach complete agreement on its text, including any and all Senate proposals that could not have been considered on the House floor because they would have violated House rules. Thus, the Senate can push matters toward the House floor agenda that did not, and sometimes would not, reach the floor through the operation of the House's own rules.

When neither house's position on a major bill is acceptable to the other, the House and Senate usually create a conference committee to resolve the differences between them. This committee is composed of Representatives and Senators who are charged with representing the position of their chamber in negotiations to reach a compromise that majorities in both houses will accept. In these negotiations, the House conferees can protect the House floor agenda from direct Senate influence if they can convince their Senate counterparts to give way on Senate proposals that are inconsistent with House rules. But if these Senate proposals are truly important to their proponents, the House conferees are more likely to accept at least some of them, although perhaps with modifications. A rigid House stance against accepting any Senate proposals that are inconsistent with House rules would doom many bills for lack of bicameral agreement and would be viewed by Senators as an attempt by one house to impose its rules on the other. Bicameralism in Congress requires compromise instead.

Thus, conference agreements can include issues and proposals that had not reached the House floor agenda and that may not even have been considered by the appropriate House committees. The usual result of a successful conference is a conference report—a proposed package settlement of all the differences between the House and Senate versions of a bill—and the House and Senate normally each vote to accept or reject the package as a whole, but not to amend it. This procedure would require the House to vote on the report without an opportunity to debate and vote separately on matters in the report that had not yet been considered on the House floor. To protect against this possibility, the House has developed rather elaborate and complicated rules by which it can deal individually, and by majority vote, with recommendations of a conference committee that bring before the House certain kinds of issues that had not been included in the House version of the bill.[21] Notwithstanding these special procedures, however, the fact remains that the Senate, through its amendments to general appropriations bills and its nongermane amendments to other bills, can force issues onto the House floor agenda, unless the House is willing to jeopardize enactment of the bills to which the Senate attaches these amendments and to strain bicameral relations generally. Thus, bicameralism limits the autonomy of the agenda-setting process in the House.

Conclusion

This report began with a summary of the constitutional context that gives the House considerable independence in setting its legislative agenda, and it ended with a brief exploration of how the constitutional position and rules of the Senate limit this independence. House procedures for setting its agenda are conditioned also by their political context—by the nature and organization of the national political parties and by the political autonomy that most Representatives enjoy. The result is a process that is far more complicated than would be necessary if a united majority party could expect its members to give consistent support to the same priorities and positions.

The conventional process of agenda-setting in the House has been portrayed as one in which the standing committees first screen the possible agenda of bills introduced, evaluating them and selecting from among them a potential agenda of bills that, in the judgment of the committees, deserve floor consideration. Priorities for considering these bills on the floor are controlled both by the operation of standing rules and by the adoption of special rules proposed by the Rules Committee. And these priorities are transformed into short-term schedules and the daily order of business through the political influence of the majority party leaders and especially through the procedural discretion of the Speaker. The House's legislative agenda is embodied primarily in the bills it considers. Individual Representatives may propose floor amendments that present alternatives or additional options, but opportunities to offer amendments are constrained by the germaneness rule, among others, and can be limited by majority vote.

Underlying these procedural arrangements is the axiom that the agenda of the House is generally for the House to decide, and the corollary that these decisions generally reflect whatever collective preferences can be assembled from the individual preferences of its Members. The House delegates great powers to its committees, powers that are exercised as much through inaction as through action. However, the House retains the power to overrule the judgments of its committees. If this power is rarely used, it is both because Representatives tend to respect the judgments of their committees and because the committees tend to respond to the will of the House.

The standing rules designate certain kinds of bills for priority consideration on the House floor, and set aside certain times for the House to consider other bills under special expediting procedures. But the most important decisions affecting the floor agenda are made one at a time, by majority vote, as the House votes on the special rules recommended by its Rules Committee. The responsibility for arranging the floor

---

[21] See clauses 5 and 10 of Rule XXII.

agenda into an orderly schedule is delegated primarily to the majority party leadership, and these arrangements are implemented and enforced through the formal powers of the pre-eminent majority party leader, the Speaker. In turn, these leaders are expected to act in ways that respond to the interests of their party colleagues and the responsibilities of the House as a whole. House leaders may lead only where and when their colleagues are prepared to follow.

The procedures of the House of Representatives, including the procedures for setting its agenda, have developed over two centuries, as have the institutional dynamics surrounding them (such as the relationship between the Rules Committee and the Speaker). The result is neither simple nor tidy, but the result also is a body of rules and practices that is generally consistent with the principle of majority control. In most respects, the House agenda is subject to control by a voting majority. But this majority sometimes can be transitory and unstable. More often than not, the House is characterized by shifting majorities—majorities that usually have their base in the majority party, but that still must be constructed and reconstructed as one issue gives way to the next. Ultimately then, the problem of agenda management in the House is the problem of developing majorities that do not necessarily emerge naturally from the imperatives of constitutional arrangements or the dynamics of electoral competition.

Related CRS Reports

CRS Report 96-684. *The Amending Process in the House of Representatives.* (Updated periodically)

CRS Report 96-678. *Committee of the Whole: An Introduction.* (Updated periodically)

CRS Report 96-708. *Conference Committee and Related Procedures: An Introduction.* (Updated periodically)

CRS Report 90-84. *The Discharge Rule in the House of Representatives: Procedure, History, and Statistics.* (Updated periodically)

CRS Report 97-552. *The Discharge Rule in the House: Principal Features and Uses.* (Updated periodically)

CRS Report 97-236. *Floor Procedure in the House of Representatives: A Brief Overview.* (Updated periodically)

CRS Report 96-623. *Hearings in the House of Representatives: A Guide for Preparation and Conduct.* (Updated periodically)

CRS Report 97-270. *House and Senate Rules of Procedure: A Comparison.* (Updated periodically)

CRS Report 97-301. *The House's Corrections Calendar.* (Updated periodically)

CRS Report 96-682. *How Measures Are Brought to the House Floor: A Brief Introduction.* (Updated periodically)

CRS Report 95-563. *The Legislative Process on the House Floor: An Introduction.* (Updated periodically)

CRS Report 96-548. *The Legislative Process on the Senate Floor: An Introduction.* (Updated periodically)

CRS Report 97-198. *Parliamentary Reference Sources: House of Representatives.* (Updated periodically)

CRS Report 97-704. *Quorums in House Floor Proceedings: An Introduction.* (Updated periodically)

CRS Report 98-696. *Resolving Legislative Differences in Congress: Conference Committees and Amendments Between the Houses.* (Updated periodically)

CRS Report 96-938. *Special Rules in the House of Representatives.* (Updated periodically)

CRS Report 98-796. *Suspension of the Rules in the House of Representatives.* (Updated periodically)

CRS Report 96-421. *Voting and Quorum Procedures in the House of Representatives.* (Updated periodically)

INDEX

D

E

F

G

H

I

J